West European Arms Control Policy

West European Arms Control Policy

Edited by Robbin Laird

Duke Press Policy Studies

Duke University Press   Durham and London 1990

© 1990 Duke University Press
All rights reserved
Printed in the United States of America
on acid-free paper ∞
Library of Congress Cataloging-in-Publication Data
appear on the last printed page of this book.

To Michael Harrison, whose untimely death
has saddened all who knew him

Contents

Acknowledgments

This project was a complicated and difficult effort. Many persons contributed to its completion and I am able to thank only a small number of them. First, on British policy, the insights of Michael Clarke, Edwina Moreton, Lawrence Freedman, Phil Williams, and James Adams were especially helpful. Second, the contributions of Jorg Baldouf, Alexander Arnot, Eberhard Heyken, and Manfred Stinnes were important in helping me understand the German situation. Third, my understanding of French issues is owed to more persons than I can possibly thank in a short section. I especially wish to thank Marc Perrin de Brichambaut for his friendship, which helped me through a very difficult period of my life and enabled me to understand the nuances of the French approach to foreign and security policy. Finally, I especially wish to note the tragic death of my friend Michael Harrison. The importance of his life for the field of strategic studies is acknowledged by dedicating this book to him.

Abbreviations

ABM	Antiballistic missile defense
ACDA	Arms Control and Disarmament Agency
ACDD	Arms Control and Disarmament Department (U. K.)
ACDRU	Arms Control and Disarmament Research Unit (U. K.)
ASAT	Anti-satellite systems
ATBM	Anti-tactical Ballistic Missile Defense
BAOR	British Army on the Rhine (U. K.)
BSR	Federal Security Council (FRG)
CAP	Centre d'Analyse et de Prevision (France)
CD	Conference on Disarmament
CDE	Conference on Disarmament in Europe
CDU	Christian Democratic Union (FRG)
CESPI	Centro Studi di Politica Internazionale (Italy)
CND	Campaign for Nuclear Disarmament (U. K.)
CPE	Centre de Prospective et d'Evaluation (France)
CSCE	Conference on Security and Cooperation in Europe
CSU	Christian Social Union (FRG)
DACU	Defense Arms Control Unit (U. K.)
DC	Christian Democratic party (Italy)
DEG	Délégation des Études Générals (France)
DGA	Délégation Général des Armements (France)
DOD	Department of Defense (U. S.)
DOD/ISP	International Security Affairs of DOD
EEC	European Economic Community
EPC	European Political Consultation

FAR	Force Action Rapide (France)
FCO	Foreign and Commonwealth Office (U. K.)
FDP	Free Democratic party (FRG)
FOFA	Follow-on Forces Attack
FOIR	Forza di Intervento Rapido (Italy)
FRG	Federal Republic of Germany
IAI	International Affairs Institute (Italy)
ICBM	Intercontinental ballistic missile
IFRI	Institute Français des Relations Internationales
IMAG	Interministerial advisory group (FRG)
INF	Intermediate nuclear forces
IRBM	Intermediate range ballistic missiles
ISTRID	Instituto Studi e Ricerche Difesa (Italy)
LRINF	Long-range intermediate nuclear forces
MBFR	Mutual Balanced Force Reduction
MIRV	Multiple Independent Reentry Vehicle
MOD	Ministry of Defense
NATO	North Atlantic Treaty Organization
NPT	Non-Proliferation Treaty
NSC	National Security Council (U. S.)
PC	Communist party (France)
PCI	Communist Party of Italy
PLP	Parliamentary Labour party (U. K.)
PPBS	Policy, Program, Budgeting System
PS	Socialist party (France)
PSI	Socialist Party of Italy
SACEUR	Supreme Allied Commander Europe
SALT	Strategic Arms Limitation Talks
SAM	Surface-to-air missile
SDI	Strategic Defense Initiative
SDP	Social Democratic party (U. K.)
SED	Socialist Unity party (GDR)
SGDN	Sécretariat Général de la Defense Nationale (France)
SIOP	Single Integrated Operations Plan
SIPRI	Stockholm Institute for Peace Research
SLBM	Submarine-launched Ballistic Missiles
SPD	Social Democratic party (FRG)
SRINF	Short-range intermediate nuclear forces
START	Strategic Arms Reduction Talks
WEU	West European Union

Introduction

This book assesses the domestic policy processes in the four major West European countries: the United Kingdom, the Federal Republic of Germany, France, and Italy. Although historical perspectives have been provided where necessary, the focus has been primarily on West European politics in the 1980s. The main focus of attention has been upon the executive decision-making systems in the four countries, although the general political framework within which those systems operate has been analyzed as well.

The book has been written in a particularly turbulent time. Just when the dust seemed to settle on the Euromissile crisis of the early 1980s, Western Europe was faced with the Gorbachev challenge and with it, dynamic movement in the arms control environment. In addition, the Reagan administration offered the twin challenges of the Strategic Defense Initiative (SDI) and the Reykjavík summit.

During this time, the West European governments have also had to cope with the collapse of the Western defense consensus. In particular, the Euromissile deployment generated a significant public protest movement across the political spectrum. Yet despite the Left's growing dissatisfaction with traditional North Atlantic Treaty Organization (NATO) policy based on nuclear deterrence, conservative governments were returned to power in Britain and Germany, and one was elected for two years (1986–88) in France. While it is clear that the Western alliance survived a significant test in the Euromissile crisis, the conservative governments have been afforded no breathing space in dealing with the superpowers and have sought refuge in revived hopes for European defense cooperation.

The focus on arms control decision making in Western Europe has necessitated extensive interviews with a wide range of governmental and opinion elites. Virtually all of the major West European political and administrative officials in the arms control area have been interviewed at least once, some several times, and these discussions have provided the factual basis for the study. Unlike in the United States, there is no extensive and accurate open-source data base for assessing security policy in Western Europe. Governments simply do not publish much documentation of their activities. The European parliaments are much weaker than the American Congress and tend to generate very few reports that provide data. The print media is much more political in character in Europe than in the United States. No premium is placed on providing factual material in the security area for West European publics. Often the media are more misleading than accurate in terms of what European governments are actually doing. Interviews are essential for the researcher to determine what material in the public domain ought to be relied upon. Finally, there is a paucity of books published in Western Europe and in the United States that address the actual character and processes of policy-making in Western Europe. Less than a dozen books that provide information on the decision-making systems have been published in the West European languages, and these publications are of varying quality and often extremely dated. Hence, it is clear that research for this book would have been impossible to pursue without extensive contacts with West European elites.

It is clear that the key European decision makers have been primarily preoccupied with the political impact of arms control agreements. Such agreements (as opposed to talks) have been primarily American-Soviet negotiations in which the Europeans have been consumers of American positions. The Europeans have sought to influence the Americans to ensure that European political objectives have been protected. Similarly, Europeans have sought with varying degrees of effort to influence the Soviets on the arms control process.

The very highest ranking European officials are not preoccupied with the details of arms control issues. What concerns them is the effect of movement or lack thereof on the East-West relationship. They seek to be able to portray to their publics that the West is seeking to reduce the East-West confrontation through a negotiated process. They do not want their governments to be placed in the position of appearing as obstacles to peace and stability. High-ranking European leaders also tend to be conservative in terms of trying to maintain NATO's traditional strategies and orientations. They seek through the arms control process to ensure that continuity is maintained in Western security policy. For example, they have used the antiballistic missile (ABM) regime to pressure the Americans not to move forward too quickly on the SDI issue.

To a large extent the debate about intermediate nuclear forces (INF) has shaped the context in which West European arms control issues have been discussed and organized. The revival of the peace movements, the debate about NATO strategy, and the decline of the superpower dialogue on arms control which emerged in the context of the INF struggle have all had a significant effect on the evolution of West European arms control policy processes.

Revival of the peace movements, which elevated concern over the legitimacy of nuclear deterrence, meant that in several countries— notably Britain, the Low Countries, and West Germany—the governments have faced a severe challenge to their security policies. This came at a time when public figures in the West, including the American president, were expressing doubts about the future of nuclear deterrence as well.

Before the debate surrounding INF, the West European governments viewed arms control issues primarily as an alliance management issue. It was a question of developing organizational capabilities in the government's executive arm to enable the head of state and his foreign and defense ministers to understand the U. S.-Soviet negotiations and to develop a language which could be used to intervene effectively with the Americans. The INF debate changed all of this. It has required the heads of state and others responsible for defending government policy to commit themselves to a political struggle over the future of nuclear deterrence. For the British and the French, there was the additional complication of carrying out significant modernization of their nuclear forces precisely at a time when the political temperature was rising because of the debate about the deployment of new American nuclear weapons. All of the countries examined in this book are heavily dominated by the executive arm of government, which has much greater latitude in the formulation of arms control policy than does the American executive. This is largely due to the domination of European executives over the legislatures as compared to the American executive versus Congress. The relative lack of expertise outside those governments is a factor as well.

A number of common dimensions of the European arms control process flow from the executive domination of policy-making. The heads of state and the foreign (and sometimes defense) ministers make the broad decisions about how the European governments will involve themselves in the arms control process. These politicians make these decisions with regard to the political basis of support in their respective political parties (and sometimes with regard to broad public opinion outside their party).

The foreign ministers are involved in regular consultations with European and American governments, and through this consultative process they become involved in the day-to-day handling of arms control issues. The making of day-to-day policy is handled by senior civil servants, who have much more power than their American counterparts. There are far fewer political appointments to the foreign policy-making bureaucracy, and career civil servants are indispensable partners in the shaping of arms control policy. The foreign ministries are the main repositories of arms control expertise. They also are given the lead in governmental decision making on arms control, coordinating inputs from other ministries, primarily the defense ministries. Unlike in the United States, the foreign ministries have unquestioned control over day-to-day decision making.

Since the mid-1970s the European governments have been strengthening their arms control expertise in the foreign ministries. A number of countries have been developing a de facto career path whereby persons who have served either in Washington or NATO have continued to work on arms control issues after returning home. In addition, the dominance of the foreign ministries has meant that embassy reporting has been an important contributor to national assessments of arms control issues. The level of accuracy of embassy reporting can have an important impact on a government's assessment of how to play the arms control game at any particular moment.

A high quality of embassy reporting, however, can become a negative factor if the American administration abruptly changes without informing its own working-level officials. For example, the British were confident that they knew what the Americans were going to discuss at Reykjavík due to the close contacts between the British embassy and various administration officials. The actual Reykjavík discussions engendered deep concern in the British government, partly due to failure of the consultation process, which was informed by constant embassy reporting concerning the preparations by the administration for the summit.

Clearly, key officials in the European governments have perceived it to be necessary to upgrade their arms control expertise both to better influence the Americans and to develop greater indigenous capabilities to assess arms control options for themselves. European governments have responded to the growing involvement and salience of arms control issues by strengthening the components of their foreign ministries that deal with arms control issues.

In 1981 the Germans created a division in their foreign ministry to deal specifically with arms control matters. This decision was a result of a series of initiatives beginning in 1977 to upgrade arms control policy. The head of this division is also the federal commissioner for arms control and disarmament. The commissioner has been granted ambassadorial rank, an indication of the post's importance.

The French formed the Bureau of Strategic Affairs in 1979, in part to implement the president's initiative in arms control in 1978, which became the Conference on Disarmament in Europe. The turnover among the players in this unit has been strikingly low. Both the head and deputy of the bureau kept their posts from the bureau's inception until the formation of the cohabitation government in 1986. A large part of the team has been there since 1979. This degree of continuity has reinforced the unit's intellectual cohesiveness, ongoing expertise, and bureaucratic weight, strengthening its virtual monopoly on French arms control policy-making on a day-to-day basis. Even though the analysts in the bureau are civil servants, they often take the initiative to shape policy or to alert political leaders to the consequences of their statements and actions.

The British government relied for a number of years on the Foreign Office's Defense Department to provide it with arms control expertise. As the salience of arms control issues increased, this arrangement proved unsatisfactory. A separate arms control unit was created to deal with nuclear issues. It is expected that this arrangement will be modified with the departure of the head of this unit, but a strong, independent arms control assessment capability will not only remain but will be strengthened. The British have also had an assistant under secretary of state dealing with arms control issues full-time since the early 1980s.

As in other European countries, the Foreign Ministry dominates Italy's arms control process. The foreign minister, however, has only a handful of officers handling NATO and disarmament affairs. The lack of personnel and the civil service's habit of rotating its officers every two to three years without regard to previous assignments has impaired the ministry's ability to develop detailed positions. Lacking the in-depth knowledge to form independent positions, the Foreign Ministry has sought to develop joint European solutions. This has amounted to accepting other NATO governments' positions. It has also increased the desire of British, German, and French experts to deal with the Italians. The joint sharing of expertise which could be enhanced by the West European Union (WEU) revitalization is a critical component of the Europeanization of arms control policy.

In addition to upgrading the capabilities within the foreign ministries, the Europeans have attached arms control advisers to the executive support arms for the head of state. The French prime minister has an arms control adviser attached to the Matignon, and the president has a diplomatic adviser who deals with East-West affairs. For the British, the Cabinet Office and the foreign policy adviser of the prime minister have provided some assistance on arms control matters. The German chancellor has relied upon a staff adviser in the Bundeskanzleramt to provide assistance on arms control issues. Under the last Italian government, Prime Minister Craxi was assisted by a four-man foreign policy team assigned to the Palazzo Chigi, and he instructed them to identify policy areas (including arms control issues) where he could innovate with a certain domestic and foreign impact.

The dominance of the foreign ministries over arms control policy, however, may be reduced as European forces become more involved in potential arms limitation agreements. The European militaries have considerable influence over European operational military policy, which is decisively affected by arms control matters. However, because these military forces have rarely been threatened by arms limitations agreements, military involvement has been much less than in the United States. This is changing as the conventional arms control talks have become more central.

In spite of the expansion of European governmental resources dedicated to arms control issues, the number of persons involved in the actual arms control process is quite small. As one French policymaker put it, "Because there are so few of us involved in the arms control decision-making process, it takes very little time—sometimes a matter of minutes—for us to coordinate a response." Although this may be an overstatement, it is clear that the Europeans do not have to suffer through a complex interagency process to establish their arms control positions.

The arms control decision-making system has operated in Western Europe within the context of a broad disarmament debate. This debate has been about the basic choices Western states ought to make with regard to strategy and their general orientation in the East-West competition. A critical dimension of this debate has been over the future of nuclear deterrence. There is spreading antinuclear sentiment in both Europe and the United States, both on the Left and in the Center. Increasingly for those espousing antinuclear views, the greatest perceived threat to peace is nuclear weapons, not Soviet military forces per se.

There will continue to be a strong commitment by many elements of public opinion and by elites, especially those from the center and the right, to maintain NATO's traditional doctrine. The vagueness of flexible response will continue to be advocated, and NATO's ability to threaten to use nuclear weapons to defend Europe in times of war will continue to be perceived as legitimate. For these elites, the Soviet conventional and nuclear threat to the alliance will be emphasized as the factor legitimizing the continued reliance on nuclear deterrence. Nonetheless, General Secretary Gorbachev's espousal of antinuclear sentiments will make it increasingly difficult to justify Western nuclear deterrence on the grounds simply of responding to the Soviet nuclear threat. Increasingly, Western leaders face the unappetizing position of justifying nuclear weapons on the grounds primarily of the Soviet conventional threat.

The intense struggle over INF and the public debate over the viability of nuclear deterrence associated with the various phases of the INF deployment have left a bitter taste in the mouth of many European leaders. They wish to avoid the expansion or modernization of NATO nuclear forces (with the exception of maintaining the British and

French programs). European political leaders will not want to reopen deep political wounds by forcing the public to consider nuclear issues. In view of the collapse of any European consensus on nuclear deterrence, it will be increasingly difficult for the United States to portray nuclear modernization in the European theater in a positive light. At a minimum, significant political costs would have to be paid for nuclear modernization, but it is increasingly difficult to be confident that such political capital exists.

There also is increasing conflict within Europe over the kinds of conventional weapons modernization that are desirable and feasible in the years ahead. In general terms there are two groups of responses to NATO's conventional modernization initiatives. The first group comes from the Center and the Right. This view favors strengthening NATO's conventional defense while recognizing the fiscal and demographic limits to NATO efforts. Tactical innovations and deliberate armaments modernization plans are favored, but not bold new strategic visions that are seen as impossible to implement in the difficult fiscal years ahead. The second group opposes NATO modernization on political grounds. Coming almost entirely from the British and German Left, there are significant forces favoring "defensive" deterrence. There is a desire to reinforce the "defensive" quality of the NATO alliance and not to procure the kinds of weapons and deploy the kinds of forces which could threaten directly, that is, in a military sense, Soviet control over Eastern Europe.

The conflict over strategy in Western Europe and within the alliance is meditated through a conflict over arms control policy. With regard to nuclear deterrence, West European leaders who favor its maintenance do not view with enthusiasm American efforts to shift alliance strategy to new defensive orientations. Because the European leaders are caught in the throes of a serious domestic conflict over the future of nuclear deterrence, they do not welcome American suggestions that it will be superseded by new technological fixes. Hence the common support for the ABM treaty by the conservative political forces in Western Europe, regardless of what noises they might make about supporting research and development in the SDI area.

The more difficult question is determining what forces will be designated to play an extended deterrent role. The British and French do not wish to play this role explicitly but recognize a de facto role.

They will resist inclusion in superpower agreements, in part to avoid the more explicit recognition of an extended deterrent role.

The British and French will be the most supportive of maintaining a battlefield nuclear role for the Americans and will resist Soviet pressures for further denuclearization. Germans of all political stripes will believe that the shorter the range of the nuclear weapon the more German the effect and will resist battlefield nuclear modernization. This will make them susceptible to pressure from the Soviets for continuing to lower levels of nuclear weapons in Europe by means of arms control agreements.

With regard to conventional forces, those who favor conventional modernization (within the generally recognized stringent fiscal constraints confronting Western Europe) will favor arms control talks that allow confidence-building measures to be put in place that suggest that new modernizations are not escalatory in character. Without some success in conventional arms control measures, conventional modernization will be more difficult politically. In addition, moderate political forces in Western Europe are increasingly attracted to conventional arms control measures as a means of reducing the burden of defense spending on their economies. They also will see the conventional arms control process as a way of reducing the Soviet threat at a time when the Americans may well reduce their force levels in Europe anyway. There will be a serious effort to ensure that any American reductions are not unilateral.

For the Left, the desire to promote "nonprovocative" strategies through various conventional arms control measures will intensify under the Gorbachev disarmament effort. Gorbachev is seen by these political forces as providing a real opportunity for significant reductions in East-West tensions. Conventional modernization of the type suggested by the Americans in the Follow-on Forces Attack policy (FOFA) will increasingly be seen as destabilizing at a time when tensions could be reduced.

Precisely because conservative and moderate political forces in Western Europe are facing a political challenge to conventional modernization, they will use the arms control process to justify desired forms of conventional modernization. They will seek, in effect, to gain Soviet acquiescence or de facto legitimization for NATO's conventional modernization by active Soviet involvement in the conventional arms control process.

It is the sense of being engaged in serious political struggle over both nuclear and conventional modernization that has and will continue to animate the actions of West European politicians in the arms control arena. In addition, this political struggle will unfold in an environment in which all the political forces recognize that Europe has moved into a less nuclear world with the achievement of the INF agreement.

The political struggle is highly structured in Britain and West Germany. In Britain the struggle between Labour and the Tories will continue over nuclear disarmament. Overlaying this struggle will be the sense of a serious crisis in the defense budget as British conventional forces become seriously underfunded. The British government will be eager to see some movement in the conventional arms control arena to help with the perception of the conventional arms spending crunch.

Similarly, in West Germany the SPD is unlikely to move away from its increasingly antinuclear stance, although it may modify its more radical positions on "defensive" deterrence to support an alliance-wide shift toward conventional deterrence. The SPD will pursue its dialogue with the East to promote the notion that a "responsible" party can reduce East-West tensions and better promote German interests. The CDU-CSU coalition will be increasingly preoccupied with enhancing conventional deterrence, reducing battlefield nuclear weapons, and gaining new assurances from its nuclear allies about weapons which could be used in a credible extended deterrent role.

The French face a similar debate in a more muted and less structured manner. On the one hand, there will be increasing pressure from the Germans for the French nuclear force to play an extended deterrent role. On the other hand, there will be increasing pressure from all of France's allies to enhance the capabilities of French conventional forces. Increasingly, French elites are recognizing the limits of nuclear deterrence and the need to beef up French conventional forces. The problem is how to do so in the context of fiscal stringencies and Frances' need to maintain its independence while believing in the continued protection of French independence by means of nuclear deterrence.

An additional problem confronting the European governments is the impact of American programs and declaratory policy. Because of the intensity of the political debate in Europe, any new programs or statements by the Americans cannot fail to become major inputs to the European debate. President Reagan's SDI program was clearly such a case. The moderate forces in Western Europe will be increasingly concerned with restraining American unilateral initiatives and will pursue an alliance arms control process as a major means for restraining the Americans. This is why the kind of Europeanization favored by European conservatives is simply one that improves the European input to an alliance process, not one that is an alternative to the American-led alliance. The Europeans do not want to pursue a Europeanization that simply spawns even more American unilateralism.

Finally, over the past ten years the public infrastructure for participating in the security and arms control debate has dramatically increased in Western Europe. New institutes or the enhanced capabilities of old ones have developed in all of the countries assessed in this book. These institutes often provide the information whereby the press and opposition parties can better participate in the public debate about strategy and arms control. These institutes also provide an important channel whereby information from the United States is transferred to the European debate. This channel is partially under the American government's control (if one includes the Congress in this formulation) by means of the information generated by American public documents and the declaratory policy the administration chooses to insert into the debate.

Nonetheless, the relationships between European and American institutes and the relationships that members of these European institutes have with a variety of American nongovernmental researchers ensure that American influence is not limited to the government alone. In fact, the pluralistic debate in the United States is increasingly reflected by the prism of European institutes and political parties.

In short, over the past decade the European governments have significantly upgraded their arms control expertise and have become more active participants in the arms control process. In addition, there is an infrastructure in place in the nongovernmental sector in Western Europe which will ensure that arms control issues will receive greater attention than in the past. As the Europeans have shifted from being passive observers to becoming more active participants in the arms control process, a difficult and as yet incomplete psychological adjustment has been required. It is increasingly necessary to define what one's objectives are in the arms control process in order to be able to participate in an active manner. Simply pressuring the Americans is not enough. Rejecting alternatives suggested by the superpowers is increasingly inadequate to protect European interests. Thus, the major challenge the European governments face is the successful establishment of a European agenda in the arms control process that is seen by their publics to protect their interests. It is not yet clear whether the processes established to date are adequate to this task. The Europeans may well have to enhance the capabilities of each major country as well as bilateral and multilateral cooperation to achieve this goal.

1

British Arms Control Policy

Robbin F. Laird and David Robertson

Introduction

The British approach to arms control issues is heavily influenced both by the serious conflict over defense issues within the political system and by the predominance of the executive in the formulation of governmental policy. The conflict between the Labour and Conservative parties on defense issues generally has created a climate in which arms control issues matter more than would be the case if the executive were left to its own devices. For Labour, the shift to a nonnuclear defense policy is the essence of its contribution to a serious Western disarmament policy. For the Conservatives, there is a necessity to have an ongoing process of arms control in the West to bolster the party's efforts in the defense area.

Executive domination of arms control policy has meant that the British government is biased toward a managerial approach to arms control policy, that is an approach that is incremental and pragmatic in orientation. Efforts by the superpowers to introduce sweeping changes in the arms control agenda are resisted by the British government, at least in part because such changes are at variance with the managerial approach.

The role of arms control policy has been a subordinate but critical component of the debate over defense policy more generally. For the Conservatives, serious arms control efforts have been critical in underwriting their nuclear efforts in the defense area. Because the Conservative party has been in charge of government policy since 1979, its arms control image has been shaped by the incremental bias of the executive system in the United Kingdom. For example, this has meant a firm commitment to Euromissile deployments to support nuclear deterrence policy in the contentious environment of British defense politics. For the Labour party, the cancellation of the Trident program has been perceived as the most significant contribution a British government might make to a serious Western effort toward nuclear disarmament.

There is a significant difference between the language of arms control and that of disarmament. The technical language of arms control is used primarily by governmental civil servants, while the politicians use the political language of the disarmament debate. The only area where these two languages overlap significantly is on the issue of nuclear weapons. Only here would the government use the technical language of arms control to justify its nuclear weapons policy. Only here has the opposition, especially the SDP-Liberal Alliance (1981–87), enter the domain of the technical language of arms control to justify its policy.

Illustrative of the impact of language is the perception that the verification problem is a technical, not a political one. Once General Secretary Gorbachev accepted a version of double zero and the principle of on-site inspection, the problem of verification became a bureaucratic, not a political issue. A good expression of how arms control is captured in political language is the title of one of Ian Davidson's columns, "The Key is Trust, not Verification."[1] In other words, to understand the British approach to arms control policy one must assess not only the political language and debate about arms control policy but the executive decision-making system and its ability to use the technical language and deal with the technical problems of arms control policy as well.

The Defense Debate and Arms Control

Throughout the 1960s and 1970s a significant defense consensus existed in the United Kingdom. This long-term consensus had three main themes. First, Britain should be a loyal member of NATO, with an "Atlanticist" rather than "Europeanist" leaning. Second, Britain should have a minimal nuclear deterrent but should integrate it as much as possible with the U. S. strategic nuclear force (and should also have a tactical/theater nuclear capacity, partly via dual key arrangements with the United States and partly independently by owning gravity bombs deliverable by Royal Air Force Strike Command aircraft). Third, Britain should have an all-volunteer force, making up in professionalism what it lacked in equipment. Defense politics simply did not count in electoral terms, and there was no good reason for the political leadership to listen to the more extreme elements in their parties that might wish to advocate other policies.

It is against this backdrop that we must consider defense politics since 1979. First, we need to establish the answer to the obvious question. What happened in the late 1970s to break up this happy state of affairs? The answer is that two otherwise unconnected issues surfaced at roughly the same time, and that the time was itself one of general realignment and confusion in British politics.

First came the Euromissile issue, which had nothing to do with a specific British defense policy at all. Britain had always been home to a major part of the NATO theater nuclear force, including since 1978 the F-111 squadrons. But by the time Europe's initial enthusiastic demand for intermediate nuclear forces (INF) upgrading turned into political doubt, the long-quiescent Campaign for Nuclear Disarmament (CND) movement had latched onto the issue, and radical elements in British politics had joined with those in West Germany and the Low Countries in a Europe-wide opposition to nuclear arms modernization.

At roughly the same time, between 1977 and 1979, the Labour government accepted the view of its military advisers and outside defense analysts that the Polaris force, which had been deployed since 1968, was nearing the end of its useful life and would have to be replaced. The cabinet appointed a subcommittee (which included Labour Foreign Secretary Dr. David Owen), and various plans were considered for replacement of the submarine squadron by the 1990s.

The third factor was Labour's election defeat in 1979. Labour not only lost the election but lost it badly. It was defeated by a Conservative party that was self-avowedly radical, intentionally rejecting what it saw as the failure of centrist policies in all areas ranging from economic management to defense. The electoral defeat tore the Labour party apart and unleashed the fury of the long-ignored left-wing elements, whose objections rested on two principal planks. First, they argued that the party had, since the 1960s, failed its working-class backers by never offering adequately radical policies in any area. Second, they claimed that a major reason for the absence of radical policies was the domination over the party of a largely self-appointed oligarchical leadership. They sought an increase in internal party democracy so that leaders and policies supported by the ordinary members in the constituency parties and the trade union leadership could predominate.

These changes did take place, and they brought the far Left to power. Their rise led to the election of a long-time unilateral nuclear disarmer (Michael Foot) to the leadership and to a serious split in the party. Some party leaders, including many highly influential and publicly known members of the previous government, left the party to found a rival, the Social Democratic party (SDP). Others, notably the ex–chancellor of the exchequer and ex–secretary for defence Dennis Healey stayed on, which suggested an effort by some to stabilize Labour policy in a more centrist direction. Their presence increased the public perception of disunity, making the Left, now nearer to control within the party than at any time in its history, even more determined that only a coherent and "pure" set of radical policies could save it from defeat.

In such an environment it was inevitable that defense should cease to be a policy area on which leading British politicians of all persuasions were going to agree. The situation was made worse during the first Conservative administration by the fact that the government itself appeared to be departing from the consensus. While trying to cut public expenditure in all other areas, and, indeed, preaching a form of monetarist economics, the government increased defense expenditure quite out of line with recent practice, until it was spending only slightly less of its GNP on defense than the United States and expanding the historical defense gap between Britain and its European allies. In fact, this was less an example of new Conservative priorities than it seemed. In 1978 the previous Callaghan government had accepted President Jimmy Carter's call for all NATO members to increase their defense expenditure by 3 percent per annum in real terms. The Conservative government was the only European one that actually carried out the promise. The public perceived that defense expenditure now had a much higher priority than in the past, a perception the government and the opposition, both newly radicalized, were happy to encourage.

The other action by the government that made a continuation of defense consensus impossible was the actual choice, announced in 1980, of the weapon system to replace Polaris. Experts had argued in public for a variety of schemes, but the general expectation was that the existing minimal deterrent would be replaced by something at roughly the same level. This expectation was not to be met. The government's first choice was the American Trident c4 missile. This purchase would have entailed a considerable enhancement of British nuclear forces, and it raised somewhat of a storm, especially regarding its cost—about £5 billion in 1980 dollars. This size expenditure obviously added serious strain to defense budgeting. In 1981, however, the government changed its mind upon learning that the Reagan administration had decided to accelerate plans to deploy the Trident d5 missile and opted for that instead. The extra missile costs and the need to build a completely redesigned and much larger class of submarine to deploy the d5 nearly doubled the cost of the program.[2]

What most incensed the Labour party, committed by its powerfully radicalized party conference to nuclear disarmament, was the huge increase in nuclear strike capacity which Trident represented. The Polaris squadron was by the 1980s capable of guaranteeing no more than one boat on patrol at any one time. Each boat was armed with sixteen missiles; each missile had three non-multiple independent reentry vehicle (MIRV) warheads. Thus Britain could not hope to launch against more that 16 targets, and realistically could only plan for a "last resort" retaliation against the USSR after Britain's own nuclear destruction. It had been the very lack of Polaris's credibility in some ways that had helped quiet the concerns about Britain's nuclear role. Trident d5 offered a possible maximum of fourteen MIRVed warheads per missile. Thus the Thatcher government was planning to increase the number of possible Soviet targets the United Kingdom could threaten from 16 to 448 (a factor of 28 times). At least, this is the calculation that can be made from a full loading of Trident, although the Ministry of Defence insisted the d5 would not carry more warheads that the c4 would have done, namely eight.[3]

The results of the 1983 general election focused largely around the deeply divided Labour party, which was officially committed to unilateral nuclear disarmament. The party lost terribly, damaged at least as much by the alliance of the new social Democratic party and the Liberals as by the Conservatives. Labour's disunity, at least in the eyes of the radicals, was the real problem, and this had been worsened by the failure of both the deputy leader, Dennis Healey, and ex-leader, James Callaghan, to support fully the unilateralist perspective. Furthermore, the SDP, effectively a breakaway Labour party, was mainly distinguished from its old friends, now enemies, precisely on defense. The former Labour leaders who split to form the SDP, especially the former foreign secretary, David Owen, were the leaders of the "Atlanticist" (and therefore "nuclear") wing.

In the aftermath of the election two things might have happened. The Labour party might have decided simply that its policies since 1979 had been electorally mistaken. Or they could have decided that it was necessary to push more wholeheartedly radical policies. They chose the latter road, elected a respectable left-wing and rather junior member, Neil Kinnock, to the leadership, encouraged Healey to step down from his deputy leadership role, and wrote an antinuclear plank even more firmly into the party manifesto.

As the election of 1987 approached, the formal issue for the two major parties became clear; one was committed to the most extensive reduction in British military power ever actually offered to the electorate, while the other was committed to a significant enhancement of military capacity. Both parties claimed that they would, at a minimum, retain the United Kingdom's conventional force strength. But it was not clear that this would have been possible in light of the budgetary problems for British defense planning, with or without a nuclear strategic force in the 1990s.

Labour tried to avoid discussing its defense policy during the campaign, while the Tories sought to use every means at their disposal to ensure that the issue came out favorably. The outcome of the June election was shaped to a significant extent not only by the Tories success in emphasizing their defense policy, but also by their use of the defense issue to portray the Labour leadership in an unfavorable light on the more significant electoral issues of the economy. If the Labour party could not be trusted on defense, they should not be trusted with managing the economy, the Tories argued.

Throughout the year preceding the election the Tory party's standing in the opinion polls steadily improved. But there was much uncertainty about how well they would do in an actual election because of the important marginal seats, especially in the Midlands. The opposition parties had either led or were dead even with the Conservative party in numerous opinion polls. Polls also revealed that the prime minister was not as popular as the party generally. The perception of her as "uncaring" or "dictatorial" had become a liability to the party. There was an important sense of uncertainty hanging over the run up to the election.

The Labour party sought to play on the personality issue by emphasizing the "human qualities" of their candidate. The party ran several successful advertising spots focusing on Neil and Glenys Kinnock as caring and sensitive people concerned with overcoming the divisiveness of Britain under Thatcher. The party manifesto was short and emphasized the essentials of party policy without providing excessive grist for the Tory campaign mill. The notion of socialism disappeared almost entirely from Labour's campaign effort.

Defense was recognized as a liability by the Labour party leadership, who tried to deemphasize it during the campaign. Healey gave a major speech at the outset of the campaign, which focused on Labour's emphasis on conventional defense policy as opposed to a nuclear disarmament policy. Of course, Healey did not help his case by an incredible slip of the tongue in Moscow, where he indicated that the Soviet leadership was "praying" for a Labour party victory.

Defense came to play an important role early in the campaign in spite of Labour's efforts. During the second week of the campaign, the *Sunday Telegraph* printed a purported "leak" of an American government document dealing with the possible American reactions to a nuclear-free-Britain policy pursued by a Labour government. The issue of the effect of Labour party policy on the NATO alliance was soon joined by the question of how Britain would defend itself without nuclear weapons. Neil Kinnock, in a television interview the same week, made it clear that he would rely on the ability of Britain to use, in effect, guerrilla tactics to defend itself against invasion. Mrs. Thatcher jumped on this gaffe to drive home the point that Labour party policy was unsound on defense matters generally.

Throughout that week as well, senior Tory leaders joined in the chorus of accusations about the unsoundness of Labour party policy. This was especially true in the case of Michael Heseltine, who in a colorful speech in Wales informed the local audience that Labour would resist the Russians by "mounting guns on the Barclays bank, on the right, and by throwing grenades from the sweet store, on the left."

Both poll data and canvassing by Tory M. P.s in local constituencies made it clear that defense was an important issue in activating Tory supporters to work in the campaign and actually to vote. In the minds of these supporters, defense was an issue which reinforced their sense that Labour leaders were untrustworthy and were heading a pack of left-wing undesirables.

The attack on labour's defense policy was abetted by the sdp-Liberal Alliance. David Owen was especially strident in attacking Labour's unilateral disarmament policy. Nonetheless, the Alliance had its own problems in presenting defense policy. There had been a long-standing dispute between the Liberals and the Social Democratic party over the issue of whether there would be a successor system to the Polaris strategic force. The Liberal party was more inclined to favor the elimination of British strategic weapons, having had a long history of favoring nuclear disarmament. The leadership of the sdp, especially David Owen, favored the continuation of the British nuclear deterrent. The dispute was to have been resolved by the Alliance Defence Commission, which issued its report on June 10, 1986. The commission, however, could not resolve the question of whether there should be a successor to Polaris. Finally, by the end of 1986, the Alliance leadership had reached a compromise which permitted the party manifesto to state the following: "In government we would maintain, with whatever necessary modernization, our minimum nuclear deterrent until it can be negotiated away, as part of a global arms negotiation process, in return for worthwhile concessions by the USSR which would enhance British and European security. In any such modernization we would maintain our capability in the sense of freezing our capacity at a level no greater than that of the Polaris system."

Nevertheless, the result of the election was to confirm the government's policy. There will, however, be an inevitable conflict in government over the priorities of conventional modernization. The Labour party has persisted in its policy of favoring the elimination of the British nuclear deterrent, but the leadership has sought to present its policy differently on the question of the role of non-nuclear Britain in the Western alliance. Perhaps the issues of American military bases will be modified dramatically in the presentation of policy. However, most party activists will continue to support such a policy at such a time when Labour forms a future government.

In short, although Trident will be a fact by the time of the next election, the controversy over the future role of Britain in European nuclear deterrence will not abate.

The Governmental Approach to Arms Control Issues

The structure of executive decision making in the arms control area is discussed in the next section. Here we discuss the general orientation of the government, primarily the executive, to arms control issues. By and large the British government reflects American positions on arms control issues and seeks to act as an important lobbying group in ensuring that British interests are as well served as possible by evolving American positions. As Phil Williams of Southhampton University has put it, "Britain, together with its European allies is a consumer of security provided by the United States and a recipient of American arms control policies. Although Britain has been a direct participant in negotiations on a comprehensive test ban, and is involved in the multilateral negotiations such as the Conference on Disarmament in Europe and the negotiations on conventional arms reductions in Europe, the negotiations on strategic and theater nuclear weapons have been confined to the superpowers, even though they have a decisive impact on British security."[4]

Thus a major thrust of British arms control policy is to ensure that the British government is in as good a position as possible to influence American positions.[5] The British prime minister, the foreign minister and his Foreign Office, and the minister of defence and his ministry are all, with varying types and degrees of access to Americans, attempting to shape U. S. policy. The British embassy in Washington plays an important role in trying to assess the process of American decision making and to inform the British government of how and when to intervene as effectively as possible.

Put in other terms, the arms control bureaucracy in the United Kingdom directs its efforts primarily toward ensuring that it brings influence to bear on the continued interagency work being done in the United States to elaborate a coherent arms control posture for both the United States and its NATO allies. This has meant repeated rounds of discussions on what NATO should propose on nuclear arms control and trying to ensure continued U. S. adherence to a number of important arms control treaties, in particular the ABM treaty. The arms control bureaucracy in the United Kingdom often acts as a lobbying group trying to influence the debate within the U. S. bureau-cracy and administration, with the specific task of opposing those who, from the British perspective, appear determined to undermine the entire arms control process.

Suggestive of the British approach was the assessment of and at-tempt to influence the U. S. process before and after the Reykjavík summit in 1986. The British embassy in Washington had made a major effort to stay abreast of the process of producing the papers being prepared for the summit, and, as a result, officials in London felt confident that they were well informed concerning what the United States would discuss. Precisely because of this, British offi-cials were especially shocked at what happened. Their response was a quick attempt to repair the damage through a visit by the prime minister to Washington to ensure that the president reversed his position. Thatcher's visit to Camp David, at which President Reagan embraced positions more consistent with British interests, was per-ceived by British officials as an important success of British policy in the arms control area. It was claimed, in fact, in the British press that the Americans in the NATO ministerial meetings in December 1986 ultimately accepted the British position.[6]

The British government has perceived the necessity of evolving a more European stance in arms control issues to influence the U. S. position more effectively. Reykjavík played an important role in this process.[7] As Ian Davidson had noted, "The lesson is beginning to be learned in London, where the idea that Britain is a European rather than a transatlantic country is belatedly making headway."[8] Anglo-French and Anglo-German relations have been important in counter-ing American positions which the British find antithetical to their interests. Since 1984 the British government has taken increased inter-est in using the West European Union (WEU) as a mechanism for coordi-nating European arms control positions. However, the harsh line Mrs. Thatcher has taken on European integration has reduced the ability of Britain to play a significant role in European defense cooperation.

Nuclear Arms Control Issues

The most significant arms control issues to the British government are those involved in the nuclear area, that is strategic forces, interme-diate nuclear forces, and ballistic missile defenses. Precisely because the British are consumers of American positions, they focus the priority of their efforts on influencing U. S. positions to take into account British interests. Above all, nuclear arms control policy is very firmly fixed by the doctrine that not only the existing Polaris force but the planned Trident force as well represent so minimal a deterrent compared with the assets of both the United States and the Soviet Union that no possible cuts in the independent deterrent can be contemplated. This line has held even under pressure from political sectors in the United Kingdom who have been influenced by the Gorbachev diplomatic offensive toward France and Britain. The furthest the government has been prepared to go, faced with Gorbachev's "deep cuts" proposal, is to say, "We never say never"—that is, if really deep cuts were to come about, there is a sense that Britain would have to take some steps to reduce its nuclear arsenal. But there is certainly no willingness to drop the Trident purchase in order to make a British move in arms control. On the contrary, the move most often suggested by the opposition parties, which is that Britain should side with the USSR on the question of nuclear testing, is hotly opposed by the government, for the obvious reason that Britain needs tests if it is to design its new warheads for the Trident missiles.[9]

It is, in fact, virtually impossible to find a positive role for Britain in strategic nuclear arms control as long as the government remains committed to retaining a U. K. nuclear deterrent. The truth is that Britain can probably only suffer from an arms control agreement at the strategic level. This would happen both because the government line on Trident would seem all the more isolated and because of a fear that the United States would agree to some kind of technology transfer ban. In fact, there was a genuine fear that the Americans, by following the logic of their positions at Reykjavík, would not provide the British with Trident. A major objective of the prime minister's trip to the United States after Reykjavík was to save Trident.[10]

The British government does have a general propensity toward strategic stability, which is to favor incremental reductions in strategic weapons with cuts that are not so deep as to put in question the role of independent French and British deterrence. It is clear that British officials oppose any inclination of an American administration to seek deeper than 50 percent cuts. They do so because they are incrementalists who believe that only small, pragmatic steps can be taken because cuts taken too deeply threaten rather than promote stability. Also, it is clear that the British government is deeply committed to nuclear deterrence, and there is a general fear that the superpowers if left to themselves might set in motion cascading denuclearization. It is thought better to pursue a "realistic" policy of arms limitations rather than a significant disarmament policy.

The British government has been deeply concerned by what it perceives to be the vision of "denuclearization" promoted by some elements of the Reagan administration. The Reagan "Star Wars" speech in 1983, the newspaper accounts of the president's position at the Reykjavík summit, and the promotion of the double zero option in INF all suggest to British officials that the denuclearization threat has increased. The prime minister's vigorous defense of nuclear deterrence during her trip to Moscow was not intended only for Soviet ears.

The adoption by the Soviet leadership in February 1987 of the NATO position on INF, namely, a reduction of long-range intermediate nuclear forces to the lowest level possible, created significant problems for the British as well as other Allied governments. The prime minister was committed to the so-called zero solution in a large part because of her struggle with some parts of British public opinion to accept American missiles in the United Kingdom. She embraced it again in March of 1987 partly because it would remove a potential campaign issue in the upcoming election. She clearly wanted to use the defense issue in the campaign, and the most controversial part of her defense program had been the installation of American missiles. The removal of this issue by means of a serious arms control process was perceived as a bonus by British officials dealing with the disarmament debate. As the prime minister argued in the Commons shortly after Gorbachev's proposals, "I believe the proposals which have come from Moscow stem from the resolve of the West to stand firm, and would never have come from any of your [Labour's] policies."[11] In other words, Britain has been able to have arms control because a unilateral disarmament policy has not been followed.

The British government has been concerned lest the INF arms control process lead to cascading denuclearization in the European theater or to significant enough denuclearization that the British deterrent would become elevated as a political issue in Europe. The government has hoped that a firebreak might be constructed between the nuclear weapons that remain outside an INF agreement and those included, and it introduced a solution to this effect in the NATO meetings in June 1987. The prime minister embraced the double zero solution in large part because it served electoral purposes and could be used to establish the firebreak as well. British officials do believe that further reductions in nuclear battlefield weapons are possible, but they wish to see other issues addressed first, primarily conventional and chemical weapons. They fear, however, that Western differences on these issues can be exploited by the Soviet leadership, which would place the West in an unfavorable position when dealing with the battlefield nuclear weapons issue.

In addition, two issues specific to Britain concern the government and are the focus of a British "lobbying" effort directed at the American government. First, throughout the SALT and START talks the British have been keen to ensure that the United States would never agree to a nontransfer or noncircumvention clause limiting the transfer of American nuclear technology to Britain. There was significant concern expressed by the British even about the protocol of SALT II. The British feared that the temporal limitations on the deployment of cruise missiles could be used by the Soviets as a precedent to build on in developing noncircumvention clauses (something which was agreed to in the ABM treaty).[12] The British are also concerned with shaping the emerging INF verification regime. This regime impinges on British interests because the United Kingdom is a base for American ground-launched cruise missiles.[13]

With regard to the question of SDI, British officials perceive their interests as best served by a narrow interpretation of the ABM treaty. To a large extent the Thatcher administration signed an agreement to participate in SDI as a research program precisely in order to influence SDI as a potential deployment program. Only with this image in mind was it possible to forge a British governmental consensus. It is accepted in Whitehall that Britain was well served by the United States during negotiations over the 1972 ABM treaty. The maintenance of the current ABM regime is perceived to preserve the viability of the British deterrent and to provide increased options for British targeting with the modernized nuclear force in the absence of Soviet abrogations of the ABM treaty. Most British officials simply do not think it likely that the Soviets would do so unless stimulated by significant U. S. advances in the SDI area.

To summarize, in the nuclear area the British government pursues four basic interests:

(1) Ensuring the continued viability of nuclear deterrence by the West; especially, protecting the modernization of the British deterrent

(2) Encouraging the United States to seek strategic stability at the lowest level concomitant with the maintenance of nuclear deterrence and the exclusion of the British deterrent from excessive political pressure

(3) Negotiating lower levels of U. S. and Soviet nuclear weapons in the European theater without the complete elimination of U. S. nuclear forces, including battlefield weapons

(4) Supporting the continuation of the ABM treaty

Non-Nuclear Arms Control Issues

In contrast to the nuclear weapons area, the British are direct participants in the conventional and chemical arms control areas. They also are important players in shaping Western positions in the relevant arms control forums. With regard to conventional arms control, the British have pursued a policy of trying to ensure that the alliance's military posture remains as robust as possible in the face of what the British consider to be clear advantages for the Warsaw Pact in conventional forces.

The British government has been at the forefront of alliance countries which characterize the Soviet conventional military threat as so serious as to require a permanent reliance on nuclear deterrence to balance the overall military equation. On the one hand, the British have sought through the Mutual Balanced Force Reduction (MBFR) talks to ensure that any American withdrawals would be met by asymmetrical Soviet reductions or, if such withdrawals proved impossible to negotiate, to encourage the Americans not to make them. In other words, the British have sought to enmesh the Americans in a web of negotiations that would deter them from making unilateral withdrawals. On the other hand, the British have pursued close cooperation with key European allies in shaping American positions. The Germans have been the key ally in formulating the European position in MBFR, while the French have been important to the British in the Conference on Disarmament in Europe (CDE).

There are clearly identifiable British-specific interests which could be pursued in the conventional arms control area. These center around the considerable costs, many of them in foreign exchange, of maintaining the European continental commitment. Between them, the British Army on the Rhine (BAOR) and the RAF Germany will account for around 55 percent of the defense budget over the next twenty years. Whatever the Americans may think about European defense budgets, it is common ground to all political parties in Britain that the country spends a disproportionately high percentage of its GNP on defense. Despite this, most defense economists and defense-minded politicians of all colors agree that the budget is seriously underfunded for the long term.

In 1981 then–secretary of defence John Nott attempted a defense review, which is British government shorthand for cutting out some major defensive function. In this case he chose to make massive cuts in the Royal Navy, with the long-term aim of permanently reducing the surface fleet. At that time the government white paper openly admitted that despite the considerable increase in defense expenditure under the Thatcher government planned for 1979–85, the existing force structure and strategic posture could not be maintained. The Falklands War intervened, allowing the Navy lobby to fight off the Nott proposals. Since then, nothing has been done to bring resources and commitments into line, in fact, the opposite has happened. Under political pressure to increase domestic public expenditure, the government announced in 1986 that the defense budget would be frozen in monetary terms for the next five years. No future government is likely to be more generous to the military.

Consequently, conventional arms control, especially along the lines of mutual and balanced force reductions on the central front, represents one of the few ways of squaring an impossible circle. There may also be increasing political pressure to do something to reduce the United Kingdom's military commitment. Certainly the idea of keeping 55,000 men permanently in the British sector of the central front is no longer as sacrosanct as it was. For several years there have been suggestions in the defense literature to reduce the continental commitment. However, the idea is no longer restricted to professional analysts. In the wake of the Defence Estimates for 1986, an editorial in the influential *Times* called for reductions in troop levels in Germany; at least some of the parliamentary Conservative party would support such a move.

In spite of the potential cost savings that a negotiated reduction in the BAOR might represent, there are clear restraints on the British side. There is the concern, already noted, that the Americans should be linked to a web of negotiations to restrict precipitous withdrawals. The British government is concerned about the future evolution of the Bundeswehr and wishes to encourage the German government to do all it can to maintain its conventional forces at as high a level as possible. Again, a proposed drawdown of the BAOR—except in conditions of significant Warsaw Pact reductions—would encourage the Germans to drawdown their forces, thereby reducing Western capability in the forward defense area.

Then Secretary of State for Defence George Younger underscored the challenge of conventional arms withdrawal for the British in the following terms:

> There is, for instance, the suggestion, not foreign to the leader pages of some of our national dailies, that we should withdraw from the central front. Consider for a moment the effect of such a move. Who would take our place in Germany? What would be the effect on our NATO allies—all of whom, whether or not they have soldiers and airmen in Germany, regard our commitment to defend Federal German territory as both politically and militarily vital? Would they continue to make their own contribution to the defense of the central front? Or might some of them take British withdrawal as a good reason for cutting their own commitment? What influence could Britain expect to retain in the councils of NATO if we did withdraw? What would be the effect on the United States—what signals would be sent to the American people about the willingness of the Europeans to shoulder the burden of their own defense? What would be the effect on the Soviet Union, and what signals would they receive about the solidarity and cohesion of the Alliance?[14]

Suggestive of the British approach was their activity in MBFR since early 1985. The British, in close cooperation with the Germans, encouraged the Americans to table the so-called December 5th proposal in 1985 at MBFR. This proposal put aside the "data question" in pursuing force reductions. The data question refers to the Western desire to have the Soviets agree to a joint calculation of the existing balance of conventional forces in central Europe as the basis for negotiations. The December 5th proposal suggested that the two sides put in abeyance the data question and proceed with withdrawals of forces on both sides. Given Soviet superiority, NATO requested an asymmetrical withdrawal of Soviet forces as part of the package.

The British and Germans sought to get the MBFR process going again through the December 5th proposal. If the Soviets accepted the proposal, it would have led to withdrawals acceptable to the British because the American withdrawals would be balanced by asymmetric reductions on the Soviet side. The British acted to invigorate the MBFR process because of their growing concern over the prospects for American withdrawals, with the proposed Nunn amendment in 1984 as a key stimulus. Also, if such reductions could be negotiated, perhaps a process could be set in motion which would allow the British to reduce the BAOR without jeopardizing British interests.

It should also be added that the British put forth the proposal without expecting dramatic action on the Soviet part. The wide range of proposals that the Soviets have made in the arms control arena under Gorbachev, especially since January 1986, have created a new concern that the Soviets might outflank the West in the conventional arms control area as well. To counter Soviet pressures for further nuclear arms control reductions in the European theater, the British hope to focus attention on the imbalances in the conventional and chemical arms areas. But this can be done effectively only if there is an ongoing arms control process in these areas.

With regard to CDE, the British cooperated closely with the Germans and the French in developing common positions to promote European interests in the conventional arms control area. The verification regime adopted in CDE was largely developed by the Europeans and was accepted by Gorbachev at least in part because of direct intervention by President François Mitterrand, who was acting on behalf of all the major West European states. The British acted to protect their specific interests as well, notably in ensuring that the West did not accept the Soviet proposal to have naval forces covered by CDE.

With the successful completion of CDE and with the lingering existence of MBFR, the West is pursuing the policy of merging the two negotiations into one. There has been an active effort to define an arms control framework within which the twenty-three major NATO/Warsaw Pact states could negotiate some loose relationship with the thirty-five nations in the Conference on Security and Cooperation in Europe (csce). Some such relationship is critical to the French government, which for domestic reasons cannot be seen to be negotiating on a "bloc-to-bloc" basis. The American and French governments were at loggerheads over how to resolve this issue. For the British and the Germans there was a clear desire to have the French involved, but not at the expense of a serious framework for negotiation, that is direct nato/Warsaw Pact negotiations. British officials made it clear that they hoped the United States would be flexible in dealing with the French. The West should not be mired in procedural controversies precisely at a time when it needs to be forging ahead on conventional arms control issues. This need would be enhanced by the successful conclusion to the inf negotiations. As a result, the British actively sought the Franco-American compromise reached in June 1987.

While there is little real confidence about mbfr, there are other possible conventional arms control moves that could slightly alleviate Britain's financial troubles with regard to the German front. Just as with the American "military reform movement," there are circles in Britain pressing for an increased reliance on reserves. The professional military are unenthusiastic about this because they feel a need to plan for the "bolt from the blue" surprise attack, with its attendant mobilization problems if reserve forces are vital. The argument sometimes heard on this point is that really effective confidence-building measures, which could minimize the possibility of surprise attack, would make it much safer to rely on ready reserves in the Territorial Army Volunteer Reserve, thus again offering budget-cutting possibilities.

The final category of arms control is chemical warfare. Chemical warfare control relates to specifically British interests in two ways. First, it catches the popular imagination almost as strongly as strategic nuclear arms control. The British have a peculiarly intense horror of chemical weapons, stemming from their experience in the First World War, which in many ways is a more vivid, though of course vicarious, experience to those middle aged and older than is the Second World War. It is notable that all British political parties, whether they approve of U.S. plans to restart chemical weapon development or not, have made it abundantly clear that they would not allow storage of such weapons in the United Kingdom in peacetime and, with the exception of the Conservatives, would forbid them in wartime as well.

Second, there is a quite practical interest for the British military. For reasons having nothing to do with arms control Britain ceased all chemical agent production in the late 1950s and retains no stocks of them. Nor is there any likelihood of a change in this situation. Four years ago, the *New Statesman* erroneously reported that the United Kingdom was planning to resume production. The resulting uproar left the government in no doubt about the level of public opposition to such a move if ever it should be contemplated in the future. The British chaired the Conference on Disarmament's Ad Hoc Committee on Chemical Weapons in 1986, and during this time the British government was active in promoting new ideas on how to conclude an accord, including a fresh proposal on how to resolve the verification problem in Article 10 of their draft treaty, which would allow challenge inspection of disputed facilities. The U.S. proposal would have permitted international inspectors to be sent to check "anywhere anytime" within forty-eight hours of one country challenging another with violating the chemical arms agreement. The British compromise focused on an extended time limit for the arrival of inspectors to seventy-two hours, but even more importantly offered an alternative under which the challenged state could offer to supply information to satisfy the challenging state within ten days. Obviously, if a challenged state refused inspection and failed to satisfy the challenging state, it would be deemed as not complying with the convention.[15] The United States however, felt that the British proposal was not tight enough, for it allowed the accused state too much freedom to reject the challenge.[16] The American-British altercation has left more than a trace of bitterness on both sides. The repeated American refusal to support or even to accept tacitly British proposals on challenge inspection have clearly angered British arms control officials.

In short, the British are pursuing several objectives in the non-nuclear arms control area. The British government seeks to meet the following objectives: (1) to involve the Americans in a network of negotiations to impede a precipitous unilateral withdrawal of conventional forces; (2) to provide a framework which might over time allow the British to draw down their forces in Germany; and (3) to reduce the conventional and chemical threat posed by the Soviet Union to Europe and to the United Kingdom.

The British Executive and Arms Control Decision Making

The British decision-making system on arms control policy is heavily dominated by the executive organs of government (see figure 1.1). On day-to-day management of arms control issues, the Foreign and Commonwealth Office (FCO) takes the lead, with the Defence and Arms Control Unit of the Ministry of Defence (MOD) playing an important role in coordinating MOD positions on arms control issues. Nonetheless, on the big questions of setting the thrust and direction of British arms control policy, the prime minister and the relevant cabinet ministers are the key players. Even here the civil service plays an important role, as the prime minister tends to rely on certain civil servants to help inform her on the details of policy. In addition, the key embassies, especially the British embassy in Washington, play an important role in keeping the government informed of actions being contemplated in key capitals which would effect British arms control policy.

The Prime Minister and the Cabinet

It is no secret that Mrs. Thatcher has been a strong prime minister, dominating her cabinet. She is a voracious consumer of briefs and relies heavily on the civil service to keep her well informed on key issues. A key to power for a high-ranking civil servant in the Thatcher administration is to produce a clever brief on an important issue and see that it is circulated to her on a timely basis. The civil servants who have been important to the prime minister have been those capable of meeting this criterion.

   She is well known for her hostility in principle to the power of the civil service and to the periodic opposition of the FCO bureaucracy to her policies. Notably, the Falklands War was not a popular cause with the FCO. Her response was to establish a foreign policy coordinator in 10 Downing Street to provide her with a more reliable perspective than that provided by the FCO civil service. The first person appointed to this position was Sir Anthony Parsons, formerly ambassador to the United Nations. Sir Anthony explained the need to which his appointment was a response: "I think that if I were Prime Minister I would feel a slight vulnerability. I would feel that I needed to be sure that somebody on my behalf was constantly on the watch for crises suddenly blowing up, which would require me as prime minister to

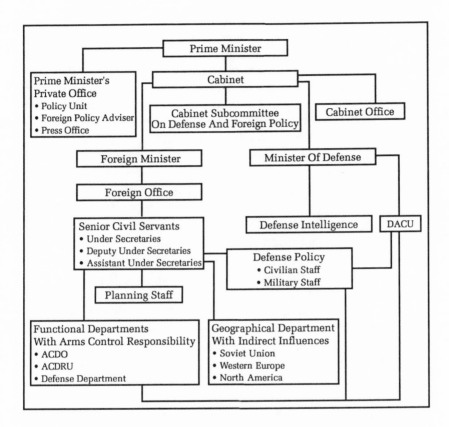

Figure 1.1 Executive British Arms Control Decision-making System

make very quick and very important decisions. I would feel more reassured if I had somebody alongside me who could give and would give a wholly independent personal view which I could match against the more formal advice which I was getting from the foreign office."[17] His appointment was only a limited success, however, and he was replaced by Sir Percy Cradock, who has been more successful up to this point in time.

The other two people who have an input are Sir Robert Armstrong, secretary of the cabinet and head of the Home Civil Service since 1983, and Mr. Bernard Ingham, the chief press secretary. Both have served in No. 10 since 1979 without interruption. Sir Robert Armstrong has a strong Treasury background, serving there in 1950–57 and 1959–64. He worked in the Cabinet Office from 1964 to 1966 and then went back to the Treasury from 1967 to 1970. During this time he was joint principle private secretary to Roy Jenkins, chancellor of the exchequer. In 1970 he became principal private secretary to the prime minister. In 1975 he became deputy under secretary at the Home Office and then permanent under secretary in 1977.

Mr. Bernard Ingham's background is as a career journalist working originally in Yorkshire and then from 1962 to 1967 for the *Guardian*. He became a press advisor on the Prices and Incomes Board in 1967 and in 1968 took his first government post as information officer in the Department of Economic Planning. He was for a time an under secretary in the Department of Energy. In his time as chief press secretary he has been most vigorous in his attempts to centralize around No. 10 the information outputs of the government. He is known to have patchy and stormy relationships with the national press, and he has never avoided controversy. His role in the Westland Affair, which led to the resignation of Michael Heseltine as defence minister, was probably the most public indication of the degree of latitude Mrs. Thatcher allows him and of the trust that she seems to place in him.[18]

Given her views on the civil service, it is not surprising that she has sought outside advice on key issues to guide her judgement on foreign policy and defense issues. The process of her preparation for the trip to Moscow in March 1987 is illustrative. Although she relied in part on the FCO Soviet Department to help prepare her for the visit, she relied as well on meetings with outside specialists, including a meeting at Chequers (the residence of the prime minister) to assess changes in the Soviet Union under Gorbachev. Not surprisingly, she has trusted outside advisers as well whom she consults on a wide range of issues, including how to assess Britain's relationship with the outside world.

As Anthony King has put it, Mrs. Thatcher's style of government is through people control rather than organizational control: *"Hers is an almost exclusively people-centered style of government. Her interest in the structure of government is minimal. She is uncon-*cerned with nuts and bolts, and organization charts bore her. Instead, she feels at home working with, through—and, if need be, around—individual human beings. Faced with a new problem or determined to embark on a new initiative, she asks, not 'How can I organize this work so that it will be done effectively?' but rather *'Who can I get to* *help me? Who would be the best person to turn to?'* Weighing people, like weighing power, is central to the way she does her job."[19]

Thatcher's views on arms control are above all a function of her views on the nature of the domestic political struggle over defense. She sees herself as leading her party in a draconian struggle with the Labour party over defense issues. From her point of view, having the Labour party in power would undercut the very foundations of British defense policy, namely, nuclear deterrence. The Trident issue is a symbol of the very struggle for the soul of British defense policy. Nuclear arms control issues are a critical component in her struggle with the Labour party. She seeks to maximize supportive positions and to reduce those positions hurting her in the struggle. The zero option in INF and ultimately the double zero solution have been useful tools in dealing with her adversaries. She has thereby sought to encourage the NATO alliance to seek such solutions. The American administration has caused her problems, nonetheless, with its performance at forums such as the Reykjavík summit, where the Americans were perceived to be questioning nuclear deterrence and more concretely threatening the Trident deal by suggesting the desirability of a nuclear-free world to their advantage. Obviously, Thatcher has not been thrilled with this development.

She had a mixed view of President Reagan and the Reagan administration. On the one hand, she clearly personally liked the president and perceived a common ideology. On the other hand, she saw the president as a leader not capable of keeping his shop in order. He was perceived to be unable to grasp important details, and he allowed subordinates to have too much power. In other words, he was the exact opposite of herself and her image of what a leader ought to be like. Also, she was quite aware of how unpopular President Reagan was in her country. She had to walk a thin line between working with the Americans (which is popular) and identifying too closely with the president (which is not). She is the most convinced Atlanticist in her cabinet, but even she has perceived it necessary to elevate the European dimension of her security policy. It has been a slow and painful evolution for her, but she has reached the point where she understood the importance in March 1987 of visiting France and Germany prior to her visit to Moscow to convey to the British public that she is a European leader, not just an errand boy for the Americans. Arms control policy can be a useful mechanism for trying to coordinate European views on security. Unlike coproduction of weapons or coordination of strategies, it is patently more possible to develop a European perspective on arms control policy.

The demise of the Reagan administration may lead the prime minister to advocate Europeanization from another standpoint as well. She considers herself to be leading a "conviction government," something she believed she had in common with the president in his effort to lead the "Reagan Revolution." She saw these two efforts as closely linked. With the election of a new U. S. administration in 1988, this link has been removed, perhaps along with some of her inhibitions about further Europeanization.

Arms control policy can be useful to rein in not only the Americans but the Soviets as well. Mrs. Thatcher's distrust of the Russians is well known, but under General Secretary Gorbachev the Soviets are becoming a more unpredictable and challenging adversary. She considers Gorbachev clearly to be interested in domestic change and likely to generate significant tactical innovations in foreign policy as well.

The prime minister is assisted at 10 Downing Street by a small coterie of advisers who function more as a unit to inform the bureaucracy of the prime minister's perspective than to try to coordinate British government policy from the office of the prime minister. Her advisers serve as well to coordinate the work of the prime minister in the foreign policy and defense area, as evidenced in her trips and major speeches.

The prime minister also is assisted by the foreign policy specialists in the Cabinet Office. Although technically at the disposal of the entire cabinet, the Cabinet Office has come to treat the prime minister as its major client. The Cabinet Office was headed by Sir Robert Armstrong, who retired in 1987 and was replaced by Sir Clive Whitmore, formerly of the MOD.

The Cabinet Office serves to facilitate the forging of interdepartmental agreements on disputed issues. For example, officials in the Cabinet Office chaired an interdepartmental group on SDI to develop a governmental position on how to participate in the American program. The British agreed to participate in SDI in order to ensure maximum British influence over American decisions with regard to future deployment decisions.

Because there is a Soviet dimension to arms control matters, the

Joint Intelligence Committee plays a role as well. Since Soviet relations have such a high security element, the intelligence services also
play a notable role in the policy process. In this case, the security
services all feed into the system directly, at a very high political level:
the director-generals of MI5 and MI6 have direct access to the prime
minister and are responsible only to her. The allied intelligence
services, the Defense Intelligence staff, the intelligence assessments
of the General Communications Headquarters in Cheltenham, the
Foreign and Commonwealth Office, and the Home Office, or Northern
Ireland Office, all feed into the system via the Cabinet Office Assessment Staff and thence to the Joint Intelligence Committee. The Cabinet Office therefore plays a crucial coordinating role. With a very
small but highly expert staff, it assesses the Soviet Union and recommends policy to the small group of ministers who will advise the
prime minister on policy. The Cabinet Office is, however, more notable for its liaison function that for its long-term planning.[20]

In general, the views of the cabinet on foreign and defense matters,
including arms control policy, are relatively unimportant. What
counts is the prime minister's opinion and, to a lesser extent, the views
of the foreign secretary and the secretary of defence. It should be noted
that in a cabinet which consists very much of Mrs. Thatcher's loyal
supporters, these two ministers are among the most loyal. Also, the
prime minister rarely holds more than one meeting of the full cabinet
per week, which does not allow it the opportunity to exercise control
over the details of conventional policy. As Peter Hennessy has noted,
"Judged by the frequency of meetings and the flow of formal cabinet
papers, full cabinet activity under Mrs. Thatcher is at an historical low.
So, too, is the workload being devolved to cabinet committees."[21]

Over the last few years it has become increasingly clear that effective political control in Britain does not lie in the full cabinet. With
regard to foreign and defense matters the prime minister relies on the
Overseas and Defence Subcommittee of the cabinet, chaired by her,
on which is represented a range of departmental interests and which
deals with most of the FCO and MOD business that requires ministerial
approval.[22] Furthermore, in crisis situations involving the prime minister it is the normal practice of the British government for the routine
machinery to be superceded by a smaller group of ministers. For
example, Peter Nailor has noted the following: "The practice was
followed for the Falklands Campaign in 1982, and clearly has instru-

mental utility in shortening the chain-of-decision between, for example, the Prime Minister and the Chief of the Defence Staff. The membership of such groups is not fixed, but is determined appropriately. The Falklands combination included the Chancellor of the Duchy of Lancaster, Cecil Parkinson, who was given a responsibility for the ministerial co-ordination of the 'information war' halfway through the crisis. It seems to have been an expedient in the sense that his responsibility was not well defined, but clearly had its origins in the confidence felt by the Prime Minister in Parkinson in so far as he was also at the time the Chairman of the Conservative Party."[23]

In addition, the prime minister relies on a key minister to form the core of a working group to advise her. As Peter Hennessy has noted: "Mrs. Thatcher will ask a particular Cabinet colleague to prepare a paper on a particular issue just for her, not for the Cabinet or a Cabinet committee. This explains why the tally of Cabinet papers is so low. The Minister is summoned to No. 10 with his back-up team. He sits across the table from Mrs. Thatcher and her team, which can be a mixture of people from the Downing Street Private Office, the Policy Unit and the Cabinet Office, with one or two personal advisers and sometimes a Treasury minister. She then, in the words of one insider, proceeds to 'act as judge and jury in her own cause.' It is this practice more than anything else which causes those on the inside to speak of 'a devaluation of Cabinet government' and her 'presidential style.' "[24]

This is not to say that the cabinet does not matter. As a senior British civil servant has put it:

> The Cabinet system has been different for Heath, Wilson, and Mrs. Thatcher. There's a reaction, which we can get in our constitution, to suit the PM of the day and his or her working relationships. The decisions get taken in the way in which people want to take them. . . . Mrs. Thatcher is very clear about her views, very much a leader. Because of that she doesn't need or want to resolve things by collective discussion. She knows what she wants to do about almost everything. But it is a collective machine because they all sink or swim with her. *She uses the Cabinet as a sort of sounding board.* It restrains her when restraint is necessary. She has her own instinct when she cannot carry her colleagues with her. She lets them know what she thinks. Then they try and adapt and mold it. She has very acute antenna. *She's very quick to take the signals if she can't carry it.*[25]

Former secretary of state for foreign policy—Sir Geoffrey Howe—is clearly more committed to the European option for Britain in the defense and security area than has been Mrs. Thatcher. His views were put most succinctly and forcefully in his speech before the Belgian Royal Institute of International Relations on March 16, 1987: "Developments in recent months, from the Reykjavík Summit to the prospect of an INF agreement, underline the need for the European countries to consult more closely among themselves about their defense interests as well as with the Americans. A Europe which gets its own ideas straight is a far more rewarding partner for the United States; and far more likely to have its views taken seriously than a Europe which speaks with a multitude of voices. If we want our particular European concerns to be clearly perceived and taken into account in negotiations between the United States and the Soviet Union, then we must argue them out clearly among ourselves and come wherever possible to a common view."[26]

The past two secretaries of state for defence have also been more inclined to take a European orientation in defense and arms control matters. Michael Heseltine resigned in part over the Westland affair, because of the prime minister's unwillingness to back him in his negotiations with Britain's key European allies in an attempt to develop a consortium to save Westland from being purchased by the American helicopter company Sikorsky.[27] The next defence minister, George Younger, also seems to have grasped that Reykjavík posed the question of the need for such a shift, but as with virtually all sitting ministers of defence he remains much more oriented toward the United States in Britain's security policy. Nonetheless, Younger too has used the Europeanization theme, for example, during the Wehrkunde Conference in 1987: "... while the other nations of Europe have followed their own various routes, we have all reached much the same destination. We have maintained strong bilateral relations with the United States; but nonetheless the transatlantic relationship is increasingly seen in European rather than purely national terms."[28]

The Foreign and Commonwealth Office

On day-to-day arms control policy the FCO is the lead department in the British government. The FCO civil servants involved in arms control issues are highly intelligent and competent analysts of the diplomatic context of East-West relations. They rarely, however, are specialists in the details of arms control issues prior to becoming involved in the area. On the average, ordinary FCO officials hold their positions for two years before they move on to new ones. Also, there is no policy of involving them in one generic area over a period of time. They are supposed to be enlightened amateurs, and they are rewarded in their careers for a demonstrated ability to move around successfully.

The practice within the FCO of circulating officials out of areas of specialization within two to three years can create problems of institutional memory in the arms control area. The civil service, particularly the FCO, is quite aware of these problems of collective memory. The consequence is to impose an even stronger drive toward consensus. Officials in the Arms Control and Disarmament Research Unit sometimes think their entire job is to act as historians—trying to work out what lay behind some phrase used in a draft treaty years before. Many of those in the FCO feel the heavy pressure of precedent on them when negotiating or analyzing positions. Had they themselves held the post for a long time, or, even better, had they or a colleague been involved in the previous discussion, they might feel freer to deviate, but instead they have to proceed with great caution. In spite of difficulties of institutional memory, the sheer intellectual capability of FCO officials who work in the arms control area has enabled the FCO to play a key role in shaping the flow of information on arms control policy. As in other areas of foreign policy, the control of specialized information in what is often an arcane area allows FCO civil servants to aid in the determination of British policy on a day-to-day basis.

In addition to his other important responsibilities, the senior minister of state is engaged in arms control matters.[29] For example, during Thatcher's second term, Timothy Renton's formal responsibilities were for the Near, Middle, and Far East, Southeast Asia, Hong Kong, defense, arms control, and disarmament, as well as nuclear energy, but his primary effort was in the defense and arms control area. In general, junior ministers do play an important role in the formulation of policy in the British government.[30] Although a great deal of work is done at the bureaucratic level, many major decisions are finally resolved at the level of junior minister, and certainly in the current government there has been a lively interaction between junior ministers in the FCO and in the Ministry of Defence on a wide number of policy issues which could be resolved at the bureaucratic level.

At the next level of significance in the FCO are the very senior civil servants involved in arms control matters. The highest-ranking civil servants in the FCO are permanent under secretaries (grade 1). Directly under these are two deputy under secretaries, one charged with responsibility for arms control and the other responsible for bilateral relations. The deputy under secretary is responsible for arms control policy and is aided by an assistant under secretary of state who has been directly charged with arms control matters. The three officials who have held this position since 1983 were, successively John Westin, Timothy Daunt, and Brian Fall. The chain of command runs from the deputy under secretary to the assistant under secretary to the arms control departments.

As of 1987 there were three departments charged directly with responsibility for arms control matters. The most significant is the Arms Control and Disarmament Department (ACDD), which with twelve administration-class officials is one of the biggest in the FCO. Prior to January 1, 1987, ACDD included the Arms Control and Disarmament Research Unit (ACDRU), but after this date ACDRU was separated from ACDD and became a Foreign Office department in its own right. It was given its own head of department (that is, a civil servant at grade 4 level), an assistant, and three administrative officers who deal with the publicity side of arms control policy. The strength of the research staff has been augmented by one further senior research officer, who is not on a contract but is rather a full member of the FCO's research cadre. ACDRU, in fact, closely monitors public interest, carrying out, for example, the sort of analysis of letters from the public that might be routine in U. S. public administration but is very rare in Britain. (Traditionally, foreign policy has been regarded as to some extent insulated from electoral politics and has certainly been of negligible importance in electoral choice.)

The major remaining department directly involved in arms control policy is the Defence Department. Most of the arms control portfolio has been stripped away, but it does retain authority over conventional arms control issues, namely, CDE, CSCE, and MBFR. The department is headed by an effective career civil servant, Paul Lever, who is of first-rate intellectual caliber.

Other departments are only indirectly involved in arms control issues but because of their responsibilities are concerned with the effect of arms control issues on their geographic or functional areas. The Planning Staff becomes involved in arms control issues primarily as an adjunct to their effort to advise the foreign minister on the evolution of the foreign policy environment and to assist him in his speech-writing tasks.

In addition to the Planning Staff, several geographic departments are involved in shaping arms control assessments. The most significant of these is the Soviet Department, which provides input in the process of assessing the evolution of the Soviet challenge to the United Kingdom and advises FCO officials on the evolution of Soviet arms control proposals. British governmental assessments of Soviet views on arms control come almost entirely from the Soviet Department. Virtually all the British Sovietologists in government work in the Soviet Department, and the government's political-military analysis comes from them. In addition, the West European and North American departments are important in providing essentially political intelligence assessments supplementing arms control evaluations. But they play only a marginal role, whereby they react to initiatives taken elsewhere in the government.

To some extent one can identify an FCO perspective on arms control. Above all, given the career pattern of civil servants who pass through the arms control area, they are not likely to be oriented toward excessively technical discussions of arms control issues. Because they work primarily in the East-West area, they are most likely to see arms control issues in broad political terms. Also, given the approach of the civil service in general to problem solving, they are likely to be attracted to pragmatic and incrementalist solutions. As William Wallace, director of research of the Royal Institute of International Affairs, has noted:

> . . . the flow of foreign policy through the Whitehall structure in a "normal" case follows well-established paths through well-worn procedures. Only major innovations or changes in direction rise to the Cabinet; the regular management of policy is conducted by officials. The number of men directly and actively involved in the management of a particular issue, writing briefs and instructions, initiating decisions, is likely to be small, perhaps ten or a dozen; but the number drawn in less actively

on any complicated issue—reading the files, commenting on proposals, attending interdepartmental meetings—will often be very considerable. The pressure of business at the higher levels operates to hold down less "urgent" matters to a lower level, to define incoming problems as falling within established guidelines and to manage them according to routine.[31]

FCO officials are concerned, of course, with shaping American positions in the arms control area. It should be noted that just as FCO officials do not think in generic terms of "arms control" but rather about specific control areas, they do not form a blanket judgment about American arms control endeavors. Nor, for that matter, do they really see the United States as having one policy or stance in any one area. Rather, the professionals in the FCO sharply distinguish among different U. S. agencies. In general, the FCO is happy with both State and Arms Control and Disarmament Agency (ADCA) but feels that the U. S. position in arms control, especially in the Reagan years, has often been too heavily, and negatively, influenced by the Department of Defense (DOD). For example, one version of verification requirements for chemical convention known as CD500 was interpreted by the FCO as a hard-line proposal by the United States, heavily influenced by DOD, which was intended to be unacceptable to the USSR.

The FCO is under no illusion at all about the strength of its influence in Washington, whatever the prime minister may believe about the "special relationship." Officials know that they have very limited political capital and see themselves using it most sparingly. The usual FCO argument is that it needs to reserve this limited capital for things that really matter.

The FCO is more than prepared, furthermore, to aid ministers in any effort to promote the European as opposed to the transatlantic dimension of British arms control policy. The FCO has become the key European office in Whitehall. The FCO is much less transatlantic than the MOD and is increasingly frustrated with American policy. The MOD thinks in Anglo-American terms; the FCO talks in Anglo-American terms but thinks in European ones.

The Ministry of Defence

Although also involved in arms control issues, the Ministry of Defence is clearly subordinate to the FCO in the day-to-day process. Its role in arms control is decisively affected by that of the minister of defence. If the minister is a forceful member of the cabinet who perceives arms control to be an important part of his role, then the organizational elements within the MOD that deal with arms control will be elevated in importance. Otherwise, MOD units dealing with arms control matters (currently the defense policy components in MOD as well as the Defence Arms Control Unit [DACU]) play their major roles not only by advising the minister on arms control matters, but in providing MOD input to the process spearheaded by the FCO. In other words, DACU and the defense policy components in the MOD deal directly with the FCO as well as with their hierarchical superiors in the MOD.

The evolution of the DACU provides some sense of the importance of ministerial support to ensuring that arms control becomes an MOD priority. DACU was created by Secretary of Defence Michael Heseltine as part of a major reshaping of the Ministry of Defence in 1985. The overall restructuring was much in line with contemporary American debates about the structure of DOD and was principally intended to centralize and unify policy-making and advice to the ministerial head. Thus, for example, the chief of the defence staff was given more authority and control and became less like the chairman of the Joint Chiefs in DOD. The creation of a unit dealing with arms control that reported directly to the minister of defence rather than via the permanent secretary was a key component of the restructuring. In the past, Section 17 of the Defence Secretariat did do arms control analysis, but this was filtered through the usual process of civil service briefing.

The necessary assumption of attaching DACU directly to the minister is a simple one: the minister of defence must actually be interested in the topic and want to take advice from DACU. Herein lies the problem, because if he does not particularly want to hear from DACU, it can very easily be isolated bureaucratically. Heseltine created the unit, apart from the reason already given, for two other purposes. First, the House of Commons Select Committee on Defence urged the MOD to take some sort of initiative in the area, because the members of the committee were concerned with Foreign Office dominance, especially under some future government where the Defence Ministry would not have the respect it has from the current prime minister. Second, it suited Mr. Heseltine's own interests, because he wished to be able to argue strongly in the cabinet, and he is well known for distrusting advice coming through routine civil service channels.

There is no evidence that his successor, George Younger, holds any of these views. In fact, DACU has not been able to play the role envisaged by Heseltine. It has gradually become bureaucratically subordinate to the deputy under secretary for policy. DACU has essentially become a secretariat dealing with arms control problems for the MOD. Although it has the formal right to deal directly with the minister of defence, it is much more concerned on a day-to-day basis with coordination of MOD perspectives on arms control issues.

DACU was created outside the usual chain of authority, which was designed to give it much more influence than in the past. In addition, it now has military officers integrated into its table of organization; before, it was purely civilian. Its organization is basically to have a civilian official as head of each section and as overall head of DACU, with military officers as deputies to each such official. As a result, there is considerably greater integration of perspective, and DACU's advice to the minister is less likely to be attacked, even dismissed, at the chief of staff level.

DACU's perception of its own role is naturally enough that of protector of MOD interests in dealing with the Foreign Office's pursuit of international agreements. It must be said at the outset that any such clashes are more likely to come about because of technical misunderstandings or disagreements between the Foreign Office and the MOD than because the FCO takes a radically different approach to the "Soviet threat." Not only is the FCO, as has been argued, not particularly "dovish," but the MOD's analyses are far from being as "hawkish" as might be expected. For example, DACU, and indeed the MOD, in general, tend not to be very interested in the sort of "worst case" threat assessment that often characterizes military bureaucracies. The reason is very simple and is freely admitted by senior British military officers—the United Kingdom cannot afford to defend against the worst case, and it makes for very inefficient planning. DACU's secondary role is to act as a counter inside the MOD to any too narrowly military perspective, to ensure that the secretary for defence does not oppose arms control initiatives in the cabinet unless there really is an overwhelming defense issue at stake. As such, it treads a rather narrow line. The civilian officials make the point that service inside DACU does indeed tend to change the perspectives of military officers themselves, and the unit ends up, whether or not it wishes it, having something of a proselytizing role.

An interesting piece of evidence about DACU's orientation comes from the attitude of its civilian officials to the various U. S. agencies operating in the arms control field. Naturally, they talk to anyone and everyone from the United States and interchange with all the relevant bureaus. They do not, however, think of themselves, as might be expected, as paired with DOD. The typical view in DACU is that it is the State Department with which they can most easily cooperate.

The final element within the MOD that has a minor role in arms control policy is the Defence Intelligence Staff. This unit is oriented toward the nuts and bolts of military intelligence and relies heavily on the NATO framework for the development and evaluation of data. It can provide an assessment of the impact of arms control policy on the military balance and upon British forces. To the extent to which this is treated as important by ministers, Defence Intelligence has a role to play. In the British system of government, however, arms control is not treated as primarily a technical task of evaluating the impacts of agreements on force structure. As a result, Defence Intelligence plays a clearly subordinate role.

It was argued in the last section that the MOD is more Atlanticist in orientation than the FCO. While this continues to be true, several senior officials in the MOD are becoming more convinced of the necessity for a Europeanization process. Certainly the Reykjavík summit has had its effect, but the process of evolution had begun before this fascinating example of the theater of American politics.

Other Governmental Players

The role of the major embassies and delegations. The major embassies provide assessments of developments in key countries affecting the political-military area and shaping arms control. The most important embassy for the British on political-military matters is, of course, Washington. The ambassador and his political counselor, as well as the specialist on political-military affairs, are the most significant members of the embassy in assessing U. S. developments. The current ambassador, Sir Antony Ackland, served for several years as the highest-ranking civil servant in the FCO. During his tenure to date Sir Antony has focused primarily on political-economic matters, not political-military ones, but his assessments of the state of the American mind have been influential in Whitehall. Stephen Bond, his political counselor, has served for a long period of time as the specialist on political-military affairs. He is well informed on U. S. developments, and his recent promotion may pave the way for him to replace Michael Pakenham in his post. The current specialist on political-military affairs, Richard Clarke, has worked for some time in the arms control area. His last posting was as the desk officer for MBFR in the Arms Control and Disarmament Department of the FCO.

The embassies in Bonn and Paris link Whitehall with developments in Germany and France. Until 1988, the embassy in Bonn was headed by Sir Julian Bullard, who has spent many years in the East-West area. Sir Julian has worked quite effectively in ensuring that close consultation occurs between the British and Germans on security matters. He has been a proponent of the importance of the Anglo-German relationship to the future of NATO Europeanization. According to a speech by Sir Julian in 1985, the Anglo-German defense cooperation relationship is a "model" for European cooperation more generally. He noted as well that "the British nuclear deterrent is the only European nuclear capability committed to the defense of the Federal Republic."[32]

The embassy in Paris is headed by Ewin Ferguson, who has worked for a number of years on Third World issues. His number two was John Westin, a former key official in the FCO on arms control matters who has recently gone to the cabinet office. This embassy obviously is interested in enhancing Franco-British cooperation, an effort officials recognized: "The United Kingdom has enjoyed a close and fruitful dialogue with the French Government on a wide range of defence and security matters, including some nuclear matters, and our policy is to continue and enhance that dialogue."[33]

Other embassies and delegations have been important as well. For example, the head of the MBFR delegation in 1985 was the initial formulator of the basic British input into what became known as the December 5th proposal. He spent a good deal of time working with his colleagues in Whitehall (that is, both FCO and MOD) to ensure that the British initiative in the conventional arms control area was kept on track.

The role of Parliament. The most important point to consider when evaluating the role of Parliament in foreign and defense matters is that it is not at all to be confused with the role of the U. S. Congress in such matters. Parliament, unlike Congress, has neither the extensive resources for assessing British policy nor the desire, broadly speaking, to do so. The parliamentary parties are not geared up to develop complex defense policies. The Commons Select Committee on Defence does not begin to approximate the House Armed Services Committee. During the 1983–87 Parliament, it had only eleven members—three Labour and eight Conservative. It is not privy to the confidential briefings a U. S. congressional committee has, and has virtually no staff. Therefore it cannot redress the lack of information and professional amateurishness of party leaders.

During the 1983–87 Parliament there were perhaps twenty M. P.s regularly involved in defense and arms control issues among the whole parliamentary opposition, and they probably had no more than a dozen staffers involved even roughly full time on these issues. Of the M. P.s, only three had government experience at all, and one, a Labour backbencher, had no influence within his party because he was marked out as an Atlanticist. The Liberal and SDP spokesmen had never held higher offices. Neither the MOD nor the FCO provide briefings for opposition party spokesmen, and neither the House of Commons nor their parties give spokesmen research help. As one of them put it: "I'm also the party spokesman on Europe, and I can't phone Germany unless I pay out of my own pocket." As a consequence, one cannot expect subtle or complex views on arms control to be expressed by British parliamentarians—the media and some research institutes are basically the only sources of information and ideas for the whole of the opposition. It is obvious, therefore, that arms control policy thinking will be crude and highly ideological, and the issues tend to be discussed in disarmament terms.

The general role of Parliament in foreign policy and defense matters is limited. The debates and question periods in the Commons and Lords do provide a setting for argument, primarily on ideological and party grounds, for or against a policy. It is not a setting conducive to raising the British public's level of understanding. Controversial subjects raised to a level of public debate can be elevated in public concern by a combination of press and parliamentary coverage. Debates on points of controversy can, obviously, have an impact on public perceptions of the nature of defense issues. The intensity of the debate on defense among the parties in the past few years has been fanned by the use of a combination of parliamentary debate and the exposure of varying party positions in the press.

Thus Parliament does not play a critical role in the determination of foreign and defense policy. As Michael Clarke has noted: "Debates tend to be generalized, ill-informed and ritualistic. Question time is not noted for its penetrating political analysis, though the volume of questions has grown considerably. And early day motions are more a reflection of the prevailing state of Government-Parliament relations. House of Lords committees are a good source of indirect influence— what the party will or will not accept from its leadership. These devices allow parliament to play some role in foreign policy, but it is an indirect one. Parliament can act as a general restraint, however, on a government's foreign policy."[34]

The Select Committee on Defence, however, has played a role of growing importance since its formation in 1979. According to a well-placed M.P., the committee has been increasingly useful as a channel of communication between the executive and the public in shaping "realistic and accurate" judgments on the issues confronting the public today in the area of defense. The role of the committee is to examine the implementation of policy rather than the options for policy. Given the hunger of the British media for facts of any sort in the defense area, the Select Committee on Defence can play a role in placing some factual data in the public domain. However, as Paul Silk has noted, "the Defence Committee—eleven M.P.s backed by a permanent staff of five— cannot hope to investigate anything more than a tiny proportion of the ministry's work."[35] According to Michael Clarke, "it is clear that the Select Committees are an evolutionary development and may be expected to gain authority and constitutional stature in the future. The fact remains, however, that eight or nine years after their introduction, these Select Committees still have no real power save the power of publicity. Their reports do not have to be debated in the Commons or anywhere else. If they fail to capture headlines, they fail to carry any real political weight. In some respects the Committee system holds great promise for an increased role for Parliament in foreign and defence affairs. But it has yet to affect the concentration of policy-making, initiative, critique and evaluation which presently resides within Whitehall and the executive."[36]

The ability of Parliament to exercise general restraint on government policy is accomplished through the Parliamentary Conservative party. The attitudes of backbenchers are canvassed by the parliamentary leadership on important issues and are clearly a factor shaping cabinet decision making. The prime minister and cabinet must be concerned not only with the reactions of the general public to government policy (which are tested on a three-to-five-year basis at election time) but with the attitudes of the backbench about the exercise of influence. The backbench Committee on Defence is one means whereby backbenchers exercise influence. This committee was chaired by Sir Antony Buck during the 1983–87 Parliament; it was prodefense but not necessarily supportive on every detail of government policy. Members of the committee have been critical of the size of expenditure necessary to fund Trident, concerned with the drawdown of conventional forces, and are especially concerned with the future of the Royal Navy. Backbench committees also facilitate contact with ministers. For example, the officers of the Foreign Affairs Group meet with the foreign secretary each month. Also, forces such as the "navy lobby," led in part by Keith Speed, the former navy minister, can affect the public debate about the priorities of defense spending.

Furthermore, past reactions by backbenchers can affect perceptions of the prospects for future policy. For example, the prime minister agreed to support the American decision to bomb Libya using U. S. bombers based in Britain primarily due to the "chit" she owed the American administration for their support of her in the Falklands War. Several backbenchers informed the Commons leadership that they would support the government's decision "this time" but not in the future. The anger expressed by Conservative backbenchers in the month after the bombing cannot be understated. In part it was due to the perceived sense of vulnerability the Tories felt over the American base issue in British politics.

The Opposition and Arms Control, 1983–87

This section analyzes the development of the opposition's views on arms control policy from the early 1980s up to the June 1987 election. The future of the opposition's perspectives on arms control and its behavior in the 1987 election is dealt with in the final section of this chapter.

The Labour Party

Before proceeding, it is essential to make one point about the internal politics of the Labour party. Everyone knows that the British Labour party suffered terrible internal division and crippling fights between Left and Right in the few years following its devastating defeat by the Conservatives in 1979. However, from 1985 onward an appearance of much greater unity was projected. In a large part this is because the leader, Neil Kinnock, systematically moved the party rightwards and stood up to the left wing and more or less defeated them in the party conferences and through party disciplinary proceedings. What is less well known is that the divisions in some policy areas have not been reconciled at all—they simply went underground, became private, or were hidden because of the need for unity in the electoral marketplace. Nowhere was this more true than in the foreign policy/defense area. Two teams of parliamentary spokesmen have been relevant to the articulation of Labour party foreign/defense policy. The defense team was nominally under the leadership of Denzil Davies, but actually it was under Kinnock's own direct control, and the foreign policy team was under the leadership of Denis Healey. The defense team has been solidly unilateralist; otherwise they could not keep their posts. In 1981 the entire team of five spokesmen on defense issues was fired because they were not committed enough to unilateral nuclear disarmament. Most of them were appointed instead to the foreign policy team. Under Healey's leadership they have remained one of the two nuclei of Atlanticist-nuclear feeling in a party whose leader, defense team, parliamentary majority, and mass membership are unabashedly unilateralist on defense and arms control issues. The rivalry is intense, though quiet. (The other nucleus has been the Labour party members of the Select Committee on Defence.)

The question for future policy formation and public opinion formation throughout the 1980s was this: Suppose a Labour government formed. Which team would dominate in cabinet; which ministry would be paramount in international negotiation? On the whole, the foreign affairs team was abler and much more sensitive to American perspectives. Politically, however, it was weak within the party and existed because of Denis Healey's protection. Healey was the most senior and ministerially experienced of the leadership group. He was secretary for defence as long ago as 1964—some Labour party members even talk of the McNamara-Healey policy of flexible response, rather than the McNamara-Kennedy policy. But he has been an elder statesman of the party and too old to be a factor if a Labour administration had been elected in 1987.

Kinnock and his defense team. There is a sense in which the Labour party has been not greatly interested in arms control, either as an American-Soviet interaction or as a British effort. This is, first, because party leaders have made no distinction between arms control policy and defense policy as far as Britain is concerned. For example, although Healey as foreign affairs spokesman naturally has spoken on arms control, it was actually Denzil Davies, Kinnock's appointee, whose official title was "chief spokesman on defence and arms control." Second, they simply did not believe that either superpower would make any genuine arms control move, that is give up a weapons system for which they would have any real use. Consequently, Labour's general defense policy for Britain is, in effect, its arms control policy. Consequently, foreign disarmament policy is the cutting edge of defense policy.

The Labour party lost the 1983 election (according to its own analysis, anyway) on defense policy. As a result, it made a very serious effort to create a more coherent policy expressing a socialist view of defense and international conflict. This was largely embodied in a National Executive Committee statement approved by the 1984 annual conference, *Defence and Security for Britain.* In its turn, this document drew heavily on a quasi-private venture by a panel of experts on defense under the aegis of the Lansbury Trust, published in 1983 as *Defence without the Bomb.*[37] Whatever one thinks of this, it certainly is the most coherent and deliberately planned policy in this area that the Labour party has had since the 1930s. The central thesis of it has been that international confidence rests on producing a "genuinely defensive deterrent," or a "nonprovocative defense." The central objective is to turn Britain into a non-nuclear state, which would require NATO to change its policy of flexible response in order for Britain to stay within the alliance. The implication of Labour's defense policy for arms control is clear. It is hard to see how a country could contribute more effectively to an international arms control effort than by: (1) giving up its own strategic and theater nuclear weapons unilaterally; (2) removing its ally's theater and tactical nuclear weapons and bases; and (3) urging the challenge of its alliance's nuclear-based general strategy to one that not only accepts "no first use" as an immediate step but aims rapidly at removing the capacity to use any form of nuclear weapon—not just the intention but the capacity. In short, what more could Britain do than give up all its own nuclear weapons? What greater pressure could it apply to the United States than expelling U. S. nuclear bases? What further gesture could it make to the USSR or to European allies?

Labour policy, furthermore, has been based on a specific theory about disarmament. The arms race, it has been argued, was never intended by anyone but has been a consequence of an action-reaction cycle. This means that any major arms reduction move by a nuclear-armed nation may well produce a matching reduction by another, which would set off its own negative action-reaction cycle, leading to a general global reduction in nuclear and perhaps conventional armaments. There is, of course, a reverse side to this—if the United Kingdom does all this gratuitously, what leverage will it have thereafter?[38] Just as there is no specific nuclear arms control policy because the independent defense plans incorporate everything that might be asked, there is no need of a conventional arms control policy. The plans for conventional arms policy, however, are very far-reaching in incorporating the idea of nonprovocative defense. They totally reject Follow-on Forces Attack (FOFA) or any version of DeepStrike/ Airland Battle 2000. Some enthusiasts want to talk about replacing main battle tanks entirely with antitank weapons, and it has been semiofficial policy to shorten the range of NATO aircraft (as well as physically removing "dual capacity" from nuclear-capable aircraft). Throughout, the argument is the same: If a nation makes itself genuinely incapable of conducting an offense, arms control is irrelevant, for disarmament will be achieved. Furthermore, if the country really wishes for general moral reasons to give up some forms of weapons systems, there is neither point nor justification in hanging on to them as bargaining chips in East-West negotiations. Perhaps nothing impresses the British Left less than the idea of building, say, an MX, missile in order to give it up to gain a concession from the USSR; as a result, the Labour party did not anticipate the double zero proposal of the superpowers in INF.

Throughout the 1980s, analysts and the electorate have wondered whether a Labour government would actually implement its defense policy. Are Labour leaders really so sure of their own diagnosis that they are genuinely uninterested in arms control events and possibilities? Do they really see no role for the United Kingdom other than implementing their separately motivated disarmament policy?

First, the role of the party leader in this area must be clear. Neil

Kinnock dragged the party from its 1983 debacle to a position where it was perceived that it could win an election by dropping nearly all its radical policies. He made it very clear, in public and privately to his shadow cabinet, that defense was the one area in which the party would not be moderate. In a letter to his senior members after the 1985 party conference, he expressly vetoed the idea that defense policy could, like all other policies, be moderated for electoral reasons. Friends and foes of Kinnock alike stressed throughout the period prior to the 1987 election that Kinnock had a very deep personal commitment to unilateralism. They all went on to say that he needed to keep this one policy "ideologically pure" precisely because it was the major left-wing policy left in the manifesto. This view, which encompassed both a faith in the individual and a slightly cynical estimate of his political requirements, was expressed, for example, by his close friend, political dependent and fellow unilateralist Denzil Davies, the ranking defence spokesman. Kinnock did not bring the party under control without making many enemies on the left, and throughout 1985 and 1986 his own position in the party looked less than secure. It is clear, then, that any change in the policy would have been over the opposition of the leader.

The Labour party itself seems solidly unilateralist as well. Apart from the leader and his shadow cabinet, the relevant actors are the mass members as they are reflected in the delegates chosen to attend the party conference and the Parliamentary Labour party (PLP), that is, the elected Labour M. P.s. Votes in the party conference in the last few years have left no doubt as to the desires of the party members— it is only with difficulty that the leadership has been able to defeat motions to withdraw from NATO altogether. As far as the PLP goes, our interviews suggest that there was a unilateralist majority.

However, what would the majority of the party look like if it increased to the three hundred or more M. P.s needed to be the largest party in the Commons? We are talking here of the sort of Labour candidates who could win in marginal constituencies. In the U. S. context this would mean, automatically, moderate candidates. In Britain the situation is quite different. Marginal constituencies are those with a relatively large middle class, and therefore a middle-class-dominated Labour party. These are precisely the constituency parties which select radical candidates. (It is a feature of British politics that working-class Labour voters are more right wing on anything but economic/welfare "bread and butter" issues than middle-class Socialists.) Unilateralism is exactly the sort of issue on which the middle-class Socialists are radical. It seems very likely that a PLP of three hundred members would have a fairly strong majority of unilateralist candidates. Some internal party commentators have guessed at a 70 to 80 percent unilateralist majority.

It is rather more fruitful to turn to the opposition inside the party, represented by the Foreign Affairs Group and the Labour members of the Select Committee on Defence. There is, however, one quite serious point of agreement between the Left and the Right that has helped bridge party divisions. Underneath the political cynicism that has been common to most British political leaders when they talk privately about arms control is an intelligent and well-taken concern. As put by the defence spokesman, it is this: All previous arms control agreements have related to past stages of weapons technology. The ABM treaty came about when both sides decided they could not build an effective system, atmospheric test banning happened after the United States and the USSR had finished designing fusion weapons, SALTs I and II came into being only after MIRVing had been accomplished. There has been a very strong sense that the important aspect of arms control refers to preventing development, and that arms control, as we have known it, has consequently been fruitless. The idea of creating limits on future development is most clearly expressed by the right wing of the party, but there is no doubt that another arms control treaty which does not enshrine the idea of stopping development will not appeal to the left wing.

Healey and the foreign affairs team. The right wing of the party made real concessions to the new policies in the defense area, however much they may regret it. Mr. Healey has been instrumental in this effort. As late as the election campaign of 1983, he was denouncing official party policy to scrap Polaris, insisting that it should be kept to negotiate at least something from the Soviet Union. In the face of the brute fact that this option was not available, he accepted, at least in public, the three main points of policy—canceling Trident, decommissioning Polaris, and sending cruise back. However, he has tried to offer a rather different interpretation of why these are sensible policies, and he has been very much more concerned with international arms control. Healey and his supporters have essentially argued for the obsolescence of nuclear deterrence. Much of what they proclaimed could be taken from another nuclear "recanter" of his generation, for Healey has sounded like the modern Robert McNamara, and his group like the "gang of four." As such, it has been vital for them both to push for specified U. S. arms control measures and to show how Britain could contribute to international arms control development.

A good example of the difference between Healey and Kinnock is that Healey was a founding member of the new British version of the "freeze" campaign, which set itself up as a more moderate, all-party rival to the Campaign for Nuclear Disarmament, while Kinnock has been a member of the CND itself, and his wife is a very public activist in it. Healey's version of arms control has been that the real risk lies not in current armament levels but in potential future developments, of which SDI is seen as the most important element. Thus he advocated a total freeze on new weapon developments and, as the major instrument of this, a complete ban on all nuclear testing. As a nuclear power still involved in testing, albeit by courtesy of Nevada, Britain could, therefore, play a role. Verification has not been seen as a serious problem, and he and his group have made much of Gorbachev's offers to allow on-site inspection.

The group searched far and wide for a role for Britain to play. One suggestion made by Healey himself, in a parliamentary debate, was to stop modernization of the Flyingdales radar station in return for the halting of the Krasnoyarsk installation in the USSR. This sector of Labour party opinion was much more concerned by SDI than by any existing development. Healey has, again in Parliament, sought to force the government to make public the terms of the SDI research agreement signed between the British and U. S. governments. In contrast, mainstream Labour spokesmen committed themselves to tearing up the agreement if they came to power, whatever the terms may be. Differences between the two groups seemed slim, but this was largely because the right wing tried to be as quiet and compliant as possible.

Attitudes to FOFA and Airland Battle 2000 are good indicators of the differences as well. Both Davies, as defense spokesman, and Healey, as foreign affairs spokesman, have opposed these programs. For Davies and the official policy document, the opposition to FOFA was a blanket one because the policy is seen as an inherently aggressive posture. For Healey, the problem has been that Airland Battle 2000 appears to involve the use of nuclear weapons and, perhaps even worse, chemical and biological weapons. Furthermore, Healey objected on tactical grounds that concentration on Soviet third-echelon forces may be inappropriate. All of this could be summed up by comparing attitudes to the classic "no first use" debate. To the Left, the argument has been pointless—they intend to work inside NATO to shift it to an entirely non-nuclear stance. Healey's people, however, accept the fact of conventional disparity and do not believe that all tactical nuclear weapons could be abandoned. Yet without some gesture they could point to as evidence of American arms control, they would have no arguments against the dominant Left. A "no first use" declaration, or even an accelerated withdrawal of obsolete and surplus short-range tactical nuclear warheads, would be at least something.

However, the real sticking point has been on nuclear testing. Given Healey's analysis of where the real threat to stability lies, namely new weapons development, a nuclear test ban treaty would be the most useful American contribution. Deep cuts, though impressive, would not get around Europe's sense that the armories are too large anyway, and in addition they invite the suspicion that smaller forces would just be all the more modernized. Of course, a test ban treaty might also imply the abandonment of SDI, but all sectors of opposition politics in Britain are formally opposed to SDI, which they have interpreted as likely to be deployed primarily to defend ICBMs.

One thing that united the Kinnock and Healey factions was their shared sense that NATO strategy, including arms control, has not been under adequate political supervision. Healey, for example, remarked, "Unfortunately nuclear strategy in the West today tends to be determined by tiny elites of middle-ranking bureaucrats and staff officers who have no personal experience of world war and are obsessed by esoteric theories. . . . These elites are predominantly civilian and are under no effective civilian control." Similarly, left-wing defense spokesmen have all commented on the U. S. graduate school output of "defense analysts."

The Alliance

The Alliance, the coalition between the Social Democratic party and the Liberal party, fought the 1987 election, as it did the 1983 one, on a common program. The two parties were committed to negotiating as a unit with other parties should there be a "hung Parliament" with the possibility of a coalition government. The two parties formed a joint commission in 1986 that tried to iron out an agreed defense policy upon which they could stand for the next election. Compromise was not all that easy because defense has been an issue absolutely crucial to the relatively Atlanticist and nuclearist SDP leadership, especially David Owen, while the Liberal membership, though not its leadership, has unilateralist tendencies.

The outlines of the positions they took to the joint commission are given in a brief section following separate discussions of the two parties. At this stage, two facts about the Alliance's electoral situation are important. First, the Alliance had an electoral pact according to which only one of the two parties could contest any one constituency. Thus, there was no chance of the electorate being offered both an SDP and a Liberal defense policy or being informed separately by the two parties about how they should view the arms control policies of the United States and USSR. The two parties were committed to fighting on a common manifesto, however bland some sections had to be. Whatever was agreed to at the center was the policy everywhere. Second, the political histories of the parties and of their likely voters are very different, so that the actual electoral performance of Alliance candidates fighting under the same defense policy represents a complex mixture of crosscurrents in attitudes. Although it may seem natural to think of a "Left versus Right" spectrum of British politics that runs Labour—SDP—Liberal—Conservative, on the grounds that the SDP is a splinter from the Labour party, this is not a good intellectual model with which to approach defense/arms control issues, for the SDP has been much nearer to the Conservative party than any other on defense issues.

The Social Democratic party. The SDP cared very much about defense policy. This more than any other single issue was what caused the split with the Labour party after the 1979 election defeat. Once the unilateralist tendency gained supremacy inside the party, Labour M.P.s who were both Atlanticist and nuclearist had two choices—get out or shut up. Even resigning oneself to lonely but vocal backbench opposition to the party policy was hardly available as an option. It probably meant loss of one's nomination to contest the constituency in the next election, so strong was the unilateralist grip on the constituency parties. There have been only two vocal opponents of unilateralism on the Labour backbenches in the 1983 to 1987 period—both are on the Commons Defence Committee, and both are lucky to have survived reelection challenges in their constituencies. One indication of how strong the unilateralist position became is that both these men hoped their party would lose the 1987 election. Consequently, the SDP represented the old right wing of the Labour party on defense issues. One secondary consequence of this development was that the "defectors" to the SDP took with them most of the party's experience in the defense area, especially with the defection of David Owen and his supporters (for example, the former shadow Labour defense minister, John Roper).

The SDP leadership has been unlike that of other parties because several of its major figures have been outside parliament. Furthermore, building a party de novo inevitably resulted in the creation of an extraparliamentary elite with a major voice in policy formulation. The SDP had a Council of 200 in semipermanent session, of which the parliamentary party had to take real note. As with the other parties, the only check on policy formulation was an annual conference in which, by and large, the parliamentary delegation had a dominant voice. As it happens, there was no contention between the council and the parliamentary party in the defense area. The mass membership of the party fell into two categories: those who were previously members of the Labour party and left for the same reasons as the parliamentary group, and those who joined subsequently, initiated into politics by the presence of this new force. This latter group, whose only real influence was in the annual conference, was not easy to characterize politically. Its members had diverse motivations and preferences but did not radically depart from the main thrust of party thinking in the defense area. Consequently, we can take the views of the parliamentary representatives in the 1983–87 period as typical of the party's, whose positions were encapsulated thus:

(1) A strong belief that Britain ought to have an independent nuclear deterrent but not Trident
(2) A very strong commitment both to NATO in general and to good defense relations with the United States in particular
(3) A general commitment to high levels of defense expenditure and general agreement with the U. S. perspective on the need to enhance conventional capacity so as to raise the nuclear threshold

(4) Ambiguity but no outright opposition to sdi, the ambiguity being a stronger version of the familiar American position of accepting research with no commitment to implementation

The main difficulty here is the sdp opposition to Trident. Party leaders opposed Trident for two reasons: first, its expense, and second, the major increase in U. K. strategic capacity which Trident represents and which is thus incompatible with the traditional British doctrine of "minimum deterrence." They sought a replacement for Polaris because of the latter's obsolescence, not a deliberate upgrading of U. K. strategic forces. The truth, admitted only in private, was that they opposed Trident mainly because if they did not, there would be no discernible difference between sdp and Tory defense policy. Their problem was twofold—both political and technical. Politically, retaining and then replacing Polaris put them in conflict with the Liberals. Technically, the problem was what it has been for British defense planners since 1978—what alternative is there to Trident? David Owen, their leader, was after all a member of the 1979 Labour cabinet which started the process of acquiring Trident. Owen's position in the sdp as a previous foreign secretary and an effective parliamentary actor was undisputed. The entire Alliance deferred to him on defense and foreign affairs, at least on a day-to-day basis. He has had a fertile imagination when it comes to thinking of Polaris replacements. In general, he favored cruise missiles, either bought from the United States or developed independently. He was in favor of a joint Anglo-French cruise missile, including the purchase of French slbms to fit into new British submarines. His defense spokesman, John Cartwright, stayed loyally silent in public about these plans, even the suggestion about placing cruise on cross-Channel ferries. Cartwright and others have been quite aware of the "sunk cost" aspect of Trident, and it is entirely possible that they would have decided to go ahead with the project in the end if they had been involved in government. The trouble was that no one has found a credible Polaris replacement with guaranteed penetrability against Soviet abm and sam capacity that costs much less than Trident. What the sdp would actually have done would be either to let the Polaris fleet go on without ever creating a replacement or to buy Trident. All they have been concerned with doing at the moment was keeping alive the symbolic existence of an independent British nuclear deterrent without either straining relations with the Liberals or looking too much like the Conservative party. If they did not keep to this policy, they would lose their identity completely.

The Liberal party. The problem for the Liberal party has been that while there is probably a unilateralist majority among party members, there is none among either their natural electorate or the party elite. Unilateralism is not, in fact, new in the Liberal party. As early as 1961, then–party leader Jo Grimond came out against Britain's having an independent nuclear deterrent. During the 1960s and 1970s the Liberals were searching for a way of being "radical" without being socialist, and antinuclear policies, both military and civil, fitted well with environmentalism, participatory democracy, and so on to give them somewhat the same aspect as the West German Green party. However, there has been a hard core of pragmatism and professionalism in the Liberal party as well, which is represented in the party bureaucracy and parliamentary elite. The leadership was not going to allow its chances for office to be damaged by single-issue policy extremism in defense or any other area. Party officials kept a deliberately low profile on defense matters in the 1980s, allowing their Social Democrat partners in the Alliance to take the lead. Only rarely did their leader, David Steel, address defense or foreign affairs matters.

The Liberal leaders essentially wanted the least possible disturbance within NATO; they did not want to pay for Trident, did not greatly care whether Britain had an independent nuclear deterrent or not, would have alienated the United States by "sending cruise back," and were above all, Europe-oriented. For example, they hoped that the question of Britain's nuclear force could be buried within some vague notion of a "European" force; historically, they were enthusiastic about the short-lived Kennedy plan for a multilateral force in the 1960s. The major concern of the leaders has been to calm the party members' fears in the area of nuclear arms. At their 1986 conference they managed to get the party to agree to retaining Polaris as a bargaining counter, which they saw as a considerable improvement on the previous slim majority for complete unilateralism. With a few exceptions, they have prevented their members from taking a more radical stance. The party has always been highly pragmatic and prone to rather carefully thought-out policy arguments; this applies even on defense policy. Thus, a major argument addressed against

Trident, for example, is not only that it is too expensive but that its dependence on American satellite navigational aids and targeting intelligence removes its independent status.

In summary, the Liberal party could be relatively easily pleased by any serious arms control offer. What they really want is dialogue between the superpowers. They believe European solidarity counts far more than anything else, and all they really care about is some sort of deal with the SDP which would keep the Alliance credible. It should be noted that one aspect of their Europeanism is that they care a good deal about the views of other European liberal parties, especially as expressed in the European Parliament and the WEU. As it happens, the party's continental cousins are fairly hawkish and somewhat dominated by the German Free Democratic party.

The Defence Commission and Alliance policy. In light of their diverging perspectives on nuclear deterrence, the Liberals and SDP found it difficult to come to some agreement on a common defense policy. In their attempt to do so, the leadership of the two parties established a Defence Commission in 1984. The commission included members from both parties as well as outside defense experts.[39]

The commission delivered its report on June 10, 1986. The report reflected much agreement on a wide range of matters, especially on strengthening the European pillar of NATO. Nonetheless, on the issue of the future of the British deterrent there was avoidance rather than the resolution of a contentious issue. The language of the agreement suggested not only the inability to resolve the issue but the absence of a need to do so: "No decision on whether, and if so how, British nuclear weapons should be maintained beyond Polaris can be made properly except in the light of: the progress of arms control and disarmament, the balance of relationships within NATO between Europe and the United States, the range and costs of the technical alternatives which might be available to maintain a European minimum deterrent, and the views of our European allies on whether new British nuclear capabilities are required for European defense."[40] The acceptance of even the hint of commitment to the idea of possibly maintaining British nuclear forces after Polaris represented a compromise from the Liberal side. As one British journalist put it, "what will strike some people as most telling in the Commission's formulation is the readiness of Mr. Ashdown and his friends to contemplate Polaris being replaced at all. This is a far cry from the early 1960s, when Jo Grimond was saying that the Liberals would have nothing to do with the independent deterrent."[41]

Even before the commission report was issued it came under attack by David Owen. He considered the inability of the commission to agree on the Polaris successor problem a fatal flaw. Not to designate a commitment to a successor system would be interpreted by the British electorate as the elimination of the British strategic deterrent. Owen heated up the political atmosphere by delivering a speech in Bonn just a few days before the release of the commission's report which provided a ringing endorsement for the need for a British strategic deterrent. In the political skirmishing in the Alliance around the time of the release of the report, the British press reported wide differences remaining; as one headline put it, "Nuclear Arms Policy Splits Alliance."[42]

In the days that followed, Steel and Owen tried to resolve differences. They settled this in part by agreeing to undertake a further study of the criteria affecting a decision on the replacement of the Polaris nuclear force. As the *Financial Times* reported, "The agreement, reached at yesterday morning's meeting of the Alliance joint strategy committee, is a further sign of the desire of the two leaders to lower the temperature of what was threatening to become a major split within the Alliance."[43]

Both leaders also experienced difficulties within their own parties. Owen's insistence on a much clearer commitment to a Polaris replacement led to a row within the SPD leadership. Shirley Williams publicly questioned whether the official position of the SDP was to replace Polaris.[44] Similarly, William Rodgers tried to tone down the effect of Owen's public insistence on a commitment to the Polaris replacement.[45] Steel's efforts were complicated by serious criticisms from the Liberal party councils.

Steel and Owen persisted, however, in their efforts to resolve the dispute. They succeeded to some extent by agreeing to a compromise on the question of the Polaris replacement. The compromise, reached at the end of 1986, involved the statement by both parties that the choice of a minimum deterrent would be left until the Alliance was involved in government. "There are a number of possible options including different ballistic and non-ballistic air and submarine-launched systems. A final choice could not be made without access to classified information and the advice of the chiefs of staff, available only when in government."[46]

The compromise permitted a more forceful statement than the one issued by the Defence Commission in June. The language of this document was carried over into the campaign in the Alliance party manifesto, which stated the following: "In government we would maintain, with whatever necessary modernization, our minimum nuclear deterrent until it can be negotiated away, as part of a global arms negotiation process, in return for worthwhile concessions by the USSR which would enhance British and European security. In any such modernization we would maintain our capability in the sense of freezing our capacity at a level no greater than that of the Polaris system."[47]

In short, although the Alliance was able to compromise on many dimensions of the defense dispute, their policy still lacked credibility on how they would maintain nuclear deterrence in the future. As Michael Heseltine taunted them on the campaign trail, "The semi-despondent party has been unable to convince the Liberals of a realistic nuclear policy. At the end of the day, we would have no nuclear weapons for there is no alternative to Trident and the two Davids know it." This taunt had the ring of truth to it, and all the efforts of the Alliance's defense experts to dispel it were unsuccessful.

The Postelection Prospects for Arms Control

The first thing to grasp is that at the age of sixty-one Mrs. Thatcher won a nearly unprecedented third term of office, and won it with her second landslide victory. In hindsight this could have been foreseen on election night 1983. The majority then was so large that the swing needed for the Conservative government to lose the 1987 election would also have been historically unprecedented. The Conservative majority in this third Thatcher administration is not much less, and it remains the case that, *ceteris paribus*, the Conservatives will be hard put not to win the *next* election as well. It should be noted in this context that a common argument against this prediction, that the Alliance vote has collapsed in favor of the Labour party, making 1987 constituency results irrelevant, is false. The Alliance vote had *already* collapsed in the 1987 election—their vote, 22 percent, is not much higher than that the Liberal party alone gained in the elections of the 1970s.' It is very unlikely that it can drop much below this 1970s figure of around 18–20 percent; this is even more likely to be the case if the Liberal and SDP wings of the Alliance merge; and at this stage it seems inevitable that they will merge. A poll of Alliance supporters published on July 5, 1987 (*Sunday Times*), showed that over 70 percent of Liberals, but more significantly 82 percent of Social Democrats, wanted a merger. Although the SDP parliamentary leader Dr. Owen opposes a merger, the rest of the leadership team are publicly fighting for it, and even Owen's closest parliamentary ally, John Cartwright, has refused to join Owen in stating that he would not join a new party. Since then the initial internal vote among SDP members has been taken, and it indicates a strong majority in favor of a merger. This is being fought by Owen and some other parliamentary leaders, and the final outcome is not yet certain. One possibility is that the merger of the SDP and Liberals would be met by the creation of yet another centrist party under Owen's leadership. However, the electoral prospects for a single party, which would become the Liberal party in all but name, would be no greater, at best, than the current state. In fact, the enormous difficulty the Alliance experienced in designing a compromise defense policy would be even greater—the unilateralist support inside the Liberal party would sit very unhappily with the multilateralists of the SDP. Those opposed to the merger insist that the outcome would be a return to the politics of the "Lib-Lab" pact of 1977–79, and it certainly is known that David Steel wanted the Alliance campaign to include a commitment *not* to enter a coalition with Mrs. Thatcher.

The other possible deterrent to a long-term Conservative government would come from the Labour party successfully ridding itself of its left-wing image and returning, not only in fact, but in the public perception, to the centrist policies of the 1960s. Again, one cannot know what will happen here, but some notes of caution about interpreting the Labour campaign need to be sounded. It is widely felt that Neil Kinnock fought a brilliant campaign and has enormously improved his standing, although this is largely a matter of media hype. As the Labour share of the polls never varied by more than 2 percent from the beginning to the end of the campaign, it is unclear in what way his personal campaigning can be judged a great success. One view is that he is now in a position of great strength vis-à-vis the

Table 1.1. Results of a Poll Conducted by The *Sunday Times*, May 7, 1987. The question was "Are you satisfied or dissatisfied with: Thatcher as prime minister, Kinnock as Labour leader, Steel as Liberal leader, Owen as sDP leader?"

	March	Now
Thatcher		
% satisfied	40	51
% dissatisfied	50	41
Kinnock		
% satisfied	28	36
% dissatisfied	58	49
Steel		
% satisfied	49	36
% dissatisfied	29	42
Owen		
% satisfied	49	35
% dissatisfied	29	42

left wing. The data do not support this idea of enhanced personal standing. A poll released on July 5, 1987, gave the rankings for the party leaders shown in table 1.1.

If Kinnock can score only the same level of support as the two Alliance leaders, who are generally thought to have fought a disastrous campaign, the prognosis is not very good. More to the point, the maneuverings in the Parliamentary Labour party at the beginning of this new parliament suggest that the sizable left-wing cohort of M.P.s does not intend to cooperate with the plans for the sort of party constitutional reform Kinnock thinks necessary to bringing the party into the center ground. The elections to the shadow cabinet have resulted in major posts being held by those who believe that the last campaign was *insufficiently radical*. In fact, these elections, and Kinnock's distribution of shadow spokesman portfolios, demonstrate the tension between him and his parliamentary party. It is true that the three or four major portfolios have been given to his supporters from the center-right. It is also true that in doing this he is flying in the face of party sentiment, because the top three M. P.s in the shadow cabinet elections were from the center-left and would normally have had the major posts. It does not seem likely that the Labour party will be a more serious challenge to the Conservative party in the future than it has been for the last seven years. In particular, the defense portfolio stays with Denzil Davies, whose indifference to modifying the public image of the party in this area was notable during the campaign. Other people close to Kinnock and implacably opposed to the nuclear deterrent, like Robin Cooke, remain powerful within the shadow cabinet. Finally, Denis Healey's resignation removes the one man who had worked hardest to moderate Kinnock's projection of Labour's policy. Recent developments inside the Parliamentary Labour party are even more ominous for Labour's chance of presenting a moderate defense policy. These include the attempt by the backbench Labour defense committee to remove the Atlanticist Labour members of the Select Committee on Defence and replace them with committed unilateralists.

Some form of Conservative administration is therefore the most likely result for 1992/3–1996/7. Ironically, this is likely to make the Conservative party more cautious rather than less. It has always been part of the Conservative party self-image that they are "the natural ruling party." As such, they will not be anxious to jeopardize the chance of ruling Britain for nearly twenty years. Signs of this were apparent very shortly after the election, when Mrs. Thatcher herself publicly took note of the widening north/south split, and particularly the inner-city problems which, despite the overall success of the party, have made large areas of Britain "no go" areas for the Conservatives. The implications for security policy of a new Conservative administration anxious to retain its political popularity for the next election, possibly in the face of an increasingly moderate Labour party and a rump Alliance, depend on one's interpretation of the role of security policy issues in the last election.

It is too easily assumed that defense issues were of crucial importance in the campaign, and that they account for Labour's defeat. Obviously, the Labour party's policies, or at least the interpretation the Tories were able to provide for them, *were* unpopular. Nonetheless, from the beginning of the campaign to the end they do not seem to have cost Labour very many votes. In the week following Mr. Kinnock's biggest gaffe, when he appeared to be advocating surrender as the main strategy for the BAOR, polls showed an increase in distrust of Labour's defense policy *but no decrease in the number of people intending to vote Labour.* This was a repeated finding in the period up to the election as well. Defense was the second most important issue, after unemployment, but it was second by a huge gap. The truth is that the Tory policy of deploying Trident has never been electorally popular in Britain, and the election has changed nothing here. A poll released on July 6, 1987, showed only a small minority of around 17 percent in favor of Trident. A clear majority of 54 percent believed that Britain should not enhance its strategic nuclear force above the Polaris level, while 29 percent were still in favor of completely abandoning the nuclear deterrent. In fact, the Conservative party was quite vulnerable on defense during the campaign because of the charges that it was weakening conventional defense. Had the combined opposition parties been more skillful, they might have made this tell against the government, especially as it is a genuine concern among Conservative M. P.s as well.

Nonetheless, Trident is bound to go ahead. On July 7, 1987, the SDP defense spokesman, John Cartwright, publicly called for the Alliance to support Trident. His argument was that Trident is the only policy that will allow the Alliance to enter the next election committed to a nuclear deterrent, because so much will have been committed to the Trident fleet by then. The long-term prospect for the government is not very encouraging, however. The international context is bound to change, with some degree of superpower nuclear arms control agreement inevitable before the next election. The danger is that the United Kingdom will come to look very isolated (along with France) as a nation that has bucked the international trend and enhanced its nuclear force in a way its own electorate did not and does not want. In addition it will probably have to go into an election with this reputation *combined* with a conventional defense record easily assailable by the opposition. This is likely because of the well-known underfunding of the U. K. defense budget and the pressing need for a defense review, which will either be very unpopular if undertaken or increasingly fraudulent if it is not carried out.

Within this scenario, it is likely that arms control will become a much more important policy area for the administration than it has been. The arms control policy will have three aims, all of which have been present in the past, but with less of a sense of urgency. The first will be to continue ensuring that no agreements between the United

States and USSR restrict technology transfer in such a way as to damage the Trident deal. This, of course, has been the essence of the policy since 1981. Second, there will be a very strongly felt need to preserve whatever theater nuclear capacity is left out of a double zero agreement. In the case of the United Kingdom, this will mean above all ensuring that dual-capable aircraft do not get into any such agreement, as Britain's *independent* theater capacity is entirely based on the Tornado squadrons with the new generation of gravity bombs being developed.

Both of these are primarily "external," or "real," security policy drives. Equally important will be a drive for the British government to look very active and very successful as a European arms control leader, for domestic consumption. If the government can go into the 1992/3 election with a solid track record on arms control, it will do much to reduce the electoral damage suggested above. This raises especially the question of conventional arms control, because this is an area in some ways of more pressing concern for European governments, and an area where a successful British initiative could most effectively alleviate criticisms of the likely Tory rundown of British conventional capacity. Similarly, the long-term ambition of the FCO to be seen as a leader on the chemical weapons convention would satisfy this political need.

The precise shape of both the public debate and actual government policy in the defense area cannot be predicted because it will be very sensitive to external events and indeed to the line taken by the opposition parties. To a large extent the shape of defense policy *within a severe cost constraint* may be left to the professionals in both the MOD and the FCO. Thus questions about European arms cooperation, or increased contingency planning and training cooperation with France and Germany, which so many *American* analysts see as unarguably rational, will come up, if they do, largely independent of ministerial and cabinet orientations.

It must be remembered that any British government inevitably has an ambivalent attitude toward European cooperation. This is not simply a matter of cultural or historical prejudices, the Washington analytic community's views notwithstanding. On the one hand is the real need for elements of the "special relationship" to be taken into account, at least as much because of economic ties as because of defense matters. On the other hand is the fact that the United Kingdom's often belligerent position inside the European Economic Community (EEC) is a rational economic policy, though European government prefer to see it as a matter of the United Kingdom lacking some morally desirable "European vision." The brute fact is that as long as the Common Agricultural Policy remains the cornerstone of the EEC, Britain will necessarily have sharp policy conflicts. With Mrs. Thatcher's perfect happiness to play a Gaullist position, these and other economic questions, such as London's returning role in international money markets, will preclude a major Europeward shift. A final example, which may well lead to a diminished interest in European defense procurement cooperation, is that the British defense industry is increasingly doing very well, but also increasingly needing to do well in international arms sales. It is currently second only to the United States, with defense sales amounting to approximately 60 percent of U. S. sales worldwide. It may become increasingly true that French and other European arms producers are the natural enemies of the U. K. industry. In short, there is little in either the objective economic environment of the attitudes or the cabinet to suggest that the United Kingdom will be much more Europe-oriented in the next four years than in the last.

In summary, a much more active arms control policy will be pursued, for all these reasons and also because of Mrs. Thatcher's increasingly evident position as the senior Western head of government. However, this policy, whatever its shape, will continue to be guided by principles of enhancing *British* security interests from a perspective actually more like that of the United States—nuclear power with at least limited possibilities for isolationism and an expensive forward deployment role that is increasingly hard to sustain.

2

West German Arms Control Policy

Barry Blechman and Cathleen Fisher

Geopolitics, history, and events since World War II have rooted the Federal Republic of Germany (FRG) firmly in the West, but the same factors have also given Bonn a substantial interest in developing good relations with its Eastern neighbors. As a significant but non-nuclear member of NATO, its relationship with the United States and the other Allies is the cornerstone of West Germany's security policy. This special dependency has enhanced West German security, but it also has meant that Bonn's security policy is tied inalterably to American and Soviet policies, and to the general climate of East-West relations.

West German arms control policy, as part of its broader security policy, is no exception. The arms control policy of the Federal Republic is shaped by a continuing interplay between domestic considerations and changes in the international context, both in the East and the West. This persistent tension between the internal and the external, and between Bonn's Westpolitik and Ostpolitik, is necessary background for understanding West German arms control policy.

In a very real sense, Bonn's arms control policy is "hostage" to Germany's commitment to a close relationship with the United States and NATO. Initially, the arms control process was seen solely as part of the superpowers' relationship, to be left in the hands of the United States. As the process expanded to include multilateral forums, however, and became more institutionalized, the FRG was compelled to develop both the capacity and the decision-making procedures to address arms control matters. The enhancement of Bonn's arms control decision-making capacity is likely to be pursued as Bonn becomes increasingly assertive in defining its national interests.

Over time, arms control has come to be linked in the West German public's mind with an ongoing process of détente, or Ostpolitik. On the whole, West Germans are inclined to give a positive assessment of the relative benefits and costs of the détente of the 1970s, particularly with regard to the value of improvements in inter-German relations. Accordingly, West German politicians and government decision makers tend to embrace a hazy notion of détente and arms control as policies serving German interests, or at least offering reassurance to an anxious public.

This general orientation notwithstanding, specific arms control policy decisions may be explained on the basis of governmental decision-making processes and the views of specific officials. In the Federal Republic, real power is lodged solely in the executive branch, and on arms control issues the voice of the foreign minister and his deputies is decisive.[1] The Federal Republic's Constitution and other legal documents, a long history of powerful bureaucracies, and the structure of Bonn's parliamentary system of government effectively guarantee the executive's predominance; legislative organs play only secondary roles. The Bundestag may provide a setting for public debate, but it cannot determine executive decisions or even influence them directly, as can the U.S. Congress, while opposition parties can only seek to educate the public on alternative views (and the talents of their security experts) in order to influence future elections and prepare for a return to power. The specialized committee that deals with arms control issues has become, however, increasingly significant as a forum for generating public exposure to arms control issues. Also, national political parties do serve to channel information on public attitudes to government officials.

This chapter explores the sources of West German arms control policies and the processes through which they are determined. In it, we review the key actors in the process, both within and outside the government, and discuss the sources of their beliefs and the specific positions they tend to prefer. This is followed by a historical assessment of West German public attitudes toward arms control and an analysis of varying party and party faction attitudes.

Decision-making Processes and Actors

Arms control policy in the Federal Republic in large measure bears the stamp of executive actors (see figure 2.1). The Basic Law and related legal documents assign primary responsibility for the conduct of foreign policy, which has been interpreted to include arms control negotiations, to the Foreign Ministry. By the same token, the Basic Law's right of concurrence (*Mitzeichnungsrecht*) guarantees the Ministry of Defense (MOD) input into the policy process. The Chancellor's Office, the cabinet, and the Federal Security Council (BSR) play secondary roles. The long-standing tradition of professional civil service and the one-sided balance of power inherent in a parliamentary system further cement the predominance of executive agencies. Consequently, although the Bundestag as an institution, all national political parties, and other nongovernmental actors may attempt to channel their views to relevant decision makers, only the parties that govern can tap directly into bureaucratic sources of expertise and power. Opposition parties and nongovernmental actors may serve to inform government officials of new ideas and changes in public attitudes, but in general they play only secondary roles.

Interagency coordination and conflict resolution are persistent problems in the decision-making process within the executive branch. Coordination among executive agencies is complicated by the generally decentralized character of the Bonn bureaucracy and the autonomy enjoyed by division heads. The level of decentralization is much greater in the German government than in Great Britain, France, and Italy. Within the executive branch, conflict often develops between the Foreign Ministry and the Ministry of Defense, or between one or the other and the Chancellor's Office. The fact that the foreign minister has been a member of the minority party in the governing coalition for more than a decade has tended to reinforce institutional conflicts. Indeed, in general, coalition politics and the competing aims and the agendas of the governing parties are an important source of friction and conflict.

The exact nature of any bureaucratic conflict and its ultimate resolution depend to a large degree on the personalities, capabilities, and priorities of persons in key positions within each agency. When conflict occurs, formal and informal mechanisms, including ongoing

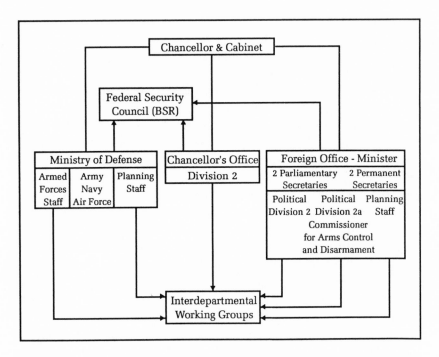

Figure 2.1 West German Institutional Structure for Arms Control Decision Making

communications at all levels or, in difficult cases, the creation of interministerial advisory groups (IMAGs), are used to iron out differences. The pressure to arrive at a consensual position is always considerable, particularly when the chancellor is known to prefer not to have to choose among competing recommendations.

A further complication derives from the Federal Republic's membership in NATO and its close relations with the United States. As was already noted, domestic decision-making processes are never insulated from the influence of American attitudes. Within NATO, a complex structure of consultative bodies and procedures has evolved to handle arms control issues; many opportunities for bilateral exchanges exist as well. In theory such channels can function as "two-way streets" to influence arms control policy either in Bonn or in Washington. In practice, NATO and bilateral channels provide more constraint than opportunity for decision makers in Bonn.

Executive Actors

The Foreign Ministry. The Foreign Ministry is the primary source of all arms control policy in the Federal Republic. The central role of the ministry is due above all to the power and political and bureaucratic skills of Foreign Minister Hans-Dietrich Genscher. The foreign minister has taken a personal interest and an active role in shaping arms control policy; the gradual upgrading of arms control issues within Bonn's security policy is partly attributable to his predominance in the policy process. The more recent emphasis on European issues in the arms control field bears Genscher's stamp as well. Moreover, during his long tenure as foreign minister, Genscher has shaped the arms control policy process within the ministry, a legacy that would likely endure even if Genscher were unable to fulfill his next four-year term of office.

Genscher believes that it is critical to the public credibility of German and alliance security policy to have a serious arms control effort. This attitude underlay his insistence that Germany accept the double zero option for INF. It also is the basis of his desire to reinvigorate the conventional arms control process. He was especially concerned when the United States and France appeared to be at loggerheads over procedural issues for establishing the new conventional arms talks.

The Foreign Ministry's central authority is based on three legal provisions: Article 65 of the Basic Law (*Grundgesetz*) establishes the principle of the departmental autonomy (*Ressortsprinzip*), which gives the foreign minister broad discretionary powers over the affairs of the ministry and limits the chancellor's interference in ministry affairs to ensuring that foreign policy is compatible with "general policy guidelines." Article 73 of the Basic Law and paragraph 11 of the rules of procedure (*Geschäftsordnung*) assign the Foreign Ministry all responsibility for international relations. In operational terms, these three principles mean that the Foreign Ministry initiates preparatory work on arms control and reserves the right to make final policy decisions. Strictly interpreted, the *Ressortsprinzip* may also block the efforts of any other executive agency—including the Chancellor's Office—to coordinate work on arms control policy.

Within the Foreign Ministry, operations are divided along the traditional hierarchical lines of German bureaucracy (see figure 2.2). In

Foreign Office - Minister		
Parliamentary Secretaries		Permanent Secretaries
Political Division 2	Political Division 2a --- Commissioner for Arms Control and Disarmament	Planning Staff
Desk 201 - NATO & Defense	Desk 220 - Global Disarmament & Arms Control (SALT/START)	Other Divisions and Desks
	Desk 221 - Security, Disarmament & Arms Control in Europe (MBFR, CSCE)	
	Desk 222 - Nonproliferation, Biological & Chemical Weapons, Verification	
	Desk 223 - United Nations	

Figure 2.2 Foreign Ministry—Organization for Arms Control Decision Making

general, the minister and his secretaries, the commissioner on arms control, and working-level officers take the most active part in arms control decisions. The foreign minister is doubtless the most broadly influential actor in the process, but his direct involvement may be limited to determining the general orientation of arms control policy. The secretaries' main function is to aid the minister; they ensure that his guidelines are carried out at lower levels in the bureaucracy. The commissioner occupies a pivotal position in the ministry; he has access to the minister and political leadership but also is in touch with working-level operations in division 2a. The commissioner may thus play a more or less active role in the process, depending upon the person and his relationship to the foreign minister. Working-level officers are responsible for interagency coordination, conflict resolution, and implementation of policy on a day-to-day basis.

Political leadership comprises the foreign minister, two parliamentary secretaries, and two permanent state secretaries. The two parliamentary secretaries (posts created in 1967) serve as aides to the minister; they are recruited largely on the basis of political affiliation. They are usually skilled political actors who serve as liaisons between the Foreign Ministry and such political bodies as the parties, parliamentary party groups (*Fraktionen*), and the Federal Council (*Bundesrat*). The two permanent secretaries have been drawn traditionally from the senior civil service, but they are selected increasingly on the basis of political criteria as well. The permanent secretaries may be more active in the formulation and discussion of substantive policies with division heads or desk officers. The ministerial staff is largely a personal task force of the minister; its members are selected by the minister, and they leave office when his term comes to an end.[2]

The direct involvement of the minister and his secretaries in policy-making is limited by the sheer volume of work; time and energy must necessarily be allocated selectively. Moreover, West German bureaucratic policy-making tends to be decentralized; most work is accomplished at the desk (*Referat*) level. Senior officials and political leaders apparently are informed, but they seldom are actively involved in the routine processes of decision making.

The degree of political-level participation, however, also depends on the foreign minister's personality and particular interests. The current foreign minister, Genscher, in office since 1974 and representing the junior coalition partner, has displayed a long-term personal and professional commitment to a continuing East-West dialogue, of which arms control negotiations are an integral part. Moreover, the political fortunes of his party, the Free Democratic party (FDP), may be linked to its ability to portray itself as the voice of experience and moderation in foreign policy matters. Consequently, Genscher takes a more active interest in arms control and security decisions than another foreign minister might assume.

At the intermediate level, the planning staff of the Foreign Ministry is only sporadically involved in specific issues, and then mostly at the behest of the foreign minister. Established in 1963 and patterned in part after the U.S. model, the planning staff is composed of approximately twelve civil servants. In the past, only one or two officials have usually been involved in arms control matters.

Also at the intermediate level, political divisions 2 and 2a are charged with the primary responsibility for arms control and disarmament decision making. The creation of division 2a in 1981 was the result of a series of initiatives since 1977 to upgrade arms control policy within the Foreign Ministry. The head of division 2a is also the federal commissioner on arms control and disarmament. The commissioner has been granted ambassadorial rank, an indication of the post's importance.[3]

The federal government's commissioner on arms control and disarmament is a central actor within the Foreign Ministry, linking the executive political leadership with working-level operations. As division head and special ambassador, the person occupying this post enjoys a significant degree of latitude to interpret his or her role and to determine the scope and nature of the post's activities. Among the more important of the commissioner's duties are the maintenance of regular contacts with allies, non-nuclear states, and international organizations; participation in the decisive directors' conferences within the Foreign Ministry (see below); under certain circumstances, participation in cabinet meetings with the chancellor; and discussions with the Foreign Affairs Committee and Subcommittee for Arms Control Questions of the Bundestag. Additionally, the commissioner may engage in public education and information programs on arms control and disarmament through a variety of press channels and can also maintain regular contacts with a number of private German international organizations working in the arms control field.[4] The commissioner thus has access to political leaders as well as contacts with all other potentially influential actors. The commissioner also maintains contacts with Allied, Soviet, and East German officials, reports to the Bundestag subcommittee on arms control, and, on occasion, may meet separately with the chancellor. Depending upon his capabilities, the commissioner can be an indispensable assistant to the foreign minister and may be instrumental in translating the minister's broad policy outlines into specific positions. Moreover, because he is connected directly or indirectly to other governmental and nongovernmental actors, the commissioner can keep the minister apprised of broad trends in attitudes on arms control.

At the working level, responsibilities within division 2a are further divided into four desks. Desk 220 is responsible for global disarmament and arms control (including the START and INF negotiations); desk 221 handles security, disarmament, and arms control in Europe (including MBFR and CSCE): desk 222, nuclear nonproliferation and verification, and the prohibition of biological and chemical weapons; desk 223 is responsible for disarmament within the context of the United Nations. These four desks routinely coordinate with two desks in division 2, which is responsible overall for all decisions with regard to NATO or East-West relations. Within division 2, desk 201 deals with NATO and defence matters; desk 212 is responsible for East-West relations and has primary authority in the CSCE process.

Working-level operations are affected significantly by limits on personnel. Currently, there are only eighteen to twenty officers of diplomatic rank in division 2a. Moreover, desk officers are concerned primarily with day-to-day operational matters. Their tasks include, for example, preparing the foreign minister or the commissioner for meetings of the Federal Security Council, NATO consultations, and bilateral meetings; and responding to specific Allied arms control initiatives. Desk officers usually have only very limited time to devote to conceptual studies or innovation; their work tends to be responsive. To carry out their tasks, officers in division 2a must work closely with desk 201 (division 2) and MOD officers.

A further constraint at the working level is the limited number of sources available to desk officers seeking information on arms control. Diplomats normally do not have technical expertise, and the Foreign Ministry's analytical capabilities are further reduced by the demands of operational matters. In addition, expertise is lost whenever desk officers, who usually are career civil servants, are rotated, on the average once every three or four years. Funds to support outside research are minimal.

The proliferation of arms control forums can be expected to further tax the resources of the Foreign Ministry. This will be the case, in particular, if increasing emphasis is given to negotiations on the reduction of conventional forces. The creation of a new arms control forum to parallel bloc-to-bloc negotiations requires complex interministerial mechanisms for consultation and coordination between the MOD and the Foreign Ministry, and between these executive organs and other unilateral bodies. Previous multilateral negotiations could provide relevant models. During the preparatory phase for the original Conference on Security and Cooperation in Europe (CSCE), the Foreign Ministry and the Ministry of Defense shared responsibility for the formulation of specific West German positions on the military aspects of security. A special CSCE interministerial working group was formed (CSCE-IMAG); informal and personal contacts played an equally important role during this initial phase.

The Ministry of Defense. A fundamental organizing principle of the Basic Law, the right of concurrence (*Mitzeichnungsrecht*), gives the Ministry of Defense a voice in the decision-making process. The concurrence principle guarantees the MOD the right to advise the Foreign Ministry and to contribute ideas and suggestions at all levels. Similar to the Foreign Ministry, arms control decision making in the Ministry of Defense follows strict hierarchical lines.

The influence of the Ministry of Defense varies according to the specific arms control issue and the power of the minister of defense within the executive branch. The Ministry of Defense may have more influence when detailed analyses of the military implications of spe-

Figure 2.3 Ministry of Defense—Organization for Arms Control Decision Making

Ministry of Defense			
Parliamentary Secretaries		Permanent Secretaries	
General Inspector --- Armed Forces Staff (FueS)		Army Navy Air Force	Planning Staff
FueS ll	FueSlll Political/Military Affairs	Other Desks	
Intelli-gence	Division 1 - General Military Policy		
	Division 2 - Military Strategy		
	Division 3 - NATO		
	Division 4 - Armaments Planning		
	Division 5 - Arms Limitation & Arms Control (SALT/START INF, MBFR, CSCE, CDE)		

cific negotiating positions are important. For example, in the case of CSCE, the most concrete proposals on military security (which originally had been formulated for the Mutual Balanced Force Reductions (MBFR) negotiations) came from the MOD planning staff. In contrast, in those cases in which the FRG's positions are determined more on the basis of political considerations (for example, the desire to develop independent European consultative procedures or positions on arms control), the MOD may play a less significant role.

Of course, the personality of the defense minister is important as well. During the preparatory phases of the CSCE, for example, it was at the insistence of then–defense minister Helmut Schmidt that the concrete MBFR positions were incorporated into the West German negotiating guidelines. More recently, former defense minister Manfred Woerner attempted to play a greater role in shaping West German policy on INF. Supported by others in the CDU/CSU, Woerner spoke against an agreement that would require the withdrawal of all intermediate-range nuclear forces, insisting that an agreement on INF must be coupled with agreements that address imbalances in conventional forces and in shorter-range intermediate nuclear forces.

The significance of its allies to German security means that players in the domestic policy process try to enlist the aid of Allied officials in internal German policy squabbles. For example, Woerner actively sought the support of Allied defense ministers in his effort to convince the chancellor not to accept the double zero option. He tried to use the Nuclear Planning Group to influence German policy as well.

The role of the planning staff may also vary depending on the personality and leadership style of the defense minister. Under former defense minister Helmut Schmidt, the planning staff played an important role in arms control policy formulation and development, providing, moreover, a counterweight to the military influence within the ministry. At that time the planning staff was headed by Theo Sommer, a prominent journalist and associate of Schmidt's. Sommer's successor was Hans-Georg Wieck, a career diplomat who served as ambassador to Moscow and, until recently, as Bonn's permanent representative to NATO. Under Defense Ministers Georg Leber and Hans Apel, the planning staff was headed by Walter Stuetzle, who is credited with the writing of Schmidt's famous 1977 speech at the International Institute for Strategic Studies, which led eventually to NATO's dual-track decision.

Some members of the planning staff complain about its growth, claiming that its larger size has made it a less powerful player in the MOD policy process. Its power has rested, in this view, on the ability of the planning staff to intervene quickly on key problems. As the staff has become larger, it has become preoccupied with managing its own affairs and less with enhancing its contribution to the real policy process.

At the political level, the defense minister exercises primary political control over all defense decision making and, like the foreign minister, is guaranteed relative autonomy in defense matters by the *Ressortsprinzip*. The minister is assisted by a parliamentary secretary and three permanent secretaries.

The inspector general performs both political and military functions. He is the highest-ranking military officer and is chosen by the minister of defense with the chancellor's concurrence. The inspector general also is linked directly to the government and political leaders. He is chief military adviser to the government, the German representative to NATO's Military Committee, and a nonvoting member of the Federal Security Council. Within the MOD, the inspector general reports directly to the minister, but he may also be called upon by the chancellor, cabinet, or Defense Committee of the Bundestag to provide expert or advisory opinions. As a commander of the armed forces staff [*Führungsstab Streitkraefte* (FüS)], he relies largely on division 2, which is responsible for all politico-military affairs.

In general, the planning staff of the Ministry of Defense plays only a minor role in arms control decision making. The staff is headed by a civilian and reports directly to the minister and his state secretaries. Its tasks include speech writing for the ministry's political leadership and preparation of the MOD's annual defense white paper. The planning staff lacks an analytical capability, however, and cannot have a substantive impact on arms control policy. It may play a small conceptual role, acting as a coordinating agent upon demand of the armed forces staff.

At the intermediate level, the armed forces staff is the most important MOD policy-making body. It links the minister, his permanent secretaries, and the inspector general with division heads and thus with the working level. The seven departments of the armed forces staff are composed mostly of military officers. One division is responsible for all political-military affairs, including military strategy,

NATO-related issues, armaments planning, and arms control. This division is further broken down into nine desks. Each desk is headed by a full colonel, who is assisted by seven to ten officers.

One of these, desk 5, is the locus of responsibility for all arms control matters within the Ministry of Defense. Staffed by seven officers, including the desk chief, the scope of the desk's activities is so broad that each staff member must routinely handle more than one issue area. As in the Foreign Ministry, working-level officers focus mainly on operational issues. Moreover, a sharp division of labor between conventional and nuclear matters further limits the capacity of the desk to complete analytical studies which might be relevant to an independent German arms control position. Rather, MOD arms control positions are described by one observer as reflecting political desires but largely lacking a sound analytical basis. Other tasks of this bureau include advising division 2a of the Foreign Ministry. Additionally, an officer from desk 5 is usually sent with the German delegation to the MBFR and CSCE negotiations.[5]

As in the Foreign Ministry, responsibility in the MOD for arms control matters is divided among bureaucratic levels. The minister, aided by his secretaries and sometimes by the planning staff, is ultimately responsible for ensuring MOD input into the decision-making process. At the intermediate level, the inspector general and the armed forces staff may be involved only marginally. Policy implementation and coordination is accomplished at the working level.

The Chancellor's Office. The third major executive actor is the Chancellor's Office, whose role is shaped primarily by the leadership style and capabilities of the chancellor and his advisers. Since the staff of the office is likely to include close personal advisers to the chancellor, it has the potential to compete occasionally with the Foreign Ministry for influence. In bypassing the Foreign Ministry, the Chancellor's Office may override sources of bureaucratic inertia, which might otherwise thwart new initiatives or departures in policy; this was the case with Chancellor Willy Brandt and his close adviser Egon Bahr's initiative, Ostpolitik. As a consequence of the 1978–83 debate on intermediate-range nuclear forces (INF), moreover, the Chancellor's Office also acts as a watchdog on political controversies, identifying the sources of likely conflicts in order to take timely countermeasures and to protect the chancellor's reputation and overall support for the government.

While limited constitutionally to established general policy guidelines, the chancellor exercises an indirect influence on specific policy outcomes in three ways. He may create or abolish ministries and define their jurisdiction without parliamentary authorization. He also recommends the appointment and dismissal of ministers. And he may issue general policy guidelines which are binding upon ministers. Additionally, the chancellor's government policy statements (*Regierungserklärung*), periodic reports on the state of the nation, and other public statements are vehicles for addressing policy issues, including arms control. The chancellor's leadership style within the cabinet also affects the decision-making process. Helmut Schmidt, for example, was not averse to taking an active hand in resolving conflict among ministers and consequently played an active role in the actual formulation of policy. Under the Kohl government, on the other hand, the chancellor prefers that conflicts be resolved, wherever possible, before reaching him.

The role of the Chancellor's Office in arms control decision making generally has been quite limited. The Chancellor's Office coordinates interdepartmental policy and oversees compliance of the various ministries with the government's general policy guidelines. Specific responsibility for security affairs lies with division 2, which is further subdivided. Three units deal in some capacity with arms control matters: desk 212, which is responsible for East-West relations and bilateral relations with Eastern Europe, the Soviet Union, and North America; group 23, which is responsible for defense, arms control, and disarmament; and the Federal Security Council. Group 23 is composed of four military officers who advise on the military implications of arms control and function as a secretariat to the Federal Security Council.

In recent years the Chancellor's Office (in contrast with the chancellor himself) has become a more visible player in security matters. Kohl's head of division 2, Horst Teltschick, has been a longtime associate of Chancellor Kohl and a key personal adviser on foreign and security policies. Teltschick attempted to carve out a greater role for the Chancellor's Office in security policy; broadly defined, "security policy" could spill over into specific arms control policy. In September 1985 he led a twenty-eight member delegation to the United States to gather information on the Strategic Defense Initiative

(SDI). Foreign Minister Genscher was highly critical of Teltschick's mission, and the resulting conflict between them was reported in the national press. Teltschick supported German participation in SDI, a position clearly at variance with that of the foreign minister. The influence of Teltschick's views on Kohl has been significant.

The cabinet's role is to approve position papers which have been prepared by the various governmental departments. As a consequence of the principle of departmental autonomy, ministers tend to identify more closely with their respective ministries than with their cabinet function. This fact, taken with the lack of an independent bureaucratic infrastructure, prevents the cabinet from acting as a collective decision-making body. The cabinet exercises influence on arms control decisions only to the extent that conflicts over policy cannot be resolved at working or ministerial levels and consequently must be hammered out at the highest political level under the chancellor's guidance.

Similarly, the Federal Security Council functions primarily as a forum to discuss political-military policy on the basis of decision papers already prepared by both the Foreign Ministry and the Ministry of Defense. Its members include the chancellor, who heads the council, the ministers of foreign affairs, defense, justice, finance, and economics, the inspector general of the Bundeswehr, and the commissioner for disarmament and arms control. The relative infrequency of its meetings tends to support the view that the council is primarily responsible for providing the stamp of approval on arms control positions which have already been taken. Between 1976 and 1980, for example, the Federal Security Council convened approximately twenty-five times. Though the council could provide a forum to resolve differences between ministerial policy positions, other mechanisms of conflict resolution usually ensure that a compromise has been reached before the issues reach either the Federal Security Council or the cabinet.

Conflict resolution and coordination. The legal and actual divisions of responsibility for arms control policy make the problems of interagency coordination and conflict resolution particularly acute. Conflicts between the Foreign Ministry and the MOD or the Chancellor's Office can and do arise. Though the predominance of the Foreign Ministry is firmly grounded, personalities may also make a difference, on occasion undermining the Foreign Ministry's power and enhancing the influence of contending agents. Mechanisms to resolve conflict start at the lowest level but, if necessary, proceed up through the bureaucratic hierarchy until compromise is achieved.

In civil-military disputes over arms control policy, the balance of power clearly favors the Foreign Ministry. As the center of foreign and security policy decision making, its voice usually outweighs that of the MOD. Most German representatives to bilateral or multilateral councils are Foreign Ministry staff members. The Ministry of Defense sends delegates as well, of course, but the instructions to negotiating teams are coordinated and transmitted through the Foreign Ministry, allowing it to monitor all incoming and outgoing information. An attempt made in 1972 by the MOD to expand its role in arms control decision-making processes by establishing a specific department responsible for security affairs (similar to the International Security Affairs division of the Department of Defense [DOD/ISP] in the United States) failed. The Foreign Ministry enjoys the ironic but nonetheless real advantage bestowed by Germany's tortured history of civil-military relations. This history provides a powerful constraint on a too-visible or too-powerful role for the military in security and foreign policy matters.

When conflicts do occur, however, the Ministry of Defense has a number of means of promoting its views. Senior officers tend to be politically sophisticated, and the MOD may be more likely to make its views known through NATO than through domestic channels. Though the Bundeswehr may be a secondary actor at home, in the NATO context it is perceived as second only to the United States, which ensures that its voice is heard.

Conflicts may also arise between the Foreign Ministry and the Chancellor's Office, again depending on the occupants of leadership positions. Under the current government, for example, disputes between the Foreign Ministry and the MOD have been less evident, perhaps because of former defense minister Woerner's preoccupation with budgetary and manpower problems. As previously noted, however, many disputes have surfaced between the Foreign Ministry and the Chancellor's Office.

Interagency coordination and conflict resolution is achieved through a complex of formal and informal mechanisms. Three instruments are usually available at the working level: First, the telephone, which is usually effective for routine matters. Second, the right of concurrence, which provides the legal basis for the involvement of

agencies other than the Foreign Ministry. Third, temporary interministerial advisory groups (IMAGS) are sometimes created for more difficult issues which may affect several departments in the ministries.
This third instrument was used, for instance, to prepare the German
position on SALT I. Similar mechanisms evolved in the formulation
of German positions on CSCE and during the course of the MBFR negotiations. The actual influence of the IMAGS on policy outcomes, however, is limited by the *Ressortsprinzip*, which safeguards the Foreign
Ministry's prerogatives in arms control matters.

The resolution of interagency conflict proceeds at all points in the
hierarchy, but there is a great deal of pressure to work out disputes
before they reach the highest levels of decision making. Through
extensive horizontal contacts, desk officers in all likelihood are aware
of which initiatives are liable to provoke objections from other quar-
ters, and they take care to preempt conflict by avoiding the more
controversial policies. The realities of coalition politics constitute
an additional source of pressure to reach compromise below the
ministerial level, as disputes, for example, between the foreign and
defense ministers automatically raise the politically sensitive issues
of the relative power of the coalition parties. The result is often
"anticipatory conflict resolution"—strong efforts are made to obtain
a consensus before policy is submitted either to the cabinet for approval or to the chancellor for his consideration.

The Bundestag

History, the nature of Bonn's parliamentary system, and party hierar-
chies place strict constraints on the involvement or influence of the
Bundestag and the political parties in the arms control decision-
making process. At the time of its creation in 1949, the Federal
Republic had no tradition of representative institutions being actively
involved in policy formulation. Moreover, the first chancellor of
the Federal Republic, Konrad Adenauer, established a pattern of
executive dominance over foreign and security affairs that would
prove hard to break. Even without these obstacles, the majority parties
will always support governmental policy, leaving only the minority
parties as weak competitors to the executive agencies.

The Bundestag, however, can fulfill a number of secondary functions in the decision-making process; for one, it provides a forum

for public debate on arms control policy. During plenary sessions, parliamentary party groups have the opportunity to challenge government policies and programs through a variety of measures: a "large inquiry" (*Grosse Anfrage*) is initiated when more than thirty deputies submit a written query to the government, which must then respond at a plenary session of the Bundestag. These public debates often are televised, and opposition parties use this device to criticize the government's current policies, suggest alternatives, and gain greater public exposure for their security experts. The "question hour" (*Fragestunde*) precedes every plenary session. One Bundestag deputy poses one specific question and two follow-up questions at each such session. Other deputies also are allowed one question, but they must be directly related to the first deputy's inquiry. The "current hour" (*Aktuelle Stunde*), introduced in 1965, is intended to encourage more spontaneous consideration of timely events and issues. It is a one-hour debate on a current political problem and may follow the "question hour" upon request of a party *Fraktion*. Each deputy is limited to five minutes of speaking time during the debate.

Though the necessary instruments exist, the Bundestag's potential as a forum for public debate and the dissemination of information is only partially exploited. The mechanisms mentioned above are designed to facilitate criticism of government policy and consequently are used seriously only by the opposition parties. The parliamentary caucuses of the government coalition usually do not provoke debate on governmental policy for fear of undermining their own support. Opposition parties have used the *Grosse Anfrage* to discuss major controversial issues, but the *Aktuelle Stunde* is used only infrequently, and then usually only by a few party experts well versed in the issues. The potential utility of these instruments is further weakened by the strict lines and procedures of party hierarchy. Only the designated security experts of opposition parties generally will be allowed to challenge governmental policy, creating a built-in bias against spontaneous criticism and debate.

The committees and subcommittees of the Bundestag give legislative actors some capacity to influence executive decision making. There are three committees broadly relevant to arms control matters: The Foreign Affairs Committee, the Defense Committee, and the Subcommittee on Arms Control and Disarmament. Committee meetings are link-up points for the parties' security experts and ministry officials, and thus offer opportunities for deputies belonging to minority parties to provide informal input into the executive decision-making process. But the committees are constrained by a number of factors. Members of the Foreign Affairs and Defense committees are responsible for a broad range of issues, typically have little training or expertise in security affairs, and have very small staffs. Furthermore, even the Subcommittee on Arms Control and Disarmament, which at present includes Bundestag deputies with extensive experience in security issues, receives only selective information at its weekly briefing with the arms control commissioner, and often the information it does receive is no longer timely. Members of the subcommittee believe that it is possible to forge a broad-based consensus on conventional arms control issues. The members are directing their resources and their efforts toward this end and are being supported in their effort by Genscher and the relevant sections of the Foreign Ministry. This could well mean that the Germans might present a tougher stance on conventional arms control issues in the years ahead, having developed much more of a consensus on conventional than on nuclear arms control issues.

The parties' most direct contribution to arms control decision making is achieved through the committee structure and the working groups that provide them with support functions. As a result of the limited resources available to individual committee members, parliamentary party groups have taken on the function of secretariat and staff. The parliamentary party group, its functional working groups, and the research institutes associated with each of the three parties' political foundations provide background information and advice on specific issues to Bundestag members. The working groups are the key link in the informational chain. Each parliamentary party group has numerous "working circles" (*Arbeitskreise*), which are further subdivided into working groups that include those deputies who sit on the Bundestag committee corresponding to the circle's area of competence. For each committee the party designates a spokesperson who has developed special expertise in the field and can decisively influence the decision-making process within the parliamentary party group. Working circles and groups meet once a week to discuss particular topics and prepare resolutions for plenary sessions.[6]

The parties also possess less formal channels for input into ministerial decision making, exerting a subtle and diffuse influence on arms control policy. Foreign Ministry staff members pay attention to ongoing security debates within the various parties, and in particular to party resolutions passed at the local and federal levels. Also, civil servants from the Foreign Ministry are periodically seconded to the party *Fraktionen* in the Bundestag. Discussions at meetings of the governing parties can have a direct impact on the perceptions and preferences of government officials, especially on the political level. While opposition party policies are not likely to be adopted by government officials, they indicate public attitudes and thus can influence internal government policy debates. The heightened public awareness of arms control and security matters in recent years may put particular pressure on ministerial staffs to ensure that their policies are acceptable; the parties' positions provide a guide to that acceptability.

In the broadest sense, national political parties influence decision making by informing government and ministry officials about public attitudes and opinions on security issues. The views articulated during committee discussions or plenary debate, as well as in party resolutions and inquiries, may be less important for their specific content than for what they convey about broader trends in public and party attitudes. The relative frequency (or infrequency) of large inquiries or use of the question hour or current hour to challenge government policies may be good indicators of security issues that have the potential to polarize public opinion. In the most general sense, national political parties may act as measures of public acceptability for arms control policy or initiatives.

Bilateral and Multilateral Channels

Formal bilateral channels between Bonn and Washington can be divided into three groups. A primary instrument of influence is the NATO infrastructure itself and, within this framework, working contacts between the U.S. military and the Bundeswehr. Second, elaborate mechanisms have evolved within the context of various arms control negotiating forums. A third obvious channel of influence is that of normal diplomatic channels at the working and executive level.

Over time, NATO has developed a complex network of consultative bodies and procedures to deal with arms control issues. The hub of Allied consultation in NATO is the North Atlantic Council. Multilateral consultations occur formally within the council, but they are supplemented by ongoing informal trilateral or bilateral discussions. In addition to inputs from national capitals, the North Atlantic Council receives guidance from other NATO bodies at the subcouncil level. The Political Committee, Senior Political Committee, and Military Committee are all involved indirectly in the process of multilateral consultations. The Defense Planning Committee provides the infrastructure for consultations among defense officials. Within this broad framework, defense ministers consult on arms control issues in the Nuclear Planning Group, which is supported by contacts at the working level. Other NATO forums for arms control consultation include the High Level Group and the Special Consultative Group. Though not formal NATO institutions, they were created to coordinate NATO positions on theater nuclear arms control. The decisions and recommendations of these additional consultative bodies are fed into the North Atlantic Council, which in turn can advise on particular arms control negotiations.

Further bilateral points of contact exist at the location of ongoing arms control negotiations. Elaborate multilateral procedures have been developed, for example, in the case of the MBFR negotiations in Vienna and for the CSCE process. In the first case, the MBFR working group and the ad hoc group in Vienna both include representatives from Bonn and Washington. The CSCE working groups provide a support function for the North Atlantic Council, helping to coordinate Allied positions. The German delegations to all of these bodies include representatives from the Foreign Ministry and the Ministry of Defense. The Foreign Ministry controls all communications and guidance to national delegations, but MOD representatives may outnumber Foreign Ministry delegations within specific negotiating forums; for example, in Brussels (NATO) and Vienna (MBFR).

Direct contacts between West German and American military personnel may help to shape MOD attitudes on arms control. Regular conferences between American and West German staff officers, joint training exercises, and service together at the operational level may facilitate the establishment and cultivation of close contacts between the two military services. In addition to American military personnel stationed in Germany, a large contingent of German military personnel is routinely stationed in the United States for military training. Coordination and joint training are especially well developed in the case of the two air forces. Moreover, in Washington German military personnel are frequently in contact with officials of the Departments of State and Defense. It is difficult to determine the exact impact of these numerous ties, but at the very least they provide military personnel with separate sources of information and may encourage a certain unity of views between the two militaries.

Though the structures of consultation described above would seem to indicate a two-way flow of influence, in fact the United States is the most important ally in this process. In the first place, NATO "consultative" bodies more often function as information clearinghouses than as true collective decision-making bodies— though in MBFR and CSCE the NATO bodies created to coordinate Allied positions probably played a more significant role in the actual decision making. In cases where West Germany has no seat at the negotiating table, such as START and INF, Allied consultative procedures more often are used to inform European allies of U.S. negotiating positions that have already been decided upon in Washington.

The overall predominance of the United States in questions of arms control gives added weight to the American input. The penetration of American views reflects not only its status as the major nuclear power in NATO but its far greater research and analytical capabilities.[7] West Germany may simply lack the necessary analytical capabilities to prevail against the United States. This asymmetry in capability could be corrected to some extent by pooling resources with other European powers.

In sum, rather than offering opportunities for forceful bargaining and lobbying for the West German position, bilateral contacts may constrain the development of independent, or at least U.S.-divergent, FRG positions on arms control. In the future, however, multilateral forums will constitute an increasingly important counterweight against American predominance in the arms control process. The CSCE process has spawned a multitude of mechanisms to coordinate with Bonn's European allies in NATO and with members of the European Community (European Political Cooperation). These have been supplemented since 1982 with frequent bilateral Franco-German consultations on a range of security matters. The WEU also appears to be of growing significance to German officials as a forum for coordinating positions with their European allies.

West German Attitudes on Arms Control

A variety of domestic and international factors influence the attitudes of all the actors in the West German decision-making process. Geopolitical realities and the division of the German nation constrain all policymakers. The lessons of German history, ideological traditions, and the perceived benefits of Ostpolitik and détente shape perceptions of security needs and policies. Additionally, such internal factors as political and sociological changes may alter perceptions of security needs and the role of arms control. The net impact of these variables is a set of broadly shared attitudes and concerns.

Geopolitical Factors

An awareness of West Germany's geopolitical situation is shared by all involved in the policy process. The fact that Germany is divided creates a perception of special security needs. Close relations with the West, above all with the United States, are seen by a majority as indispensable to West German security, but at the same time the FRG has special interests in maintaining good relations with the East. The result is an underlying tension between policy components, sometimes more apparent than not, which poses problems for all West German leaders, regardless of their party. In the 1950s this tension took the form of a domestic debate over rearmament, which, the Social Democratic party (SPD) argued, would cement the division of Germany and eliminate any hope of reunification in the short run.

A more recent example has been the controversy over the deployment of INF; one of the arguments put forward by critics of the NATO dual-track decision was that deployment would threaten the gains of the inter-German détente of the 1970s. Upon returning to power, the Christian Democratic Union (CDU), which otherwise supported the decision, took parallel actions to prevent a deterioration in Bonn's relations with East Germany and Eastern Europe as the missiles were being deployed, granting trade credits to East Germany to coincide with the beginning of deployments. The division of Germany and Bonn's special interest in an East-West climate conducive to inter-German dialogue does not necessarily mean that a desire to continue Ostpolitik will override all other security considerations, but any party in power will be at least concerned about the atmosphere of East-West relations.

The border running between East and West Germany obviously divides NATO and Warsaw Pact countries as well. This "frontline" position contributes to an acute sense of vulnerability; even the public's dim awareness of the presence of large numbers of Allied troops and weapons on West German soil heightens Germany's sense of being the most exposed member of the alliance. This frontline position influences attitudes toward arms control in a number of sometimes contradictory ways. For many West Germans it underscores the importance of the American connection and creates concern lest any specific arms control agreement be "decoupling" or introduce tensions into the relationship. This concern was reflected in the Kohl government's critical reaction to the arms control agreements discussed at the November 1986 Reykjavík summit. Similarly, Gorbachev's offer in February 1987 to delink an agreement on intermediate-range nuclear forces from negotiations on strategic defenses led Kohl, Alfred Dregger, and other figures in the CDU to caution the West against concluding an agreement on INF unless measures were taken to address imbalances in shorter-range systems and conventional weapons.

The general sense of exposure and vulnerability among members of the German electorate also may prevent any party, once in office, from implementing the more extreme aspects of its program. It is not certain, for example, that even an SPD majority government could proceed decisively with arms control policies that caused difficulties within the alliance and thus were perceived to run counter to the current majority's pro-NATO sentiments. On the other hand, a latent angst, brought to the surface primarily during times of increasing international tension, causes even CDU governments to press hard for progress in arms control, if only for its reassurance effects. In this sense, the arms control process itself may be more important to many West Germans than the specific terms of particular agreements. Many West Germans share the view that as long as the superpowers are talking, things cannot be all bad.

Historical Factors

No matter what their party affiliation, all West German arms control actors share a common historical legacy, which may influence attitudes on security and nuclear weapons in the broadest sense. The experience of combat, devastation, and occupation during World War II undoubtedly continues to affect views on the role of force and the relative efficacy of military defense and détente. The impact of the war was most evident in the first decade of the Federal Republic's existence. Resistance, first to rearmament and subsequently to the deployment of U.S. nuclear weapons in Germany, drew strength from antimilitarist sentiment. Civil-military relations, though generally good, can still be a point of contention. Though many of the West German leaders now in power are less affected by direct exposure to war and its aftermath than their predecessors were; even for them, there are sufficient reminders of the past. While younger West Germans may not feel the deep aversion to the use of force that was typical of the immediate postwar period, they are likely to be at least ambivalent, all the more so when the issue concerns the use of nuclear weapons. The German electorate's recognition of the implications of any war, conventional or nuclear, for West Germany is linked to their perception of the relative utility of arms control for West German security.

The German ideological tradition continues to influence the policies of the political parties toward arms control. In its most basic form, an ideology may color a party's entire outlook on security. The Social Democrats' historical tradition of antimilitarism and internationalism was doubtless a factor in the party's opposition to rearmament in the 1950s. In one sense, the SPD's rejection of INF deployments in the 1980s, as well as its current departures from NATO's existing policies, are a return to normalcy—a revival of older SPD notions about security and German interests.

The Christian Democratic Union/Christian Social Union's (CDU/CSU) attitudes toward arms control are rooted in a strong tradition of anticommunism. Among conservative West Germans, anticommunism retains its potency, magnifying perceptions of a persistent Soviet threat and underscoring the importance of military readiness. Any departure from tried-and-true Adenauer-style Westpolitik, any venture that is seen to lead down the path of neutralism or "Finlandization" is rejected. Anticommunism feeds the sense of primacy afforded the American connection. As a result of this more or less latent ideological underpinning, the CDU/CSU views arms control as an uncertain variable and is particularly uneasy about the possible decoupling effects of many actual or prospective arms control agreements, including SALTs I and II and the separate negotiations seeking the total elimination of intermediate nuclear forces from Europe.

Internal ideological disputes may affect the priority which parties assign to military defense and détente or arms control as well. The Social Democratic party, for example, has suffered from internal tension between its doctrinaire socialist and reformist social democratic factions. While such ideological disputes are primarily a response to domestic political and social changes, they sometimes have spilled over into security issues. For example, the emergence of the Greens as a national political force in the late 1970s threatened to steal away voters from the SPD's left wing. Internal wrangling over whether to move the party leftward in response to changing social conditions led to the emergence of a counterelite (Gegenelite) that challenged Helmut Schmidt's leadership of the party. Eventually, this Gegenelite also began to explore alternative security conceptions, such as the "security partnership" with the East, as means of regaining the support of these defectors.

A third, more recent historical experience was the successful Ostpolitik initiated under the Brandt-Scheel government (SPD-FDP) between 1969 and 1974 and consolidated by the Schmidt-Genscher coalition of 1974–82. For many West Germans, and above all for West Berliners, the Soviet-American and inter-German rapprochement of the early 1970s was not merely an ephemeral phase of East-West good feeling but resulted also in concrete, visible improvements. Few would deny, for example, that the security of West Berlin was well served by the 1971 Quadripartite Agreement. Today, West Germans may disagree about the cost of further improvements in East-West relations, but few would favor a return to the hostile truce of the 1950s and 1960s.

This generally positive assessment of the détente period causes West Germans to view the arms control process more favorably than do most Americans; there was no widespread sense of disillusionment about the process of détente in Bonn, as there was in Washington. In fact, both FDP and the SPD currently proclaim hopes for a new phase of détente. Many, though certainly not all, West Germans have come to view arms control as part and parcel of détente and support it as such.

One of the most dramatic changes in West German strategic culture over the past decade, however, has been the steady muting of the perception of a Soviet military or political threat. The postwar security consensus rested upon the foundation of a strong concern about the threat posed to German security by the USSR. This view has been altered substantially over the past decade. While specific events which have involved the use or threatened use of Soviet military power (i.e., military actions in Hungary, Czechoslovakia, and Afghanistan) have resulted in short-term increases in these threat perceptions, the long-term secular trend has consistently reasserted itself after a period of a few months to a year. The result is that by the mid-1980s only between 9 and 16 percent of West Germans felt the Soviets would attack Western Europe in the next five years. Thus the Germans tend to be somewhat less concerned than other Europeans about the Soviets as a military and political threat. In fact, more West Germans were concerned about American pressures on their nation's policies than Soviet pressures.

This diminishing perception of threat has occurred in a military environment which is perceived to be far less favorable to the West than it was in the 1960s. By the early 1970s, more West Germans consistently believed that the Warsaw Pact was superior militarily. The fraction holding such beliefs declined somewhat in the early 1980s, and by the end of 1985 there had been a substantial erosion of the Soviets' perceived lead (although 20–25 percent still viewed the Soviets as ahead). The recent trend reflects increasing numbers of West Germans who believe that there is rough parity between East and West. German views are in the mainstream of European assessments; similar attitudes pertain to the conventional balance as well.

Moreover, evidence suggests that many West Germans tend to prefer a state of parity to one of U.S. superiority. This represents a marked change from the 1950s, when 73 percent preferred the United States to be militarily stronger than the USSR.[8] Parity is seen as a more stable condition conducive to arms control, while the superiority of one side is viewed as an incentive for an arms race.

Internal Changes

Domestic sociological and political changes may cause shifts in attitudes toward security and arms control. Two recent outgrowths of the INF debates—concern over security matters and the revival of the German national question—have fostered a newfound sense of legitimacy for specific "German interests" and may lend security issues a lasting salience on the nation's political agenda. Following the extensive mobilization of antinuclear groups in the early 1980s, some analysts suggested that security policy-making in the Federal Republic had been "democratized." But the controversy over the NATO dual-track decision has not changed the process of arms control decision making in the manner implied. There is little evidence that new channels for popular influence have been opened up or new means created to check the predominance of executive agencies. Existing mechanisms for legislative input have not been exploited to their fullest due to persistent constraints on resources and know-how and the inherent limitations of a parliamentary system. Security policy-making, in this sense, has not been "democratized."

The true impact of the INF debates may be the lasting "securitiza-tion" (concern over security matters) of politics in the Federal Repub-lic. Elections may continue to turn on economic issues—growth, unemployment, and tax reform—but security issues have greater saliency than before. Public acceptability has become a more impor-tant criterion of arms control decision making. West German officials have become more attuned to any policy's perceived impact on the overall *process* of arms control, though public understanding of and interest in negotiating positions remains sketchy and therefore of less significance.

Within the Foreign Ministry, more careful attention is being paid to the various barometers of public opinion—party resolutions and platforms, Bundestag debates on security and arms control policy— to determine the likely public reaction to any specific policy posi-tion.[9] The Chancellor's Office, always concerned about the impact of policy decisions on the chancellor's popularity and on support for the government, seeks to ensure that a repeat of the INF tensions does not occur. An ongoing arms control process is seen to be desirable if only to reassure Germans that the East-West dialogue continues and dialogue with the GDR can proceed.

Securitization of the decision-making process has been reinforced by the evolution of interest in the German question. The latter is no longer posed primarily in terms of reunification but has taken on a number of forms. Whether the talk is of German identity or a shared "community of fate" between the GDR and FRG, a common element is a newfound confidence in the legitimacy of what are perceived as specifically German interests. This may help to explain the SPD's slogan in the 1983 elections: *In Deutschen Interesse* (in the German interest). Four years later, the SPD, from the more conservative Helmut Schmidt to spokesmen of the party's leftwing, called for the "self-affirmation" (*Selbstbehauptung*) of Europe.[10] The CDU/CSU, once an ardent opponent of Ostpolitik, in essence has continued the social-liberal policies with only cosmetic rhetorical changes. The concern for protecting the inter-German dialogue from escalating tensions between the superpowers translated into conciliatory policies to parallel the beginning of INF deployments, including a DM 1 billion trade credit deal with East Germany facilitated by Franz Josef Strauss. For the FDP, German national interests tend to be cast in the guise of renewed enthusiasm for the European "pillar" of NATO, or talk of the Europeans taking a more independent and united role in arms control vis-à-vis the United States. The common theme running through each party's policies is a readiness to press what are perceived as special German interests.

The most direct link between arms control issues and the inter-German dialogue, however, would be official arms control negotiations between the Federal Republic and the GDR. The Social Democratic party and the East German ruling Socialist Unity party have already completed the outlines of draft treaties to ban chemical weapons in central Europe and to create a corridor free of tactical nuclear weapons along the interbloc border. While the Liberal party (FDP) has excluded the possibility of a separate arms control dialogue with East Germany, Foreign Minister Genscher does favor consultations between the two Germanies within existing multilateral arms control negotiating forums. In addition, former special commissioner Friedrich Ruth met on occasion with his East German counterpart to discuss arms control issues.

If it proves to be a lasting trend, the securitization of politics and discussion of German identity and interests may cause West German governments to become stronger advocates of positions perceived to be in the German national interest, even when such positions diverge from American policies. In some instances this may mean pressuring the United States to conclude arms control negotiations; in others it may mean an emphasis on new forms of European consultation and cooperation, with the goal of devising independent positions on arms control. Foreign Minister Genscher has been especially keen on enhancing European security cooperation in order to increase German room for maneuver vis-à-vis the Americans.

General Concerns and Attitudes

The factors discussed above shape the attitudes of all of the actors in the arms control decision-making process: they shape public concerns as well. A number of broadly shared views are discernible, not all of them mutually compatible.

Support for the process of arms control. Whether out of pragmatism or conviction, a majority of West Germans support the arms control process. In the case of the CDU/CSU, support may be most closely related to an awareness that an arms control dialogue dampens public feelings of vulnerability. It may also be seen as a way to sustain a consensus behind what the CDU/CSU perceives as the vital component of West German security—the American nuclear guarantee and the NATO connection. In contrast, the Social Democrats perceive the arms control process as an integral component of détente, a necessary concomitant of successful Ostpolitik. Similarly, the FDP is committed to the arms control process for its intrinsic merits and, increasingly, for its utility in the push for greater European independence and autonomy in the security field. In each case concerns may arise with regard to particular provisions of a negotiated agreement, but support for the process is a view shared generally by all parties.

Fear of decoupling. West German defense experts and CDU/CSU party leaders believe that poorly conceived arms control agreements undermine the credibility of the American nuclear guarantee. The fear that reductions in arms could "decouple" U.S. strategic forces from the FRG may help to explain why some CDU/CSU leaders initially supported the United States' so-called zero option proposal, made in 1982, to remove all intermediate nuclear forces; after the 1986 Reykjavík summit, however, and again in February 1987 with Mikhail Gorbachev's initiative to conclude an INF regime separate from other strategic issues, they became alarmed that such an agreement appeared within reach. While CDU/CSU leaders may reject the military utility of nuclear weapons, they recognize that American weapons deployed in West Germany are stark symbols of the U.S. commitment to the FRG's defense.

Importance of public opinion. Public attitudes on arms control matter when it comes to the formulation of arms control policy. Increasingly, any West German government feels great pressure to appear to be promoting the arms control *process* and advancing German interests. Simultaneously, however, public attitudes may prevent any government from taking extreme positions or attempting radical departures. Admittedly, it is no longer taboo to question the terms of existing West German security arrangements, but there is still a generally shared sense that détente and Ostpolitik are not sufficient to guarantee national security, as seen in the fairly unwavering support for NATO. The public thus embraces membership in NATO and, in a broad sense, support for its existing policies, but also demands Ostpolitik, détente, and arms control, even though all elements may not be compatible at all times. This contradiction compels all parties at least to pay lip service to all their elements. Thus, the CDU/CSU may consider military defense and the American connection of overarching importance, but it feels compelled to support, at least rhetorically, the arms control process. The SPD suggests far-reaching changes in NATO military policies but insists on its continued allegiance to the alliance and support for cooperation with the United States.

The Parties and Arms Control

Divergent attitudes on arms control are discernible among the partisans of the FRG's several political parties. Moreover, the more politically active portion of the population, represented by actual party members and leaders, is split into factions within each party. Party positions on arms control are rooted fundamentally in ideological traditions, but they also reflect alternate views of the German-American relationship and the requirements of West German security.

CDU/CSU. Positions on arms control within the CDU/CSU can be grouped into two broad factions. Since late in Adenauer's era there has been an underlying division between union "Gaullists" and "Atlanticists" over how much Bonn should depend upon its American, as opposed to its European, partners. These terms, though rarely used in recent years, retain their validity if the Atlanticist-Gaullist split is understood, in Waldemar Besson's words, as a dispute over the implications of bipolarity. Since the early 1960s Gaullists have feared that accepting U.S.-Soviet preeminence unhesitatingly makes Europe a marginal force in world politics, thus unable to shape its own destiny; they also have questioned the permanence of America's commitment to Europe. Atlanticists, on the other hand, have always regarded bipolarity as irreversible and have argued that Europe must adapt to that fact or else risk alienating its American partner while provoking its Soviet adversary. Both groups have feared that, in the long term, the wrong choice could isolate Bonn from those upon whom it must rely for protection; both thus have had security uppermost in mind.

This basic disagreement has led to a permanent difference of emphasis and frequent disputes on foreign policy issues within the union. Gaullist instincts have been most compatible with strong anticommunism and, more importantly, an uncompromising political style; thus the CSU and many notable CDU conservatives have been considered Gaullists, while most CDU leaders fit the Atlanticist label.

Nuclear weapons have long played a key role in CDU/CSU security policy. The party has always contended that a conventional military balance must be achieved, but, given the need to offset the peacetime effects of Soviet power, the West cannot merely equip itself for victory on a possible battlefield. Instead, it must strive to make war such an unthinkable risk as to exclude it as an option, thus rendering Soviet military forces irrelevant. In this view conventional weapons are not suited to a goal of such far-reaching deterrence; they play an ancillary role. The effort to build up forces matching the Soviets' would in any case turn the FRG into a garrison state, tearing at its social fabric and opening the way for externally directed subversion.

From Adenauer's day until the present, the key variable in the CDU/CSU security equation has been America's nuclear guarantee. German nuclear weapons are an unthinkable option on historical grounds alone and have been unilaterally renounced by the party. A multilateral European nuclear deterrent built around Franco-British forces also has been viewed generally with skepticism by the union's Atlanticist majority. The Atlanticist perspective regards any potential European nuclear force as inherently incapable of matching the value of U.S. central systems as a dissuasive force because Europe lacks the large land area and low population density necessary to make an entirely autonomous deterrent threat credible.

To be sure, former CSU chief Franz Josef Strauss implied, and the

CDU's Alfred Dregger still occasionally implies, what union Gaullists openly stated in the early 1960s: that Paris, not Washington, is the FRG's most reliable partner.[11] Even in the late 1970s the CSU's newspaper carried columns arguing that with ongoing modernization programs, "Paris understands its 'force de frappe' as an atomic shield for Europe." Aside from providing a more reliable security partner, in Gaullist eyes, a European deterrent would end over-dependence on the United States, revive Western Europe's will to defend its own interests, and restore Western Europe's status as an actor in, rather than merely an object of, world power politics. Yet, in the short term, Strauss in particular was also concerned with finding a realistic, credible nuclear "partner" rather than a nuclear "patron." In the early 1960s, and again late in the 1970s, when he and his spokesmen assailed the Carter administration, he often thus emphasized the European deterrent idea. In the 1980s, however, with a more assertive America and a more cautious Europe, the Bavarian boss talked more enthusiastically of a German "second key" for U.S. nuclear forces and less favorably of European options.

In any case, even union Gaullists have been frank in their skepticism about the possibility of real progress toward creation of a European deterrent; national rivalries and political inertia have come to be seen as intractable obstacles. Strauss and Dregger expressed their frustration with the sluggish pace of European integration and Europe's skittishness about power politics quite bluntly. Moreover, both openly criticized the discrepancies between talk by French politicians of an expanded deterrent and the French government's jealous treatment of the independent deterrent as an exclusively national asset. Atlanticists like Manfred Woerner and Helmut Kohl have been more diplomatic but even more certain in their view of inherent limits on European cooperation in the nuclear field.

Still, the Gaullist critique points to the central problem of traditional CDU/CSU security policy: the need, for lack of alternatives, to rely on a U.S. nuclear guarantee which can never be considered unquestionably viable. Despite commitments and verbal reassurances, the U.S. guarantee inherently lacks certainty; the vulnerability of U.S. cities beginning in the 1960s, the subsequent removal of U.S. missiles from Europe, the bilateral superpower modus vivendi, the acceptance of strategic parity—all of these developments have nourished doubts. Despite public expressions of confidence that America's stake in Europe and a transatlantic "community of values" reinforce the U.S. nuclear guarantee, even CDU/CSU Atlanticists harbor concerns. Periodic American pressures to cut troop strength in Europe or to remove nuclear weapons are taken as additional signs of waning U.S. interest in Europe. Atlanticists wonder whether it could ever be widely enough believed, above all in Moscow, that the United States would risk nuclear war on Europe's behalf.

In CDU/CSU eyes, arms control has long been the most uncertain variable in the security equation. No CDU/CSU party program since 1949 has been without an expression of commitment to the general proposition that negotiated arms reduction can reduce the risks and damage of potential conflict, minimize tension, enhance FRG security, and, ideally, make peace more secure.

Yet just as clearly, the basic premises and implications of CDU/CSU security policy have created a misconception about arms control. Party leaders have always feared that poorly conceived arms control could weaken the credibility of America's nuclear guarantee, or even sever Bonn's alliance ties altogether. In the union's view these would be the logical aims of Soviet arms control initiatives, and they could just as easily be the unintended consequences of Western initiatives. Consequently, there has been a tendency on the union's part to treat weapon limitations as desirable and possible only within the limits set by Bonn's reliance on U.S. nuclear protection and its alliance commitments. Negotiated reductions can never replace, or even really supplement, German security policy, they argue; they must be subordinated to it.

As a result, CDU/CSU arms control policy has been exclusively defensive, its primary aim lying not in arms reduction but in risk reduction—the risks arising from the arms control process itself. The party has given scope for arms control proposals only under certain circumstances: that the U.S. guarantee preempted an undesirable alternative, did not isolate the FRG, and did not weaken the credibility of transatlantic coupling. Union Gaullists applied still another condition: East-West arms control must not discriminate against the non-nuclear FRG. In addition, the union has stipulated that arms control proposals should demonstrate a biased stance on the German reunification question, which will be discussed below.

The CDU/CSU has feared that Moscow would use arms control talks to isolate Bonn from its allies. Throughout recent decades, the party has worried that the limited area covered by the Vienna troop-reduction talks (MBFR) could create separate zones of security within Europe, splitting Bonn from Paris and London. This is seen not only as risky militarily in its direct effects but likely to handicap West European integration. The union also has resisted notions of an arms control dialogue with East Germany (even after it had tacitly recognized that state); it has feared that Moscow would use the lure of East German concessions on the national problem to win West German compromises on arms. This would split Bonn from its Western partners, weaken the alliance, undercut the credibility of America's nuclear guarantee, and hasten the process of Finlandization.

Of even graver concern to the CDU/CSU for two decades, however, has been the prospective decoupling impact of arms talks. The union worries that U.S.-conducted arms control talks, under certain circumstances, could reflect or cause an erosion of the credibility of the U.S. nuclear guarantee. Specifically, in the 1960s the CDU/CSU saw the Non-Proliferation Treaty (NPT) as likely to cause, perhaps by design, cancelation of the multilateral force (MLF). Washington had just persuaded Bonn to accept the MLF as a vital step in offsetting Soviet medium-range missiles and restoring the credibility of NATO's nuclear deterrent. CDU/CSU Atlanticists obliquely voiced their concern about U.S. willingness to permit "an erosion of the alliance"; Gaullists were characteristically more blunt. But both were concerned with the U.S. nuclear guarantee and thus made German support for the NPT strictly conditional: It must leave the MLF untouched (Schroeder), or it must leave open the option of U.S. help in constructing a multilateral *European* nuclear deterrent force (Strauss). Although the MLF was indeed scuttled, union Atlanticists were eventually satisfied by creation of the NATO Nuclear Planning Group, which formally brought Bonn into alliance nuclear decision making.

Like its security policy, the Union's Ostpolitik has long been a major determinant of the party's views on arms control. For two decades this factor reinforced the conviction, arising primarily from CDU/CSU security policy, that the scope for negotiated agreements was circumscribed. But whereas the party's security policy has not changed fundamentally since Adenauer's time, its approach to Ostpolitik necessarily has undergone a transformation.

For over two decades the CDU/CSU contended that German reunification remained a priority goal. Under Adenauer, to be sure, it had deferred national unity so as to integrate West Germany into the West European community. But the party then argued that this would make reunification more likely by solidifying Western unity and military power so that Moscow would be compelled to give up its control of the nation, and the two Germanys could then be integrated into the emergent West European federation. This argument was largely an expedient rationalization for Westpolitik decisions made on the grounds of security interests, but it also reflected the genuine determination of Adenauer and his successors to avoid closing the door on German unity altogether. While by and large not traditional nationalists, they felt that accepting Germany's division was tantamount to accepting the first phase of Soviet hegemony over central Europe. Consequently, the CDU/CSU maintained that, Westpolitik notwithstanding, Bonn had not and could not indefinitely accept the existence of East Germany or the overall division of Europe. The status quo was said to be entirely provisional.

The implications of this traditional Ostpolitik for CDU/CSU arms control preferences were profound. The party remained wary of superpower, pan-European, and, above all, German arms initiatives which explicitly or implicitly accepted the territorial and political status quo in Europe. Union leaders instinctively resisted proposals in which Europe's division, including Germany's division, was the point of departure. Even the promise of actual arms reductions thus implied risks from the union's perspective. It long sought to modify any such initiatives or rechannel them in a direction that would not result in a "cementing" of the status quo.

A much more complicated question is whether the CDU/CSU, like the SPD, has come to believe that arms control is a necessary concomitant of successful Ostpolitik. The party had accepted that dealings with the East, most notably the GDR, were necessary to secure "humanitarian relief measures"; this, not reunification, had become the CDU/CSU's central aim in day-to-day affairs. Does this mean that preserving and pursuing Ostpolitik has increased the CDU/CSU's stake in East-West arms control? Within limits, yes. As an opposition party, and especially since returning to office, the CDU/CSU has come to see East-West arms talks as a necessary element of smooth relations with the Eastern bloc and the GDR. In practice, the Ostpolitik imperative has generated a preoccupation with the "proper atmosphere" for arms limitation that would not be warranted by strict adherence to CDU/CSU security policy. Especially after deployment of INF in late 1983, some union leaders urged steps to improve the East-West, and thus the inter-German, atmosphere. CDU/CSU leaders share in the general consensus of West German elites that détente is intrinsically valuable for the FRG and should be preserved.

Moreover, the union leadership has begun depicting its Ostpolitik as part of an overall policy designed to ease tensions. While this stops short of explicitly linking Bonn's own arms control policy with its Ostpolitik, the connection is often implicit. Some have suggested that the CDU/CSU's desire to show that it can conduct dialogue with the East better than the opposition SPD, and even better than its FDP coalition partner, adds a new impetus to its arms control endeavors, even though it is precisely this tendency in the SPD that union leaders criticize.

Yet there are clear limits to the role that Ostpolitik plays in CDU/CSU thinking on arms control. The party still gives security policy clear precedence over détente considerations and does not believe that the latter significantly enhances the former. This is reflected in surveys which reveal strong support for deterrence among union elites, little faith that détente can complement security, and no confidence that détente could ever replace it. Unlike the SPD then, the CDU/CSU has never espoused a concept of East-West "security partnership" or a "pan-European peace structure." In other words, it does not envision gradual demilitarization and extensive political cooperation across the East-West divide, as does the SPD. For the union, these scenarios are unacceptable on security grounds, represent an unthinkable concession to Moscow's design for Europe, and would Finlandize West Germany—the very scenario its heads of foreign policy since Adenauer have sought to avoid.

But actual CDU/CSU support for arms limitations can be derived from neither the security policy it shaped nor the Ostpolitik it grudgingly inherited. At most, those policies permit a cautious tolerance of arms limitation under restrictive conditions. The primary positive impetus for the CDU/CSU with respect to arms control is concern about public attitudes toward both of these policies. Party leaders have come to see the promise of serious arms control as vital in sustaining a consensus for nuclear deterrence, as well as for co-opting sentiment for pursuing Ostpolitik without careful regard for alliance commitments. The extent and nature of CDU/CSU support for arms limitation are largely functions of its implicit concern about the fragility of West Germany's foreign policy consensus. In short, the party sees arms control, or at least arms control talks, as vital means of reassuring a population that lives on what Helmut Kohl calls the geopolitical fault line between East and West.

If there is little rank-and-file influence on major policy decisions such as arms control, the CDU is far from centralized. On the contrary, its heterogeneity, its diverse interests, and its pragmatism make for a very loose organization. Above the level of party activists (those who attend party conferences and work at the local level), there is considerable factionalization. Party executive committee members, parliamentarians, and regional government leaders have often fallen into different factions. As a rule, genuine factions do not crystallize around issues, let alone conflicts between ideological purity and political pragmatism (as is often the case with the SPD). There is no basic CDU/CSU leadership, particularly for foreign policy. Rather, the CDU/CSU is most often rent by factions grouped around rival leaders or rival strategies. And this form of factionalization has often had clear implications for party decisions on policy.

Arms and arms control issues have often been fodder in intraparty leadership struggles. The debate between Gaullists and Atlanticists over the Test Ban Treaty and the NPT was in the larger sense a struggle for the succession to Konrad Adenauer; most CDU Gaullists did not consider Ludwig Erhard fit for the job. The CDU/CSU's deep divisions over détente, including its response to SALT I, CSCE, and MBFR, were also part of a leadership struggle. Even after Helmut Kohl prevailed and began his long tenure, the problem persisted. Despite having waged an effective campaign in 1976, Kohl was compelled not to run for chancellor in 1980; this undercut his hopes of gradually encouraging the party to adapt its security policy, even modestly, to Ostpolitik. Factionalism and its consequences have thus handicapped any effort to have CDU arms control policy take the need for reassurance more fully into account. Whatever the party leader's own inclinations may be, he must defer to the imperatives of unity in a party still dominated by cautious conservatives. But the latter's leverage would not be nearly so strong without the unique relationship between the CDU and the CSU. Indeed, while it is a separate party, the CSU in a sense is the CDU's strongest faction. The Bavarian sister party's compositional and philosophical cohesiveness greatly exceeds that of the CDU; its homogeneity and unique ideology have forged a bond between leaders and activists so integral as to preclude factional and doctrinal disputes—except in rare, but notable, instances.

This has meant not only that party activists fall in line behind the party leadership but that the CSU leadership acts as a unit, with resulting disproportionate leverage over the CDU in intraunion policy-making. The sister parties nominate one candidate for chancellor; since Bavarian votes will provide the parliamentary majority, the union candidate must run on a platform which satisfies the CSU. He also must appoint CSU members to cabinet and subcabinet posts. More important, before the CDU/CSU parliamentary group votes on legislation, the Bavarian members caucus informally to determine their position and confront their CDU partners with a bloc vote.

CSU leaders frankly concede their assertiveness with the union, justifying it as an effort to provide Bavarians with a voice in federal politics. "Critical loyalty" to the CDU and a confrontational political tone go down well in Bavaria. Strauss also proclaimed that in its uncompromising defense of traditional Adenauerean policy, the CSU is "the hope of millions outside Bavaria."[12] In government, as in opposition, Strauss and his CSU colleagues hectored the CDU, ridiculing its strategy and tactics, deploring its (Kohl's) indecisiveness. The CSU has insisted that a harder, more forthrightly conservative CDU/CSU approach would win more votes. It routinely cited the CSU's 60 percent appeal in Bavaria as proof of the success that such a strategy offers.

Under certain conditions, the necessity for a compromise between its two factions may force the CDU/CSU to adopt untenable or contradictory positions or even to reverse itself on specific arms control issues. There is an inherent tension in the party's arms control policy between efforts to further the process of arms control and positions which, in the CDU/CSU view, would undermine the American-German defense connection. In the case of INF, for example, the party, in an appeal to the popular desire for a continuing arms control dialogue, initially endorsed the zero option but later made clear that it preferred an agreement that would leave some intermediate-range missiles in place. Similarly, the CDU/CSU supports German participation in the Strategic Defense Initiative, but has also argued that participation guarantees Bonn a channel to influence the evolution of SDI and a means to ensure continued adherence to the ABM treaty. In the end, so long as it remains in office the party will support whatever position ultimately is adopted by the U.S. government on both issues, although it may make clear certain nuanced differences in reasoning.

The SPD. The SPD is more seriously divided over security issues than the CDU/CSU. Through the late 1970s there existed in the FRG a consensus on security issues between the dominant moderate wing of the SPD, the FDP, and the majority centrist elements of the CDU. With the exception of the bitter ratification debates over Willy Brandt's Eastern treaties ("renunciation of force" agreements with Moscow and Warsaw that tacitly accepted the postwar boundaries of Germany), this security consensus was based on the twin goals of deterrence (i.e., military parity with the East) and détente, as enunciated in the 1967 Harmel Report of NATO. Yet this consensus was made possible precisely because of the confluence of the détente policies of the FRG and the United States. As long as Willy Brandt's Ostpolitik was in step with U.S. efforts to negotiate arms reductions with the Soviets and lessen political tensions in central Europe, the more leftist elements in the SPD found themselves isolated. Once superpower détente began to sour in the mid-1970s, however, the SPD found itself increasingly divided over pursuing Ostpolitik, on the one hand, and supporting U.S. and NATO policies that at times conflicted with West Germany's deepening relations with the GDR and Eastern bloc, on the other hand.

By the late 1970s this split within the party had been exacerbated by the neutron bomb affair, as well as by the growing political challenge posed by the Green party. Long before the rise of the West German peace movement in the early 1980s, a growing segment of the SPD left wing was voicing its concern with the centrist policies of the Schmidt "government wing" of the party. At the Hamburg party conference in 1977, for example, Schmidt was confronted with widespread SPD opposition to any deployment of enhanced radiation weapons.

This growing split between the Schmidt-led "government" wing of the party (which included Defense Minister Hans Apel and Schmidt confidant Hans-Jürgen Wischnewski) and the "party" faction of Willy Brandt, Egon Bahr, and others was then exacerbated by the debate in early 1980 over an appropriate Western response to the Soviet invasion of Afghanistan. The need for party unity prior to the national elections in September 1980, given that Schmidt's popularity with the German electorate was much greater than that of the SPD, maintained a semblance of order within the party only until the election had been held.

Following the 1980 election, in which the SPD-FDP government actually increased its plurality in the Bundestag, the SPD found itself increasingly divided over three main issues: alliance security policy (especially the INF issue), economic policy differences within the SPD-FDP government, and the electoral challenge posed by the Greens. It was a combination of the first two issues that led FDP leader Hans Dietrich Genscher to bring down the Schmidt government in September 1982, while the growing strength of the Greens manifested itself in the March 1983 national election in which the SPD suffered a devastating defeat, winning less than 40 percent of the vote for the first time in twenty years.

The final breakup of the West German security consensus occurred during the campaign for the 1983 election, when the SPD was advancing the concept of an East-West "security partnership" (*Sicherheitspartnerschaft*). The SPD sought to give equal weight to the FRG's relations with East Germany, the Soviet Union, and other Warsaw Pact countries, which for many Germans seemed to call into question the party's allegiance to NATO and the West. As set forth by Egon Bahr, Horst Ehmke, and others, the security partnership concept, to the extent that it went beyond generalities regarding the primacy of politics over conflict in the nuclear age, implied a greater role for the FRG in stabilizing East-West relations, in large part because of West Germany's special relationship with the GDR and other Warsaw Pact countries. While Bahr and Ehmke asserted that the security partnership concept was predicated on continued West German membership in NATO and the Western alliance, rising SPD criticism of INF deployment plans and U.S. arms control policies suggested to many that the SPD was seeking a quasi-neutralist third way for West Germany between the superpowers. Such fears in the United States, and in France especially, were fueled during the electoral campaign by statements from the SPD chancellor candidate, Hans-Jochen Vogel, and other party figures, including Brandt, Eppler, and Oskar Lafontaine.

Following the election, the SPD continued its leftward drift on security issues. At a special party congress held in Cologne in November 1983, SPD delegates voted overwhelmingly for a moratorium on the soon-to-be-deployed Pershing intermediate-range ballistic missiles. In addition, many members of the SPD participated in, and helped to coordinate, the mass demonstrations against the NATO INF systems that took place in Bonn and other German cities during this period. Perceptions that the party was embarking on an increasingly unilateral security policy were further fueled when the SPD announced in the spring of 1984 that it would hold talks with the East German Socialist Unity party (SED) regarding the creation of a chemical weapons–free zone in Europe.

The failure of the West German peace movement and its supporters in the SPD, the Green party, and other political groups to block the initial deployments of the Pershing IIs in November 1983 signaled the cresting of public concern with the INF issue. The stated willingness of the Reagan administration to negotiate a global ban of intermediate-range ballistic missiles, set forth in the president's "Zero Option" speech that same month, dampened some of the West German opposition to the Pershing and cruise missiles, even though the Soviets made good on their threat to walk out of the Geneva INF negotiations. By the time the United States and the Soviet Union resumed arms control negotiations in March 1985 on a wider range of both offensive and defensive weapon systems, the antinuclear movements in the FRG and elsewhere in Western Europe could no longer mobilize the hundreds of thousands of citizens for public demonstrations that they managed during the 1981–83 period. Yet the activist core of the West German peace movement remained strong, and in conjunction with its allies in the SPD, the Green party, the Evangelical church, the media, and several research and peace institutes, continued to seek strategies with which to rekindle public concern with nuclear weapons, as well as to formulate alternative security strategies for the FRG.

There is little question that, beginning in the early 1980s and especially with the fall of the Schmidt government, the Brandt/Bahr wing of the party has been gaining the upper hand. The influence of the older party moderates (former defense ministers Hans Apel and Georg Leber, Wischnewski, and Löwenthal) has waned in recent years, and Schmidt himself is more influential in international circles than in SPD party politics.

Thus the SPD has found itself at an important transition point in its long-standing attempt to reconcile its socialist and social democratic factions. The SPD Commission on Basic Values has worked on a new basic program for the party that would continue the tradition of generational reevaluations of the party's ideology and political strategy. As with the Brandt-Löwenthal debate over political tactics vis-à-vis the Greens, the battle over the new basic program has divided along the lines of those moderates who favored modifying the Bad Godesberg program and those on the left wing who favored a return to fundamental socialist principles that would clearly distinguish the SPD from the FDP and CDU/CSU.

No security issue more aptly characterizes the leftward drift of SPD policy in recent years than its position on intermediate-range nuclear weapons. From the late 1970s, when the SPD-led government of Helmut Schmidt was a prime architect of the NATO dual-track decision, to 1983, when SPD delegates at the Cologne party conference voted overwhelmingly to postpone deployment of Pershing and cruise missiles in order to allow more time for arms control negotiations, party debate on security issues has become increasingly dominated by the Brandt/Bahr search for ways of constructing an East-West security partnership, which often is at odds with NATO policy.

A group of younger members of the party who were taking a special interest in security issues joined the SPD old guard in the late 1970s. Among the more important of these are Andreas von Bülow, a parliamentary state secretary for the Defense Ministry from 1976 to 1980 and minister for research and technology from 1980 to 1982, and Alfons Pawelczyk and Hermann Scheer, members of the Bundestag. Other SPD officials, such as Karsten Voigt, a former chairman of the Young Socialists (Jusos), and Erwin Horn, like Voigt a member of the Bundestag, have shown more of a preference for working within NATO as opposed to advocating unilateral initiatives. Yet it is fair to say that the views of all of them represent a departure from the Schmidt policies of the 1970s and an increased questioning of U.S. policy, especially during the Reagan administration.

Nowhere was this more evident than in the draft report on security authored by von Bülow in the fall of 1985. Von Bülow had been put in charge of a party commission on security that was instructed to draft a report in advance of the SPD party congress to be held in Nuremburg in August 1986. Entitled "Strategy for a Confidence-Building Security System in Europe: The Way to a Security Partnership," von Bülow's draft raised a storm of protest, both within the party and from the ruling CDU/CSU, when it appeared in September 1985. The report was controversial to many for what was seen as its sense of "moral equivalency" in portraying NATO and the Warsaw Pact as being equally responsible for the military confrontation in

Europe. Taking its cue from the security partnership concept, the report stressed the need to eliminate the nuclear threat that is a central component of the NATO deterrent, to reduce the presence of U.S. and Soviet groups in Europe, and eventually to dismantle the opposing military blocs. Predictably enough, the report was not only castigated by the CDU/CSU but became the subject of a full-scale Bundestag debate, as well as raising objections from some party members. In seeking to downplay the more radical elements of von Bülow's report for SPD policy, the party leadership instructed the party commission on security to submit a new draft before the Nuremberg party conference. However, it was by no means certain that the majority of the SPD was dissatisfied with von Bülow's report.

The von Bülow report indicated an important trend in SPD security policies. In April 1986 the SPD executive released the revised draft of the security platform that would be debated in Nuremberg, and it indeed contained many of the unilateral initiatives advocated by von Bülow and his co-author, Bruns, for breaking the East-West arms control stalemate. It is true that the document also forcefully acknowledged West Germany's role in the Western alliance, saying that its concept of an East-West security partnership could only be carried out with an FRG firmly anchored in NATO. In doing this, the document sought to answer the criticisms made by many in the SPD that the original von Bülow draft had gone too far in espousing a unilateral role for West Germany in mediating East-West tensions. Nonetheless, the platform contained numerous items that were greatly at odds with official NATO policy, the more important being: (1) a reaffirmation of an earlier SPD call for an immediate halt to INF deployments and the withdrawal of those Pershing and cruise missiles already deployed; (2) a freeze on all deployments of nuclear weapons, on nuclear testing, and on development and testing of antisatellite weapons and other space-based weapons, for the duration of the arms control negotiations in Geneva; (3) the withdrawal of battlefield nuclear weapons and the creation of a nuclear-free corridor in central Europe, as proposed by the Palme Commission; (4) the withdrawal of all chemical weapons from central Europe and the establishment of a chemical weapons–free zone in Europe; and (5) the rejection of NATO deep-strike strategies, such as Airland Battle 2000 and Follow-on Forces Attack.

The revised draft of the party's security platform that was distributed prior to the Nuremberg conference contained most of the policy initiatives raised earlier in the von Bülow draft, even though the revision was more moderate in tone and paid more attention to the FRG's role in the Western alliance. Little was said, or could be said, about how and whether the GDR and other members of the Warsaw Pact could exert the kind of pressure on the Soviets that an SPD-led West Germany could be expected to wield within NATO. The one-sided criticism of U.S. nuclear weapons policies that earlier had characterized the West German peace movement led many, both within the FRG and elsewhere, to feel that the SPD was indeed searching for a third way between the superpowers that was in fundamental conflict with NATO policy.

Nowhere was this more clear than at the party conference in Nuremberg in late August 1986, where the more than four hundred delegates approved, with virtually no dissent, the electoral platform on security. If anything, many delegates felt that the security platform adopted by the SPD for its campaign for the January 1987 election was not militant enough. Of the approximately one hundred amendments and motions offered from the floor, most called for more radical security initiatives.

Party defense experts hope to ride the crest of concern within the German elite over conventional arms control issues back to respectability on security issues. At the forefront of this effort is the work of Karsten Voigt, who has recently outlined a range of conventional arms control proposals reflective not just of SPD thinking but of a broader consensus within the German elite. It is clear that the Sub-committee on Disarmament will seek as well to develop a consensus on conventional arms control issues.

It is hardly surprising that the current security partnership concept of the SPD can trace its origins to the Ostpolitik initiated by Willy Brandt when he became chancellor in 1969. In tandem with U.S. efforts to promote superpower détente, the Brandt government concluded renunciation of force agreements with the USSR and Poland, and then the Basic Treaty with East Germany, in an attempt to normalize the FRG's relations with Eastern Europe.

In the beginning, this *Deutschlandpolitik* between the FRG and the GDR focused primarily on issues of "low politics"; that is, trade, transportation, energy, and common environmental concerns. More politically sensitive issues, such as West German recognition of GDR sovereignty, questions of German citizenship, access by West Germans to friends and family in the GDR, and the ability of East Germans to emigrate to the FRG, were discussed as well but not resolved to the satisfaction of either state. Regarding common security concerns, it was only in the later 1970s that *Deutschlandpolitik* began, slowly and tentatively, to include such issues as arms control and confidence-building measures that up until then had been handled primarily within the context of NATO and the Warsaw Pact.

A breakthrough of sorts on security issues was achieved at the Schmidt-Honecker summit in December 1981, when the two heads of government agreed to try to formulate a joint initiative that could break the deadlock at the MBFR talks in Vienna on conventional forces. The fact that Foreign Minister Genscher met in early 1982 with his East German counterpart, Oskar Fischer, to try to reach agreement on a common position was a departure from the usual FRG practice of entrusting such contacts to its minister for inner-German relations (in this case, Egon Franke). By the same token, the GDR had usually avoided participating in talks with the FRG that went beyond strictly German concerns for fear of compromising its status as a sovereign state (since the FRG has refused to recognize the GDR as a sovereign, legal entity). In this case, however, the opportunity to deal directly with Genscher on an issue of such importance overcame East German hesitations.

This attempt by the Schmidt government to at least open up lines of communication with East Berlin served the double purpose of seeking ways to end the stalemate on arms control (particularly on the MBFR talks, a particular concern of Schmidt's) and dampening criticism within the SPD over the chancellor's support for INF deployment. A firm believer in pursuing the twin tracks of arms control and force modernization, Schmidt's policy has been continued by the Kohl government, albeit with reduced visibility.

Once out of power, however, the SPD decided to initiate its own talks with East German officials. In March 1985 the SPD held its first talk with officials of the East German Socialist Unity party on ways of creating a chemical weapons–free zone in central Europe. Strictly speaking, these party-to-party discussions were little different from the contacts the SPD had followed while in power, given the confluence of party and government in the GDR. At the conclusion of the first round of talks in June 1985, the SPD and SED reached agreement on a draft proposal.[13]

The fact that the SPD has negotiated directly with the SED (that is, the East German government), an act that would have been an immense political liability in the 1950s, passed with little additional comment from the Kohl government. Nonetheless, the talks did raise political sensibilities within the United States and NATO (not least because the only chemical weapons in the FRG are American) that the party was undermining the alliance through its independent initiatives. Similar discussions between the SPD and SED on nuclear weapons in central Europe, as well as SPD talks with the Communist parties of the Soviet Union, Poland, and the GDR on ways of reducing defense expenditures, will only further increase fears that the SPD has embarked on a unilateral course that will undermine NATO cohesion.

The FDP. For over two decades the Free Democratic party (FDP, or Liberals) has been instrumental in shaping Bonn's foreign policy, exercising an influence disproportionate to its small size. Since 1949 it has participated in all but two cabinets at the national level and it has served to check the more extreme factions of its larger coalition partners. Moreover, the FDP has been assured a decisive input into the foreign policy-making process through its sustained control of the Foreign Ministry; since 1966 the FRG's foreign minister has been an FDP politician—first Walter Scheel, then Hans-Dietrich Genscher.

The FDP's power derives from its unique role in the postwar German political system. Though the party has continually sought a more substantive profile, the FDP's political and electoral support has been achieved less from its program than from its perceived actual function as coalition maker, safety valve, and corrective. Though the party continues to espouse liberal themes—free market economic principles and individual rights—the FDP has long recognized the electoral advantages which accrue from its image as guarantor of stability, continuity, and moderation. This image neatly matches the German electorate's apparent preference for avoiding drastic departures from the statue quo, whether the radical change was proposed by the left wing of the SPD or the hard-line ideology of the Christian Democrats' right wing.

The FDP's continued participation in national governments is matched by the continuity of its attitudes on security and arms control. Its fairly unwavering support of arms negotiations is rooted in its overall perception of the desirable condition of East-West relations and is evidence of the controlling hand of Hans-Dietrich Genscher within the party. Without exaggeration, one can assert that Genscher's policy is FDP policy. Under Genscher's leadership, continuity and predictability have become the catchphrases of FDP foreign policy. As in the days of the social-liberal coalition (1969–82), the FDP sees strong ties to the West and NATO (Westpolitik) and cooperation with the East (Ostpolitik) as two indispensable and complementary components of West German foreign policy. The party has supported Genscher's initiatives to bring about substantive progress in arms negotiations and European security conferences, along with his calls for a vigorous European and German role in the East-West dialogue.

The FDP's influence has been inextricably linked to its power as the swing party, its access to crucial leadership positions, and Genscher's long tenure as foreign minister. Whether the FDP can continue to play this corrective role will depend both on the evolution of the party in the post-Genscher period and on developments in the West German political system as a whole. Since 1982 and the FDP's realignment with the CDU/CSU, the party has been in a state of transition. A large turnover in membership and leadership has left the FDP without potential leaders who are well versed in foreign affairs and security issues. Genscher's strategy appears to be to stay in power as foreign minister long enough for this next generation of leaders to acquire the necessary expertise to ensure continuity of the party's current policy. But struggles over leadership succession within the FDP, an intensifying conflict with the CSU, or a usurpation of the FDP's traditional functions by the Greens as a result of the next election could undermine Genscher's efforts. The combined effects of these factors make it unlikely that the post-Genscher FDP will exercise as great an influence in the formulation of Bonn's security policy as it has in the past.

The FDP's attitudes toward arms control are rooted in the original elements of the social liberal coalition's program: maintenance of a firm foundation in NATO coupled with dialogue and cooperation with the East. Over time, this prescription has undoubtedly been shaped by Genscher's own perspectives on the requisites of German foreign policy. The result has been a view of arms control, and more generally of East-West relations, which has remained largely unchanged over the past two decades. Only the nuances of emphasis have altered, with an increasingly important role assigned to a European pillar within the alliance as a counterweight to the influence of the United States. While Genscher emphasizes the importance of alliance and German-American cooperation, he also has attempted to preserve the fruits of détente, including the inter-German dialogue. The recurring themes of continuity, predictability, continuing cooperation and dialogue with the East, and substantive progress in European security have been the hallmarks of Genscher's tenure as foreign minister. They also have become mainstays of the FDP's foreign policy agenda.

In Genscher's scheme the purpose of European endeavors is continuing and expanding cooperation with the East, above and beyond arms control negotiations. Such broad-based cooperation is necessary because security can no longer be guaranteed unilaterally, but only through cooperation. And while Genscher has not gone so far as to use the SPD's term "security partnership," he has spoken of a "survival partnership" (Überlebensgemeinschaft) and of the goal of creating global and European "cooperative security structures." Further, while he does not echo the Social Democrats' call for a "second phase of détente," in July 1986 Genscher expressed his hope for a "new phase of East-West relations, of détente."

The European framework is also the only permissible context for German initiatives. In this vein, Genscher rejects unilateral actions by Bonn, arguing that Bonn should work together with its European allies for progress in arms control.[14] Genscher supports efforts by the two German states, within their respective alliances, to improve East-West relations, promote cooperation, and accelerate progress in disarmament and arms control. But he draws the line at unilateral initiatives such as the SPD's ongoing dialogue with the SED. He has cautioned the SPD against going beyond the limits of party activity and intruding upon governmental prerogatives or undermining the defense consensus. But he has tempered his condemnation of the SPD's "parallel foreign policy" (Nebenaussenpolitik) by welcoming the comprehensive exchange of information. It is not an inter-German dialogue per se that Genscher seemingly rejects but the attempt to pursue negotiations with the GDR outside the existing alliance system.

The FDP's attitudes on arms control and its ability to influence governmental policy will depend on the party's leadership in the post-Genscher period and on its ability to retain its function in the German political system. The party must first find successors to current leaders, who, in turn, may determine whether the party would realign itself with the SPD or remain firmly allied to the CDU/CSU. The further evolution of the Greens is a factor beyond the FDP's control, but one which may bear on its political future.

Though the questions of leadership and future alignment remain open, there are few indications that the party's attitudes on arms control, East-West relations, or defense will undergo drastic changes. The party has displayed remarkable continuity in its policies; the only change has been the appearance of a greater emphasis on the European component of arms control as an alternative to an unquestioning pro-American line. The party's 1986 program, in fact, reads much like the original proposals and goals of the early foreign policy of the social-liberal coalition. It is a moderate course with familiar elements.

The FDP's emphasis on modernization, continuity, and predictability in foreign policy may prove to be one of its strongest assets in its fight to retain its function in the German political system. The FDP's steady but independent course in foreign policy is likely to appeal to German voters who are wary of both the strident ideologies of the Right and the radical departures from the status quo advocated by the Left. And the FDP has proved itself adept at playing on these fears, depicting itself as a factor of stability, an advocate of arms control, a promoter of European cooperation, and watchdog of the inter-German dialogue. The portrayal of the FDP as a loyal ally to Bonn's European partners and the United States, but one with an independent and forceful voice as well, may carry enough electoral appeal to secure the FDP's future as kingmaker and corrective, and safeguard its channel for influencing arms control policy.

The Greens. Of all the West German parties, the Greens hold the most radical positions on arms control and security. Rooted in their commitment to the principle of nonviolence, the party advocates an "active peace policy" to replace the FRG's current military commitment to NATO. Arms control plays little or no role in this view because it has not gone far enough and has failed, along with all conventional notions of security, to bring mankind closer to a demilitarized, disarmed world. The Greens propose a number of radical measures, including withdrawal from NATO, unilateral disarmament measures, dissolution of Europe's bloc system, and the eventual dismantling of the Bundeswehr.

Though generally viewed as utopian and thoroughly impractical, the Greens' program nevertheless may have a marginal impact on the future evolution of West German arms control policy. The Greens' pronouncements on security—perhaps the one issue upon which most factions can agree—give vent to more generally shared reservations about the presence of nuclear weapons in West Germany and appeal to underlying sentiments of pacifism and antimilitarism. Further, there is an explicit linkage between German security and the fundamental issues of autonomy and national interests. Finally, the Greens' radical program is a constant reminder to voters in the SPD's left wing who may be dissatisfied with the Social Democrats that another alternative exists, a factor that is certain to figure into the SPD's calculations in choosing the party's new leaders.

Conclusion

The arms control decision-making process of the Federal Republic reflects the continuous interaction between internal and external factors in the formulation of Bonn's security policies. Arms control policy is caught between West Germans' commitment to a special bilateral relationship with the United States and their interest in good relations with the East, above all with the GDR. Progress in arms control depends ultimately on the U.S. commitment, an external factor. At the same time, West Germans increasingly view arms control as part of a European détente process that should be more independent of the great powers' behavior.

This common thread of internal/external tensions runs through all aspects of West German arms control policy. The decision-making process has a few clearly domestic components: conflict among executive agencies, public debate in the Bundestag, the impact of domestic changes such as the securitization of politics, and the resurfacing of the German question. But bilateral channels also exist and ensure input from the United States.

Similarly, the broader factors that shape the attitudes of all actors and public views are both internal and external. Thus, some things are unique to the German experience—division, the experience of war, the rewards of Ostpolitik. Others are part of the broader international context: Soviet and U.S. policies, East-West relations, the progress (or lack thereof) in arms control negotiations.

The future evolution of arms control policy likewise will depend not only on election outcomes or coalition strife but also on developments at the international level. Whatever coalition is in office, the policies of the West German government will be strongly affected by the evolution of Soviet-American relations.

If the INF debates have had any lasting impact, it is the new importance of domestic interests in the security policy-making process. Unquestioning support for NATO has broken down. The splits within the SPD and the defense policy alternatives put forward by the party are evidence that national interests and new domestic perceptions of security needs are given more weight. This evolution is certain to continue.

Nevertheless, change in arms control policy is likely to be incremental. Geopolitically or historically derived feelings of insecurity and vulnerability persist. A majority of West Germans continue to support membership in NATO. But attitudes can and do change. Indeed, the growth of support for détente, Ostpolitik, and the arms control process occurred gradually, yet undeniably. Taking a longer-term view, increasing polarization on security issues, a slow but evident erosion of support for NATO, a different perspective on the prospects or benefits of security alternatives, and, above all, a newfound sense of the legitimacy of questioning current arrangements and their service of German national interests are likely to influence West German security and arms control policies.

3

French Arms Control Policy

Robbin F. Laird and Dinah Louda

Introduction

Until recently, French policymakers have rarely taken nuclear-age arms control seriously. The typical French reaction when talking about arms control would be a shrug of the shoulders and possibly a comment on the naïveté of American diplomacy. Arms control efforts have generally been viewed as irrelevant at best, if not positively dangerous for French and European security. Bilateral U.S.-Soviet negotiations have been perceived, especially since de Gaulle, as a way for the superpowers to impose their supremacy without enhancing European (or international) security. Meanwhile, multilateral arms control discussions have more often than not cast France as the villain and sought to prevent France from pursuing its independent nuclear program.

Recently, however, French attitudes have begun to change: President Reagan's "Star Wars" speech of March 1983 sent shock waves through the French defense community. Since then, the multiplication of Soviet arms control proposals, the controversial Reykjavík summit, and the INF agreement have heightened French concern about U.S. intentions and Soviet objectives in Europe.

France has increasingly appeared to be the last true believer in nuclear deterrence. Skepticism about arms control remains, yet there is growing awareness that a purely negative stance will no longer adequately protect French security interests. It is not enough to dismiss Western or Soviet arms control proposals as propaganda, nor to warn that nuclear disarmament proposals would leave the Soviets with a military advantage in Europe. France must have something constructive to say lest it be isolated in a Western defense posture that is increasingly based on conventional deterrence.

The new interest in arms control talks stems primarily from attempts to protect France's nuclear option from political erosion and to prevent the isolation of France within the alliance. As such, French arms control policy continues to pursue political objectives rather than the less practical military objective of preventing a Soviet attack which few experts believe likely. The main goal is to win European, in particular West German, backing for France's independent nuclear posture. In exchange, a growing number of French analysts appear willing to commit France's conventional and tactical nuclear forces to the defense of Europe.

The trick, of course, is for France to become increasingly involved in the ongoing arms control process without eliminating its independent defense posture. France refused to be included in INF negotiations on the grounds that its nuclear forces were all central systems, designed not for counterforce strikes and war fighting but for massive strikes against Soviet cities and industrial centers. Yet it refuses to include its forces in strategic arms limitation talks, given the huge disproportion between its nuclear arsenal and those of the superpowers. Many French analysts agree that the French position is becoming increasingly untenable. At the same time, the Soviet Union's apparent willingness to respond positively to recent French initiatives, especially in the conventional area, has placed French policymakers in an awkward position.

The related and equally difficult issue is how to cultivate public opinion. French policymakers and politicians, long shielded from any serious public debate on defense issues, suddenly fear that the cohesion of the defense "consensus" based largely on nuclear confidence may indeed be unraveling. But attempting to rethink and recreate that consensus in an increasingly antinuclear Europe may be a Pandora's box.

Factors Affecting French Arms Control Policy

The most significant factor affecting French arms control policy in the mid-1980s has been the evolution of French security policy since the mid-1970s. The title a 1986 book edited by Robbin Laird (*French*

Security Policy: From Independence to Interdependence) is suggestive of the shift in French policy. The splendid isolation of the classic
Gaullist synthesis has ended.[1] Increasingly, French policymakers
have sought to accommodate their policy of independence with the
security concerns of their allies. They have done so primarily by
pursuing a more interdependent course with regard to their conventional forces while remaining as independent as possible with regard
to their nuclear forces.

The pursuit of a more interdependent course with regard to conventional forces has not been an easy one. The major barrier remains the
absence of France from the integrated military command of NATO.
Because of public opinion and the interpretations of public opinion
crystallized in the political parties and their leadership, the French
remain unable to broach the subject of reintegration into the military
command. However formidable a barrier this remains, the French
have sought various ways to cope with it. Above all, the French have
pursued military cooperation with the West Germans as a way not
only of furthering their European security objectives but also of ori-
enting their conventional forces toward a greater role in the alliance
without confronting the question of their relationship to American
forces.[2] The formation and utilization of the Force Action Rapide
(FAR) is an important case in point. Many factors contributed to the
formation of the FAR; one clear motivation of the French government
was to create a military instrument useful for the diplomatic purpose
of reassuring its allies while maintaining as much independence as
possible.

French nuclear forces remain ostensibly outside this effort toward
promoting greater interdependence between French and alliance security. On the one hand, the French have sought to discourage their
allies from expectations that French nuclear forces exist other than
to protect French territory. When some German officials have called
for the French to extend nuclear deterrence to West Germany, the
French have emphasized the limited capability of their forces. The
French president has, however, provided increased assurances of
consultation with the Germans on nuclear issues, most notably tactical nuclear matters. On the other hand, in the alliance debate about
the future of nuclear deterrence the French have emphasized that
their forces play an important de facto role in alliance defense. In
effect, the argument has been, please do not ask France to protect

other Europeans explicitly; in a de facto sense the French forces already do so.[3]

The evolution of French security policy has affected its arms control policy in several ways. First, it has created the perceived need to end its empty-chair policy and become an active player in the arms control process.[4] Second, as French security policy has become more interdependent in orientation, the French government has had to pay more attention to trying to coordinate French arms control policy with European and American allies. Third, the French government has been paying more attention to the arms control process as a threat to their independent position, or, more bluntly, as a threat to the tensions between independence and interdependence in their policy. As the evolution of their security policy proceeds, French officials seek to avoid situations which threaten to highlight tensions inherent within French policy.

Closely associated with the evolution of French security policy as a factor influencing arms control policy has been the question of the attitude of the French defense consensus on that policy. Compared to their allies, the French clearly have a much greater degree of consensus toward their security policy, but one cannot avoid a sense that it is much more fragile than the casual visitor or commentator on the French scene might assume. The consensus revolves around the priority of French independence and the equation of nuclear deterrence—especially in the form of France's possession of nuclear weapons—with that independence. French policymakers seek to reduce pressures from the foreign policy environment which threaten nuclear deterrence in large part because of this equation between independence and deterrence. It also is clear that if this close relationship were broken, a wide range of alternatives would struggle for supremacy in the French security concept.[5]

The French government has sought in every way possible to ensure that its defense consensus is not endangered by the arms control process. Above all, France will not permit its nuclear arms to be included directly in a U.S.-Soviet agreement. This has meant that the government has been tough with the superpowers as well as with its European allies on this issue. It also has led the French to seek cooperation with the British on nuclear arms control issues to protect their joint interests. In addition, the French have sought in the conventional arms control area to ensure that France is not perceived by its public to be involved in bloc-to-bloc negotiations, which would imply reintegration into NATO. Although it is generally true that France has had greater room for maneuver than its allies have in the arms control process, the defense consensus has been an important factor in constraining the actions of French policymakers.

In addition to domestic factors, the evolution of the foreign policy environment and French interpretations of that evolution have had a critical impact on French arms control policy. Above all, the French have been preoccupied with the evolution of West German security policy in particular, and European policy in general. The collapse of the consensus on defense policy in Western Europe has been particularly threatening to the French security concept, a concept which has presupposed the ability of France to remain somewhat aloof from European developments, or, alternatively, has assumed solidarity in Western Europe on security matters. Ironically, the French could leave the integrated military command based on the assumption that NATO was solid. When questions about the solidarity of NATO are raised, however, the desirability for French aloofness becomes more questionable.

The collapse of the Western defense consensus has required a restoration of the language of alliance solidarity in French defense discourse. In theoretical terms, the French position is like that of the operation of an interest group in Mancur Olson's *Logic of Collective Action*.[6] France could act with benign neglect as long as the United States, as the force shaping the alliance, could primarily by itself provide for the "public good" of collective defense. When the United States's ability to do so declines, the "public good" of Western defense has eroded. The French are left in the position of either remaining aloof and watching further deterioration in collective capabilities or contributing directly to the enhancement of the "collective" or "public good" of Western defense capability. The French are increasingly finding themselves in the position of having to link their "independence" more directly and publicly with the efficacy of overall Western defense capabilities in order to deter the Soviets.

The French perception of the West German situation in the 1980s has occasionally bordered on the hysterical. French concern during the debate about Euromissile deployment in the early 1980s focused on the "pacifism" rampant in West Germany.[7] It has since focused on the growing pressures for denuclearization in West Germany, a pressure evident across the German political spectrum. The concern for more securely anchoring West Germany in the Western security system, a system solidly based (the French hope) on nuclear deterrence, has been a major motivation for the evolution of French security policy, including arms control issues.

French arms control policy has become a critical component of France's general West European policy. It has provided a language and a framework within which general security issues can be discussed with France's European allies. The French experience in the Conference on Disarmament in Europe (CDE) has been critical for learning how to deal more effectively with their European allies in the arms control area. A major French motivation for being involved in arms control forums today is simply to ensure that they are in a position to lead Europe in the "right" direction on security issues, that is, a position commensurate with the French defense consensus.

Also, unlike the British, the French have sought to work primarily with their European allies to influence the Americans. From the French perspective, the way to Washington has been through Bonn and London. The French have pursued a European effort to support their long-range strategic assessment as well. France more than any other European power expects the United States someday and somehow to draw down its forces in Europe. The French are, of course, concerned to delay the inevitable as they understand it, but it is necessary to prepare for the day that it happens. The critical effort to prepare for that day is thus to foster European security cooperation. Increasingly, French policymakers recognize that the arms control process is a critical avenue in which to enhance such cooperation.

A final element in the French assessment of the foreign policy environment and its impact on arms control has been the evolution of the Soviet effort. The French sense that the Soviets are maneuvering themselves to be in a position to pressure the French defense consensus and to fragment the European as well as transatlantic components of the Western alliance. This French perception dates at least from the early 1980s and was reinforced by the Andropov proposal for the inclusion of their nuclear forces in the INF talks. Naturally, the Gorbachev phenomenon has only deepened their concern. Although there are some French Sovietologists who welcome in a positive sense the rise of the general secretary, the French government has not been among his enthusiastic admirers. French officials perceive more of a change in Soviet tactics than strategy, but they are clearly worried about the innovativeness of Gorbachev's tactics. Given Soviet ingenuity and Western inability to deal with it, the French government perceives it to be necessary to become more involved in arms control issues in order to ensure that the West is not tricked into going down the garden path to unilateral disarmament or unwittingly negotiating to Soviet advantage. French leadership is required when the West must be vigilant.

The domestic and foreign policy factors converge on one important point for French arms control policy. The French seek to prevent or avoid problems rather than to achieve a positive arms control agenda. Domestically, they seek to avoid pressures on their defense consensus. Internationally, they hope to avoid the collapse of the alliance, to foster Europeanization, and to deter the Soviets from successfully pursuing their anticoalition strategy.

Perspectives of the French Executive on Arms Control

For the French policymaker, the arms control process has been about the politics of Western strategy much more than it has been about the technical question of how to limit arms. Not insignificantly, the French government's arms control expertise is primarily located in the Foreign Ministry's Service des Affaires Strategiques. The French by implication consider arms control to be a component of strategic affairs, not a separate entity.

The French talk about disarmament issues rather than arms control issues. The term *arms control* is Anglo-Saxon and is viewed as an alien entry into French—a case of strategic Franglais. The typical language French officials use in dealing with arms control issues publicly is evident in the interview former defense minister André Giraud gave to *L'Express*. In this interview Giraud referred to "a good and a bad" form of disarmament—"the first accentuates peace, the latter accentuates the disequilibriums which increase the risk of war."[8] Specialists in the French government, however, have learned to use the technical vocabulary associated with arms control issues as a means of influencing the debate among France's allies.

The debate about arms control is, then, an inextricable component of the debate about the future strategy. The French approach pays enormous attention to the presentation of policy in the strategic and arms control area. Declaratory policy is considered to be an absolutely essential dimension of general policy. French policymakers simply cannot comprehend the carelessness of American policymakers' use of language. Linguistic gaffes by American policymakers which go almost unnoticed in the United States often become major issues for the French. The French intellectual culture plays an important role in elevating the importance of declaratory policy in the security and arms control area as well. The intellectual plays a much more significant role in public life in France than in America. French politicians seek to be seen as men of letters in addition to being men of power.

The propensity for the French to take declaratory dimensions of policy seriously is further enhanced by the fact that the French role in arms control policy has been largely symbolic and declaratory. The French followed an "empty chair" policy until 1978, and since that time have been directly involved in the Conferences on Disarmament and the Conferences on Disarmament in Europe (CD and CDE) talks. Nonetheless, on the other major arms control issues, especially the nuclear ones, the French have been involved primarily by developing their declaratory stance on these issues. This might change, however, as the French become more involved in conventional and nuclear arms control issues in the years ahead.

Nuclear Arms Control Issues

Above all, the French have been concerned with protecting the viability of nuclear deterrence. Discussions of arms control issues have been pursued to underscore the continued legitimacy of nuclear deterrence in the face of various threats to its continued future, ranging from Soviet denuclearization efforts to claims that NATO "excessively relies" on conventional deterrence.

The French have sought to enhance the support of their European allies for independent nuclear deterrents. The problem has been that in the absence of providing an explicit extended deterrence or an explicit involvement in a NATO nuclear planning process, non-nuclear European powers have been reluctant to be enthusiastic about French nuclear forces. Reykjavík has heightened the appreciation of some European officials—especially West German conservatives—for the de facto role of these forces, but it has simply led to greater pressure by these officials for an explicit nuclear guarantee from France.

A French official involved in security-issue discussions with the West Germans, however, has made it clear that there are definite limits to the prospects for providing a French nuclear guarantee to West Germany. As André Adrets (a pseudonym for a former MOD official) put it, "At the very moment when the U.S. guarantee seems to be weakening, it would undoubtedly be presumptuous to want to replace it in its most ambitious functions. [Also] . . . the demarcation of an extended sanctuary would have the drawback of guaranteeing the opponent nonnuclear combat in regions that would not be explicitly covered by the extended sanctuary."[9] The French seek, in short, to avoid being forced into reassuring the Germans by means of formally extending the French deterrent to cover German territory. They wish to avoid arms control pressures which imply that the French would have to make this shift in their policy.

As mentioned briefly above, the French have sought to involve the British in a strategic dialogue as well in order to enhance common positions on nuclear issues, especially on an arms control basis. The Anglo-French discussions of nuclear issues date from the 1984 Avignon meeting between Thatcher and Mitterrand and have covered arms control issues and the joint production of an air-launched attack missile.

Most important to the French, of course, has been the question of superpower competition in nuclear weapons, a major component of which has been the arms control relationship between them.[10] The French were enthusiastic supporters of the ABM treaty and cautious supporters of the SALT II agreement. French officials, especially President Mitterrand, were concerned with the political consequences of the breakdown in the superpower strategic dialogue.

The political conflict over Euromissile deployments led the French president to make the political decision to support publicly the emplacement of American missiles in Europe. This was seen as necessary partly because of the Soviet effort to gain strategic superiority at the European level but even more so because of the "pacifist" reaction of the peace movements against nuclear weapons. It was, above all, the threat to nuclear deterrence that motivated the French president to make his January 1983 speech in the Bundestag.

The American president's speech on SDI and the entire rhetoric surrounding the immorality of nuclear deterrence was perceived by the French as snatching defeat from the jaws of victory. On the verge of defeating Soviet efforts to delegitimize nuclear weapons in the Euromissile struggle, why would the American administration seek to support that political objective? For the French, the Euromissile struggle was primarily about political objectives, not about technically evening the military balance.

From the French perspective, the meaning of the Reagan administration's actions became clear at Reykjavík. According to an article by a French Foreign Ministry official, the true problem revealed at Reykjavík was "the Soviet-American convergence on the delegitimization of nuclear deterrence, basically on the Old Continent."[11] The French concern was simply to try to influence the Western strategic debate to ensure the continued vitality of nuclear deterrence in the face of disregard or carelessness by its American ally in dealing with a Soviet adversary dedicated (as the French saw it) to denuclearization.

The arms control framework within which this issue was debated became clear when Gorbachev announced in February 1987 that he accepted, with some reservations, the NATO proposal of zero long-range INF weapons. The French government's reaction was shaped by the diversity associated with cohabitation, but the differences that emerged were on the level of tactics, not objectives. Former defense minister Giraud characterized the Soviet action as creating a "new Munich."

Gorbachev soon outflanked the French and others by proposing to pursue a so-called double zero option whereby short-range intermediate nuclear forces (SRINF) would be eliminated as well. It soon became clear to France that its American and British allies were willing to proceed with the double zero option. It was clear as well that the German government could not resist the double zero in front of their public. When the German government sent its various representatives to request French support for resisting the second zero, the French president refused, largely on the grounds of that German government's inability to commit itself to modernization.

The question of how to reassure the Germans in this "new" strategic situation has become a critical one for the French government. How can a firebreak be constructed at the tactical nuclear level without providing explicit assurances to the Germans? How can France defuse

Soviet pressure for further denuclearization? How can France ensure that the Americans will not go further down the road toward replacing nuclear with conventional deterrence in Europe? These critical strategic questions shaped the French stance on nuclear arms control issues in the mid-1980s.

The final nuclear issue of great concern to the French is SDI. The French, like other Europeans, began to have a major debate about the future of nuclear deterrence in a defense-dominated world. This debate was reflected at the public level in a television program, a special magazine issue of *Le Point*, and a book published by Pierre Lellouche. The thrust of these public presentations was that the future for nuclear deterrence was grim.

The French government, however, was reaching different conclusions. Specialized assessments began to probe the problem of shifting to a defense-dominated world. The consensus began to emerge that France would continue to have significant ability to counter any probable Soviet defenses for many years to come.[12] This assessment was made by a carefully coordinated team of French technical, strategic, and military officials. More sensitive French documents show greater concern with the future of the French deterrent, presaging the public statements by François Fillon of the National Assembly about the need for a military reconnaissance satellite in order to better organize attacks on Soviet strategic defenses.[13]

Two arms control issues became increasingly critical as the French conducted their assessment of the future strategic environment. First, the reaffirmation of the ABM treaty and the need to maintain a "narrow" interpretation of that treaty was underscored. Modification of the treaty to provide for counterforce protection was also considered unacceptable to the French, given the location of Soviet ICBM belts. The Soviets could buy both countervalue and counterforce protection with the deployment of land-based defenses. Second, the French began to step up their effort to gain support for an anti-satellite systems (ASAT) and other space-based weapons ban. The French assessment that their deterrent would remain viable for the indefinite future rested squarely on their ability to degrade Soviet radars associated with defense. If the Soviets began to deploy space-based radars, the viability of the French deterrent would be brought into question.

Non-nuclear Arms Control Issues

The French government has paid the greatest attention to nuclear issues, but, increasingly, conventional arms control issues have become of greater importance. The French refused to participate in the Mutual Balanced Force Reduction (MBFR) talks for a variety of reasons, most notably because it was a negotiation between the Warsaw Pact and NATO "blocs." Also, the French believed that the talks were too narrowly focused on the central front rather than on the broader issues of the conventional balance. The French believe that there is a more significant asymmetry in conventional forces than their German and British colleagues perceive. They tend to believe that the asymmetry is too great to overcome, although some military officials privately believe that greater French involvement and more significant modernization of French forces could shift the balance more in NATO's favor. It is clear, however, that for the conventional imbalance to be rectified the French would have to become more interested in conventional rearmament and closer coordination of their forces with NATO.

The major innovation the French have introduced in the conventional arms control area is, of course, the proposal for the Conference on Disarmament in Europe. The French were motivated by three key concerns. First, the discussions should cover forces from the Atlantic to the Urals; that is, Soviet forces in European Soviet territory must be included in any agreement. Second, the discussions should not be bloc-to-bloc but should encompass all of the European states affected in a potential conflict; in other words, the neutral states should be included as well. Third, European discussions on conventional forces should not include limitations on theater nuclear weapons systems. The French totally opposed an expansion of MBFR to include such limitations.

There were other motivations as well. The French hoped to enter the conventional arms control process on the terms most favorable to their interests. They were concerned with the West German involvement in and American management of MBFR and wished to be in a position to influence their allies more directly. Above all, as the INF arms control process unfolded in the 1980s, the French wanted to become more involved in the conventional arms talks to ensure that tactical nuclear issues would not be handled in that forum. They want to see these issues handled separately with the exception that the prospects for an agreement limiting tactical weapons would be much worse than if the possibility of such an agreement was included as a bargaining chip in conventional talks. The obvious Western ploy would be to seek significant Soviet *conventional* reductions in exchange for serious reductions in NATO battlefield *nuclear* weapons. The French wish to make this ploy as difficult as possible to pull off.

Involvement in the Conference on Disarmament in Europe has been an important experience for the French. An agreement was reached that increased Western security while not reducing Western conventional forces. The French have sought Soviet conventional reductions with as few reductions as possible on the Western side. In their view, the West barely has sufficiency and should not seek or allow dangerous reductions. The process allowed the French to work more closely with their allies and prepared their own bureaucracy to work more effectively in the future on arms control issues.[14]

Soon it became obvious that France's allies sought to merge the CDE and MBFR talks into a single forum with French involvement. The German foreign minister was especially eager to ensure French involvement, and the Franco-German relationship was on the line in French handling of the follow-on negotiation issue. The French remained adamant, however, about avoiding involvement in bloc-to-bloc negotiations. At stake was an agreement between the United States and France to define the relationship between the twenty-three NATO and Warsaw Pact members and the thirty-five CSCE members in follow-on negotiations. This relationship would provide for negotiations on force reductions to be handled by the twenty-three, with confidence-building measures to be handled by the thirty-five. The French wanted to ensure that there were clear linkages between the two groups, and that these linkages made it plain that the French were not involved in bloc-to-bloc negotiations. After a rocky road, such an agreement was announced in June 1987.

With the procedural questions of the relationship between the twenty-three and the thirty-five resolved at least to some extent, what will be the substantive focus of the negotiations? The French sense that they are going to be the most recalcitrant players in the conventional arms control process and have worked quite hard to generate ideas which will take pressure off themselves. In part, the problem is simply that the French have been nay-sayers on conventional arms control issues for so long that it is not clear that they are capable of generating positive ideas.

The other arms control issue of import to the French has been the question of chemical arms control. The chemical issue has been in the background for some years. Public discussion of the issue was enhanced by the publication of General Étienne Copel's first book on defense issues.[15] General Copel had just become chief of staff of the air force when he sought publication for his book, and he resigned in order to publish it. The book is a bold challenge to the French defense consensus in which he lays out in much greater detail than ever before to the French public the nature of the chemical threat.[16] Soon after its publication, Defense Minister Hernu indicated in a televised interview that French policy was to respond to a chemical attack with the use of nuclear weapons. Although this is French declaratory policy, French officials have been uneasy with this position and realize the need to have alternative responses.

The French government decided to modernize its chemical arsenal to respond to the Soviet challenge in chemical weapons. The basic idea was simply that deterrence of Soviet chemical attacks requires the possession of chemical weapons by France and the alliance. This fundamental political-military judgment has guided their subsequent arms control behavior. The French government is perhaps the only one ever to send its foreign minister to a disarmament conference in order to announce the production of new weapons.[17] This action and the general French position have caused definite tensions with British and German allies, and at the same time have drawn France closer to the Americans.

In short, the French action in the chemical area is typical of the general French approach to arms control. The French think in strategic and political terms first, and pursue disarmament efforts second. They use arms control language to influence their allies but not to guide their own decision-making process on security matters.

The Executive Decision-making System

French decision making on arms control policy is characterized by the very small number of key players and by the informal nature of the interaction between those players (see figure 3.1). There are, of course, formal bureaucratic setups and standard operating procedures for drafting proposals. But aside from routine diplomacy, the main arms control initiatives in recent years have been elaborated by a handful of politicians, civil servants, and military officers in ad hoc working groups or other informal settings. French diplomats, indeed, pride themselves on the "flexibility" of their decision-making process. As one Foreign Ministry official has pointed out, "We are the pragmatists. We don't have arms control agencies working in a vacuum, or constant interagency disputes leading to paralysis, the way the Americans do."

In 1978 the French considered, and rejected, the idea of establishing a separate arms control agency along the lines of the United States' Arms Control and Disarmament Agency (ACDA). Neither the Foreign Ministry nor the Ministry of Defense (MOD) relished the thought of having a bureaucratic competitor. More important, however, is the deeply rooted belief that arms control is part and parcel of East-West policy and should not be dealt with separately—conceptually or institutionally.

Figure 3.1 The French Executive Decision-making System on Arms Control

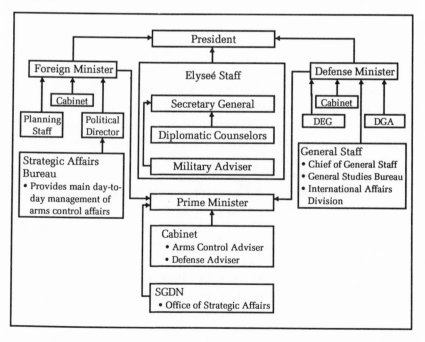

The small, informal, tightly knit network of arms control players allows for quick, consensual decisions. There is usually no need for carefully crafted position papers to wend their way through the bureaucracy to the political leaders. Several participants have pointed out the effectiveness of the system during the Euromissile crisis. "The handful of people involved in the issue at the Elysée, the Foreign Ministry, and the defense minister's cabinet (his direct staff) were constantly on the phone. It took five minutes to coordinate our positions and statements," says a former MOD official.

The CDE was invented and is followed by a small number of players. It was the brainchild of the Foreign Ministry's policy planning staff, the Centre d'Analyse et de Prevision (CAP, established in 1973), with some input from the military. Now two institutions clearly stand out as the central players in the arms control game: the presidency (the president and his diplomatic advisers) and the Foreign Ministry (the minister's cabinet, the Bureau of Strategic Affairs and Disarmament in the ministry, and the CAP). The MOD and the Secrétariat Générale de la Defense Nationale (SGDN) clearly play a subordinate role in the arms control process, although this may change with greater French involvement in arms control talks which directly affect French forces.

The Primacy of the Executive

The Fifth Republic, established in 1958, adopted a constitution fraught with ambiguities and inherent tensions. There was no clear delineation of the responsibilities of the president and prime minister; however, both positions were invested with considerable power. Only the subsequent combination of de Gaulle's personality, the Algerian War crisis, and the more direct presidential elections helped to establish the president as the real and almost unchallenged head of state. This is particularly the case in matters of defense and foreign policy, where they have become informally designated as the "reserved domain" of presidential prerogative.[18]

The "modus operandi" of the Constitution became firmly entrenched over the years as voters consistently returned the president's political party to a majority in the Parliament. Thus, the French electorate has allowed the system to follow the same pattern from de Gaulle to Mitterrand. If anything, presidential powers have increased over time to such an extent that most political observers, in France and abroad, have described him as the most powerful chief executive in the Western world. He alone can decide to activate French nuclear forces, and he is unquestionably the main French foreign policy player on the international scene. Unlike his American counterpart, he does not have to worry about expert questioning coming from a powerful, well-staffed Congress, excessive pressure from public opinion, the lobbying of well-organized interest groups, or bureaucratic heavyweights.[19]

This kind of primacy and freedom of action in foreign affairs is so well established that in the summer of 1985, when the conservative opposition, anticipating victory, began to claim a foreign policy role for the next prime minister, President Mitterrand exclaimed, in a most Gaullist fashion: "If the Prime Minister were to confiscate foreign policy, that would be a coup d'état."[20] In fact, the entire battle between Mitterrand and Prime Minister Jacques Chirac throughout cohabitation has been largely muted by the desire of both sides to see presidential supremacy restored after the 1988 election.

Presidential power is supreme on nuclear issues, and by extension on arms control issues. It is the president who sets the direction for French security policy, including the launching of arms control initiatives. The president also has the final say on weapons development (military) programs that have implications for arms control negotiations (chemical weapons, tactical nuclear weapons, the mobile missile sx, etc.). The president is usually not concerned with the details of day-to-day policy but rather with the strategic direction of policy. He does not have a large enough staff to become excessively involved in managing day-to-day details. Unlike the American president, the French president does not have a National Security Council staff which allows him to manage the bureaucracy on such details. The French president relies on the bureaucracies themselves for such efforts.

The president has considerable room to improvise and innovate on his own initiative or at the suggestion of one of his close personal advisers. Because the bureaucracies—in the arms control case this means primarily the Foreign Ministry—dominate day-to-day decision making, the French decision-making system has been largely incremental in nature. It has required presidential initiative for French policy to move in substantially new directions. It is therefore necessary when analyzing French arms control policy to keep in mind the important dimensions of that process. On the one hand, it is important to gain a sense of the president's preferences and the views of his closest advisers, for the president may choose to intervene in the policy process to establish a new direction. On the other hand, it is necessary to assess the instincts and preferences of the arms control bureaucrats whose activity will predominate in the shaping of arms control policy on a normal basis.

The influence of diplomatic advisers (some seconded from the Foreign Ministry but others recruited directly) has varied, depending partly on their personal qualities and access but primarily on the president's willingness to listen to them.[21] Under de Gaulle, for instance, a formal hierarchical system was set up whereby diplomatic advisers with clearly defined responsibilities reported to the secretary general of the Elysée, who then acted as a screen between them and the president.[22] This system was maintained by Presidents Pompidou and Giscard d'Estaing, although Pompidou's entourage, or "kitchen cabinet," played a key role in the negotiations for Britain's entry into the Common Market, and the Jean François-Poncet/Gabriel Robin team had unprecedented influence over President Giscard d'Estaing's foreign policy—especially on East-West relations.[23]

The general secretary of the Elysée usually has been the principal aide to the president on foreign affairs issues. He devotes much of his time to it, follows decisions closely, calls the Quai d'Orsay directly for information or to transmit presidential decisions, has frequent contacts with the aides of foreign heads of state, receives ambassadors, and sometimes serves as an emissary to foreign leaders. In addition, in an international crisis situation all the information from the different ministries is coordinated through the secretary general.

Nevertheless, despite intense activity in the foreign policy area, the influence of the secretary general, with a few rare exceptions, has remained limited for two reasons. First, the Elysée has no independent organization able to prepare or make decisions—these belong to the different ministries. Second, the president must make foreign policy himself, without publicly prominent intermediaries. Foreign policy control has been critical to the image of the president as the embodiment of France itself; to allow a powerful functionary to usurp that role would be to undercut the president's image.[24] It is clear, however, that the secretary general can have extraordinary de facto power simply by being closely identified with the president and understanding the president's proclivities and propensities. He can also act as a shock absorber in dealing with foreigners and the bureaucracy, thereby insulating the president from pressures whose existence he would not wish to acknowledge.[25]

The role of the "entourage" has increased markedly under President Mitterrand since May 1981. The rules have become less clear and the system more complex. "Mitterrand, a bit like Franklin D. Roosevelt, put up with overlapping attributions, even encouraged them. He liked to have several different advisers follow the same issue, so much so that their counterparts outside the Elysée, high civil servants and foreign ambassadors . . . often did not know who was in charge of what."[26] The relatively unstructured system also led, or nearly led, to some incoherence (on SDI) and blunders (on France's silo-based missile force on the plateau d'Albion) as different advisers caught the president's imagination with a new idea before the normal channels managed to reassert the official line.

Mitterrand's positions on arms control, as they are articulated in his public statements as president, are well summarized in the overview to a collection of his speeches published shortly before the 1986 election. According to Mitterrand, the major problems which disarmament should address are: "the overarmament of nuclear weapons, the strategic destabilization which results from military reliance on new technologies, the conventional disequilibrium and the threat of chemical war."[27] He added that although France favors disarmament, "it is not willing to place the issue of its national defense at the mercy of Russo-American negotiations, negotiations in which it is not a participant."[28]

Although he remains a protector of French independence, Mitterrand is more aware than many of his conservative rivals of the need to include French nuclear forces in arms control talks. Mitterrand's one public reference to the possibility of inclusion when the 50 percent reduction in superpower strategic forces threshold is met (as long as the ABM treaty is maintained) was heavily criticized by Quai d'Orsay officials but does reflect Mitterrand's greater awareness of the changing diplomatic context facing France. Also, the insistence Mitterrand placed on accepting the zero solution to the long-range INF forces reflected his understanding of the political pressures on the alliance as opposed simply to maintaining doctrinal purity.

The diplomatic counselors to the president are formally known as *conseillers technique;* they have the responsibility to coordinate relations with the Foreign Ministry. The diplomatic counselors are always diplomats, usually high-ranking ones. Their major function is to process and distill incoming information for the president. They synthesize the dossiers sent by the Quai to prepare the president for meetings with foreigners or trips abroad, they prepare drafts of presidential addresses on foreign policy, and they organize the contacts between the president and foreign ambassadors.[29]

An additional adviser of significance to the arms control process in the Elysée is the military adviser to the president. It has become traditional for the military adviser, on leaving the Elysée, to become chief of the General Staff.[30] The military adviser is, of course, primarily concerned with operational matters important to the president, but the close personal relationship which develops between the president and his military adviser has been critical in shaping the president's judgments of Soviet capabilities and intentions.

The Foreign Ministry

Though the president may take the initiative to launch a new idea or full-fledged plan, responsibility for the actual content of the arms control proposals, as well as the management of France's arms control policy (or nonpolicy), lies squarely with the Foreign Ministry, known as the Quai d'Orsay. Although the Defense Ministry has recently taken steps to reinforce its expertise in this area, the Quai's leadership in policy formulation and implementation has been undisputed because arms control has been primarily a diplomatic rather than military activity.

Thus the Foreign Ministry fleshed out President Giscard d'Estaing's disarmament plan, despite its misgivings, and used the CAP's expertise to bolster President Mitterrand's tough stand on the Euromissile issue, partly against the advice of other more traditional-minded bureaus ("services") in the ministry. The Quai, as we argue below, has been the prime mover in the decision to focus on conventional arms control.

The foreign minister himself can give only a small part of his time to arms control issues. He is aided by a cabinet of civil servants whose task is to help him manage the day-to-day affairs of the ministry. The chef du cabinet is the director of the secretariat serving the foreign minister, and it is his task to keep the relevant bureaus informed of the minister's agenda and to coordinate information flows upward and downward. A close personal relationship with the foreign minister (in this case Dumas) puts him in a position to influence policy by reinforcing or discouraging flows of information, but he is not in a position actually to make decisions.

The political director is responsible for initiating and coordinating policy on East-West relations in the Quai, and as such is concerned with arms control policy. In general, the political director follows the lead of the Strategic Affairs Bureau on day-to-day policy, but his continual contact with the Elysée, and now with the Matignon, makes him an important conduit to the bureaucracy of the presidential or prime ministerial perspective, or, conversely, a conveyer of problems and information to the presidential or prime ministerial advisers. The political director is an important point of contact for foreign governments, as well. The EPC and the WEU have provided increasingly important forums where the political director can deal with his European counterparts in shaping general perceptions and approaches to strategic and arms control problems.

Inside the Quai, expertise on arms control is concentrated in the service des affaires strategiques. The turnover among the players in this unit is strikingly low. A large part of the team has been there since 1979. This degree of continuity reinforces the unit's intellectual cohesiveness, ongoing expertise, and bureaucratic weight, strengthening its virtual monopoly on French arms control policy-making.

Even though the analysts in the Foreign Ministry's Bureau of Strategic Affairs are bureaucrats, they often take the initiative to shape policy or to alert political leaders to the consequences of their statements and actions. On several occasions diplomats have been distressed by what they saw as presidential willingness to break with traditional declaratory policy. Giscard's decision to halt atmospheric nuclear tests in 1974 and to formulate an arms control "doctrine" in 1978 struck many of them as heresy. For the first two years of Mitterrand's presidency, the Quai worried about the "imaginative things" the new Socialist president might do. "We felt that the dominant line of thinking within the Socialist party was dangerous," a senior diplomat recalls. "As a result, the Bureau of Strategic Affairs and Disarmament produced countless educational papers for the Elysée to make sure that the president would not go off in any new and nutty directions."

Despite a few close calls (the suggestion that Albion might be negotiable, the momentary interest in nuclear-free zones), many professional diplomats breathed a sigh of relief when it turned out that "Mitterrand accepted the basic premises of traditional French nuclear policy," and that "despite the Socialist rhetoric about total disarmament in the seventies, the realistic line prevailed among the president and his closest advisers." The relief was all the greater as they felt that the bureaucracy had the power to thwart some proposals and catch some slips, but "not to make the president change his course."

Yet in the final analysis, most of the "new departures" in French arms control policy, like the policy itself, are essentially declaratory. "One must not exaggerate the importance of the president's ability to improvise," says a diplomat who has himself shuddered at some of President Mitterrand's public and private statements on arms control negotiations. "After all, it has always been rhetoric and has never modified France's long-standing refusal to negotiate on its strategic nuclear forces unless its conditions were met."

The Quai perhaps more than any other ministry has been impregnated by Gaullist concepts (national independence; nuclear sanctuarization; distrust of the superpowers but even more of the Anglo-Saxons, especially the United States). Within the Quai, the diplomats in charge of strategic affairs and disarmament, whether out of personal conviction or professional obligation, often have a particularly Gaullist, "sanctuarized" mind-set.

In addition to the Bureau of Strategic Affairs, the ministry's planning unit, the CAP, follows arms control issues, analyzing and sometimes actually participating in ongoing negotiations.[31] It built its reputation on the quality of its political-military analyses in the middle and late 1970s and played a key role in formulating the 1978 disarmament plan for President Giscard d'Estaing. Since the disarmament process actually started, however, power has shifted more to the service des affaires strategiques et du disarmament (Strategic Affairs and Disarmament Bureau), some of whose members arrived from the CAP. The CAP has played an important role in shifting the Quai toward a position more sympathetic to an interdependent rather than an excessively independent role for France.

The Defense Ministry and the General Staff
The Foreign Ministry clearly has the leading role in the arms control area. The MOD's concern, to the extent that its technical

expertise is required and requested by the Quai, is merely that some of these diplomatic exercises or pirouettes endanger French military programs, or that new developments in an ongoing negotiation (CDE, MBFR, INF) raise the level of military concern. Beyond this, there has been little or no interest on the part of defense officials in becoming more involved in the process, often to the irritation of some foreign defense officials who would prefer the practical approach of the military to the imagination and subtlety of the diplomats.

Indeed, some foreign and French analysts believe that greater involvement by the MOD in strategic affairs would further the process of adapting France's nuclear doctrine to the realities and requirements of the Allied defense. Not that they expect any major strategic rethinking on its part: "The military, on the whole, defends the Gaullist orthodoxy, or at least pays lip service to it, some out of discipline, some out of conviction," says one diplomat. However, he adds, the MOD's real concern is elsewhere: to hold firm, "to prepare for the engagement in Germany, to set up early warning systems that obviously can't be individual systems." The idea is that MOD defense choices taken for purely pragmatic reasons are more likely to change French security policies than any rethinking of declaratory policy by the "keepers of the flame" at the Quai.

There is clearly some truth to this view. Most agree that the MOD is spontaneously far more Atlanticist than the Quai. "Anything that will increase cooperation, coordination, and exchange of information interests the military: if they had their way, they would integrate the NATO command tomorrow," says a diplomat, echoing a widely held opinion. "What is also obvious is that they are convinced that there is no French sanctuary," he adds. Although few officers admit this, even off the record, some military officials have indicated that such views are now being expressed more frequently in military circles than in the past.

Until recently, Defense Ministry officials paid little, if any, attention to arms control issues. "We concentrate on armaments, not disarmaments," is the position articulated by many of them. France's direct security interests did not appear to be at stake in most arms control negotiations, although its indirect security interests have been. None of France's disarmament proposals threatened any vital French security interest or military program. The Defense Ministry, through its representative in the policy formulation process, made sure this was the case. In recent years, however, arms control activity with potential implications for France has prompted a growing awareness that the French defense establishment must be able to play a more active role in this area. The U.S. Strategic Defense Initiative, in particular, has forced some rethinking as has the creation of several MOD committees and study groups on space issues and directed-energy weapons. France's own nascent military observation satellite program, for example, has given France a new stake in the outcome of ongoing negotiations on the militarization of space, although the Quai and the Elysée were the prime movers behind France's June 1984 proposals on antisatellite weapons and prevention of ABM systems.

New developments in the conventional arms control area have also raised concern and recognition of the need for greater military involvement in the policy process. The Defense Ministry and General Staff participated, if skeptically, in the 1977–78 decision to promote the Conference on Disarmament in Europe "from the Atlantic to the Urals." The discussions were expected to drag on for years with few concrete results. But the Soviet decision to participate, the activization of the Stockholm talks, and the apparent progress toward discussion of actual troop reductions have heightened awareness of the need for greater involvement by French military officials.

These factors have led to an enhancement of arms control expertise, especially within the General Staff. But by most accounts, the steps taken thus far, while necessary, are still too limited to enable the Defense Ministry to become an active rather than reactive player. The civilian side of the MOD is relatively small, and civilians leave most of the details of military operational planning to the uniformed military.

The defense minister's role in shaping security policy varies widely; it is based both on his personal ties with the president or prime minister and on his personal abilities and proclivities. The defense minister is aided by his cabinet, within which there is a civilian diplomatic adviser who traditionally plays the classic diplomatic role of preparing the minister's speeches on international issues and organizing his visits abroad and those of his foreign counterparts to France.

In addition to the cabinet, there is the powerful Délégation Générale des Armaments (DGA). The DGA is one of the largest employers in France and is directly responsible for weapons development and deployment. Its orientation is clearly toward armament, not disarmament, but its technical expertise is critical in assessing the impact of arms control proposals on force structure development. The DGA has been involved primarily in the area of assessing the impact of SDI on French nuclear forces.

Like the Foreign Ministry, the Ministry of Defense has a planning office that provides assessments relevant to arms control issues. For many years the Group de Planification et d'Études Strategiques (known as Groupes), previously the Centre de Prospective et d'Evaluation (CPE), was the closest equivalent in the French Defense Ministry to the U.S. Department of Defense Net Assessment Office. The CPE was a prestigious department when it was created in 1965. Its first director, Hughes de l'Estoile, was an important figure in the strategic community. The very success of the CPE prompted Michel Debre to suggest creating a policy planning staff within the Quai when he took over as foreign minister in 1968, though the actual creation of the CAP did not occur until 1973. The high point of the CPE's influence came during 1975 to 1980, when it was actively involved in formulating French security and disarmament policy.

At a technical level part of Groupes's job was to evaluate the effectiveness of ABM systems and their consequences for French nuclear penetration capability. Though the actual analysis might be done by other divisions (the Direction Générale des Armaments or the Missile Directorate, known as the Direction Technique des Enfins Tactiques), Groupes was responsible for the overall synthesis. Its final report was sent to Ministry of Defense officials, to the president, and to the head of the General Staff (and sometimes to the foreign minister).

Groupes's indirect influence was clear in the SDI debate. The head of Groupes (later a member of Paul Quilés's cabinet when he became minister of defense) represented the views of a lobby of anti-SDI engineers and played a key role in helping Defense Minister Hernu's closest aides dampen Hernu's initial enthusiasm for SDI. "The Groupes is not as devoid of influence as some people claim," says one diplomat. "While it is clearly less influential than in the past, here is a case, however, at a crucial point in time, in which its director played a very major role." Other observers do not rule out a revival in the near future. In 1987 Groupes was disbanded and included in a new body, the Délégation des Études Générales (DEG). This new body was charged with providing the minister with a planning function, similar to the CAP in the Foreign Ministry. The DEG is to play an important staff role in aiding the minister in arms control matters.

The État Major des Armées, or the General Staff, provides the overall leadership for operational military matters. It is concerned with the implications of arms control discussions or agreements on East-West military force levels as an adjunct to military planning. The état major is the highest-ranking French military official. In the past few years he has been appointed after serving as the president's military adviser. Although a high-ranking officer, the état major is usually well attuned to politics and the changing political environment.

Within the General Staff, disarmament issues have been followed by the small bureau d'études générales (Bureau of General Studies), essentially a single officer. The position was first filled by an admiral, who represented the General Staff in the preliminary discussions for President Giscard d'Estaing's disarmament plan in 1978 and in the delegation to the U.N. Special Session on Disarmament that same year. Both of his successors have also been from the navy. Personal interest was the key factor in explaining General Staff's involvement in disarmament issues; they themselves built up contacts with the other ministries, mainly the Quai. "We were more like free-lancers than bureaucratic players; we had no orders, we were on our own," one officer explained. The handful of officers who held this position at the General Staff were the rare military experts in the small world of French policy-making on arms control issues.

The bureau d'études générales monitors the Geneva arms limitation talks and analyzes the repercussions of the discussions and their effects on France's defense posture and programs. Information is drawn from military sources, especially the network of military attachés in the major capitals, from the DEG, and from the Quai. "It is primarily a rewriting office, putting together internal armed forces information with memos from the Quai for the head of the General Staff," a diplomat explains. Beginning in 1986, the General Staff enhanced its arms control expertise by expanding the international affairs division of the bureau d'études générales. Although it is still very limited, its growth has been a sign of the increased interest of the professional military in ongoing arms control talks.

More sustained attention to arms control negotiations has been prompted by the acceleration of Soviet and U.S. nuclear disarmament proposals in recent years, especially those focusing on intermediate-range nuclear weapons. But it is the movement in the conventional arms control area that seems to have been the driving force behind the new awareness. As French forces became potentially more affected by agreements, the uniformed military wishes to become more involved. The General Staff has been forced to participate in policy-making in this area, especially since the Stockholm talks on confidence-building measures in Europe appeared to be making progress. It has been increasingly called on by the Quai for technical input into French negotiating positions. "We pushed the military to organize for the negotiations. The Defense Ministry had no organization in this area. Now there are several individuals within the General Staff who liaise with us on a daily basis."

At the same time, the military establishment itself seems to have recognized the need for greater involvement in arms control processes, because they are felt to have potential implications for French security. The Stockholm talks focused on concrete proposals such as thresholds for notification of troop concentration and on-site inspection of military installations by foreign observers in signatory countries. "We viewed our role as one of damage limitation," one officer explains. "It was crucial for us to constantly make clear to the Quai what we considered to be unacceptable."

Diplomats involved in the Stockholm negotiations were keenly aware of military concerns. The achievements made during this phase of the talks, they believe, were limited, because Stockholm was "primarily a way to show Western public opinion that leaders of the democracies are willing to reach mutually beneficial compromises on a key issue with the East bloc." Nonetheless, French diplomats believe that military concerns precluded further possible compromises; for example, on exchanges of military information. Soviet on-site inspection of French military installations is not an attractive idea to French officers, and the Quai seems to have been forced to do some serious convincing.

The ambiguity, or at least the complicated nature of France's relations with NATO, may also have played a part in the reinforcement of the General Staff's international department. Greater rationalization of the process was necessary, according to a diplomatic observer. "The French military delegation to NATO includes generals, colonels, and many armaments engineers. No one in the bureaucracy knew exactly what they were doing and saying," he explains, referring to the recent decision to reinforce the bureau d'études générales. "It was therefore reasonable for the General Staff to set up a unit to recentralize the instruction and control process."

The SGDN: An Institution in Search of a Role

Theoretically, the prime minister can draw on the strategic expertise of an institution that is administratively linked to Matignon—the Secrétariat Général de la Defense Nationale (SGDN). But the very fact that the prime minister has traditionally not played an important role in strategic affairs has in turn reduced the influence of the SGDN. Most analysts and even members of the SGDN agree that its key weakness has been its lack of an effective political power base.

Even the greater involvement of Matignon in defense and foreign policy matters during the cohabitation period (1986–88) did not significantly increase the SGDN's role, as might have been expected. "The prime minister could have said: The SGDN is mine. I will take charge of it, bolster it, and use it," a high-ranking official at the SGDN explains. But that has apparently not happened: "We are a bit more involved than in the past, but not much," he admits. The SGDN is an interesting example of an administrative think tank that has been insufficiently used, largely because it has rarely been plugged into the political power network. It has been most effective when it has been in tune with the president, says a diplomat. "After all, even if it is organizationally tied to Matignon, it's the Elysée that counts."

Personal relationships have also been important in determining the influence and effectiveness of the SGDN under various presidents. "It was relatively effective under Secretary General Reinter, who hunted with Valéry Giscard d'Estaing, while the deputy secretary general was a close friend of Jean François Poncet, the secretary general of the Elysée." Whatever the explanation, the SGDN did indeed play a key role in preparing the 1978 disarmament plan presented to the United Nations by President Giscard d'Estaing.

"We continue to play an important role in defense policy, through the Office in Charge of International Relations, who is in touch with the defense minister," explains an official of the SGDN. But the SGDN's contribution to arms control discussions is relatively minor, he adds. "Arms control remains the Quai's private domain" as far as the government is concerned—that is, until the president takes an interest. "The direct consequence of having eliminated the Defense Ministry and the military from arms control policy-making is that they really have no say," says a civilian researcher at the SGDN. "We have an arms control specialist here who follows new developments on a day-to-day basis. It is terribly frustrating. Every time he tries to have some input, the diplomats say, 'Stop! Hands off!'"

On at least one occasion the Quai has been willing to listen to the SGDN's arms control advice and to act on it. In 1985 the SGDN, with outside help from international legal experts, produced a study on the specific provisions of the 1972 ABM treaty. Their conclusions differed from the Quai's. According to the SGDN, though the spirit of the treaty clearly limited the development of defensive systems, the actual letter of the treaty forbade very little. It did not, for instance, forbid the development of new anti-tactical ballistic missile (ATBM) defense systems, they felt. The Quai subsequently adopted this interpretation, much to the surprise of the SGDN staffers.

Over the years, the SGDN has become primarily a bureaucratic instrument of administrative coordination. Its main role and justification is to act as the secretariat for the Defense Council, the highest decision-making body on security issues. Yet its resources could make it a useful source of strategic thinking and rethinking. First, it collects considerable information from various sources. In its role as secretariat of the Defense Council it synthesizes information from the various bureaucratic agencies and political centers of power. Access to military intelligence gives it geographical expertise and a useful capacity for crisis analysis. The SGDN also has technical expertise useful in the arms control area. Second, the SGDN is in closer touch with civilian defense specialists than most other defense-related institutions. One of its main goals is to bridge the gap between the government and the universities and to foster greater interest in strategic studies among students. Moreover, a position for a "strategic affairs adviser" was created in 1985.

Nonetheless, the SGDN's hybrid nature is a drawback when it comes to positioning itself bureaucratically. "We are neither a strictly diplomatic nor a strictly military institution," says a top official, "and this is a problem." In fact, the specter of a U.S.-style National Security Council (NSC) seems to lurk in the minds of the SGDN's main bureaucratic partners, and rivals. When asked for their view on the SGDN's current and future role, several diplomats and defense officials imme-diately responded: "It has never, and will never, become an NSC." According to a Foreign Ministry official, "the SGDN plays no role at all and no one wants it to. Every so often, the idea of creating a French NSC pops up; Presidents Giscard d'Estaing and Mitterrand toyed with it. But it cannot be done; there is no pool of expertise, not enough experts with different political views for different governments to build a full staff, nor is an NSC desirable." Even SGDN officials cannot foresee such an evolution. "We are the embryo of an NSC, we could develop into one, but nobody wants us to, least of all the presidents," explained one official. "There is a need for one, especially to coordi-nate intelligence. There is no 'intelligence community' in France; the various agencies fight among themselves. Yet no president has wanted a strong intelligence community," he added.

In short, French arms control policy has been dominated by the executive arm of government. Above all, it has been dominated by the president's ability to innovate and the Quai d'Orsay's dominance of the day-to-day management of arms control matters. As French forces have become potentially more affected by arms control agree-ments, military officials have become more involved as well.

The French Decision-making Context

French public opinion is strikingly absent from the policy-making arena. Defense issues in general and arms control issues in particular provoke little public debate. This low level of interest is illustrated in a February 1987 poll on defense issues carried out in France, the United Kingdom, Italy, and West Germany. France had by far the largest proportion of respondents who expressed "no opinion" on most issues: 11–21 percent, compared with a mere 1–2 percent in West Germany. Twenty percent had no view about the likely conse-quences of U.S. military disengagement from Europe, while 21 per-cent expressed no opinion on whether France should participate in SDI. This relative indifference to defense issues is all the more striking when compared to the level of concern, or "angst," in most of France's neighbors, especially in the United Kingdom and Germany. The French also share their leaders' skepticism about arms control pro-posals. A poll for Le Figaro in April 1987 showed that 45 percent of the public viewed Mr. Gorbachev's zero option as a trap which would leave the Soviets with a clear military advantage in Europe (35 percent saw it as a positive step toward disarmament). And an overwhelming majority (61 percent) believed that France should not lower its nuclear guard.

Since they are relatively free from the day-to-day pressures of public opinion, French decision makers have far greater leeway in defining France's security policy and arms control positions than their allies do. They are keenly aware of the benefits they derive from the inability of other powers, primarily the Soviet Union, to influence government policy by playing on the French public's fears and hopes or to encourage antinuclear movements, as they do elsewhere in Europe.

The absence of public pressure to reach arms control agreements also gives French officials what they see as a "special responsibility" to defend French and perhaps European security interests in arms control negotiations. At the same time, however, this relative freedom of action complicates attempts to draft common European positions on arms control issues. Many French officials, whatever their political views, are often shocked by the need for their British or West German counterparts to cater to the fears of arms control–minded voters and politicians.

The French consensus concerning France's independent nuclear posture and its consequences for arms control policy is commonly attributed to the perceived need for nuclear self-reliance and confidence in France's leadership. "A large number of Frenchmen have confidence that these issues are well managed and prefer to leave them to others. With a certain sense of modesty they feel that they are not competent in this area," explained former defense minister Giraud, commenting on the Le Figaro poll findings.[32]

France's major political parties have, for their own reasons, adopted identical or similar positions on nuclear issues over the past two decades. The Gaullist-Communist alliance on the force de frappe, followed in 1978 by the Socialist party's conversion to the nuclear faith, have put France's parties on a parallel course. This has occurred partly because the political parties have so few defense experts, which in turn partly explains the limited role of the French Parliament in shaping defense policy. In general, French politicians only begin to study strategic issues when they become presidential aspirants. Valéry Giscard d'Estaing ostensibly displayed his boredom during strategic discussions when he was finance minister. Socialist candidate Michel Rocard publicly explored them only when he began to set up his 1981 election campaign.

The main reason why French political parties adhere to the nuclear doctrine without really participating in its formulation is the dual Gaullist legacy. According to de Gaulle's definition, parties were not to be involved in managing nuclear issues. He treated nuclear policy, including the disarmament aspect, as a "domain réservé" where decisions were made by the president and a few key advisers, mainly military. This was part of his design to make the nuclear program acceptable to the military after events in Algeria ended the military's colonial role. It is no wonder, then, that so few politicians have any real expertise in strategic nuclear affairs.

Also, de Gaulle used the nuclear deterrent to gain political prestige for France. In the minds of the French, France's nuclear stature in the 1960s coincided with a period of stability and growing prosperity. While the British government had to contend with the Campaign for Nuclear Disarmament, international criticism of France's nuclear policies effectively consolidated French public support for the country's independent posture. Even in the 1980s, in an era when the French are more consciously part of Europe, the nuclear angst prevalent in neighboring countries has never been echoed in France. This is also because the French peace movement is tainted by its identification with the Communist party.

The parties were, then, locked into the consensus. The growing power and credibility of the Socialist party, for example, could only be achieved by reversing its traditional rejection of the force de frappe, despite some pacifist and antinuclear segments within its rank and file. As a result, the parties now see no advantage in opening the strategic debate. They will use their powerful party apparatuses to quell any attempt by dissident groups to raise antinuclear issues and put them on the political agenda. In reality, however, many specialists view the solidity and durability of the consensus in somewhat less rosy terms. Despite their public expressions of confidence, French officials have worried about the solidity of the defense consensus since the beginning of the Euromissile crisis, and even more so since President Reagan's "Star Wars" speech. The few, largely unsuccessful, attempts to generate a debate on France's defense options—mainly Pierre Lellouche's book, *L'avenir de la Guerre*, and a television show hosted by Yves Montand, "La guerre en face"—were viewed by the nucleus of policymakers as dangerous exercises that could undermine the credibility of the French nuclear deterrent.

Traditional cleavages on attitudes toward NATO remain, with possible long-term consequences. The SOFRES poll taken in April 1987 shows that the French can be divided into three roughly equal groups: Atlanticists, Europeanists, and neutralists. While 32 percent still viewed military alliance between the United States and Europe as the best way to protect French security interests (especially conservative voters), 28 percent preferred an independent Western military alliance (mainly Socialists), and 27 percent chose neutrality (mainly Communists but also many Socialists). According to a poll taken for *Liberation* in 1987, 26 percent of the French chose NATO, while 35 percent preferred an independent European defense system and 20 percent opted for a purely neutralist course. These underlying differences subsist simultaneously with the "consensus," but could resurface if France were to rethink its defense options.

In the foreseeable future the French public will not spontaneously provoke a public policy debate or push for any arms control agreements. The policy-making process will remain dominated by the technocrats and politicians. Moreover, it is unlikely that either of the two main political forces on the left, the Parti Socialiste (PS) and Parti Communist (PC), will be able to recant on their commitment to nuclear weapons despite the reservations of some of their membership.

At the grass roots level the Socialist party remains divided on defense issues such as the value of nuclear weapons, the size of the military budget, and the need for NATO. The antimilitiarist, antinuclear tradition remains strong among rank-and-file party members, who only grudgingly accepted the Socialist president's hard-line defense policy, including his policy on INF deployment. Even party leaders, despite a general endorsement of France's nuclear posture, differ in their perceptions of Europe's future security needs.

Indeed, many past and present members of the Mitterrand administration privately express little confidence in the solidity of the Socialist party's defense consensus and worry that an open debate within the party might not be manageable. In the meantime, debate on defense and disarmament issues within the PS, to the extent that it exists, is controlled by a handful of "experts" (including the two Socialist former defense ministers, Charles Hernu and Paul Quilés, as well as Jean-

Pierre Chevénement) who remain committed to France's nuclear strategy.

The Communist party also favors maintaining France's independent strategic nuclear force, although according to a recent policy shift it no longer approves of the nuclear modernization program. Communist voters' hostility to defense spending and even to nuclear weapons is evidenced in recent polls. Yet the dramatic decline of the Communist party—to about 10 percent of the vote—reduces its importance as a political player. On the other hand, it should be noted that the decline of the PC may also, in the long run, open the way for more effective representation of antinuclear, antimilitary views. In the past, and throughout the Euromissile debate, the French peace movement remained tainted by its association with the Communists. The decline of the latter, coupled with a Soviet "charm offensive," could eventually make pacifist or neutralist views more respectable.

For dissident voices to influence the policy process, however, they would first have to organize effectively. The few attempts to create influential counter–think tanks have failed. This illustrates the limited nature of the French strategic debate and the control of the policy-formulating process by a small group of technocrats and politicians. For there to be counter–think tanks there would first have to be legitimate influential think tanks with a say in defense matters. Yet their virtual nonexistence in France is a widely recognized and increasingly bemoaned fact.

The few outside experts on strategic affairs, drawn from the national research institutes, the universities, the defense industries, France's main institute on international relations (IFRI), and the press (a handful of journalists), can be brought into the decision-making process. This happens informally, of course, since the small world of defense specialists meets often at conferences, seminars, and Parisian dinner parties. On a more formal basis, outside experts can be involved through consulting work for the Foreign Ministry (CAP), the Defense Ministry (DEG), or the SGDN. They have also testified before parliamentary work groups on such issues as SDI and French plans for a mobile missile (SX).[33]

Conclusion

French interest in disarmament issues stems primarily from the desire to protect France's nuclear deterrent from political criticism and erosion rather than from a belief in the military benefit of arms control agreements. French officials have sought to avoid a replay of the 1960s, when France was singled out as the troublemaking nuclear proliferator in a world seeking to control and reduce nuclear weapons. For French policy-making circles, the Euromissile crisis, President Reagan's Strategic Defense Initiative, the Reykjavík summit, and Mr. Gorbachev's double zero option ushered in a new, dangerous era in international relations. Most dangerous of all, many believe, is the trend toward the denuclearization of Europe.

The Euromissile debate of the late 1970s and early 1980s heightened the fear of "decoupling" between the U.S. strategic nuclear arsenal and the defense of Europe. French policymakers objected to the very concept of a "Eurostrategic" balance—which could only accredit the dangerous notion of a separate "European" balance. They also regretted what one official called the "absurd decisions" to hold separate negotiations on medium-range forces (INF) and strategic arms reductions (START), endorsed by the North Atlantic Council in April 1981.

Soviet arms control proposals under Gorbachev have been viewed primarily as attempts to advance a Soviet objective dating back to the 1950s—that of dividing Europe from the United States. Ironically, recent Soviet willingness to discuss conventional disarmament as well, originally a French idea, has generated even greater apprehension. The Soviets, it is felt, have considerable leeway to make an empty gesture that can nonetheless capture the European, especially West German, imagination. As a result, French leaders have sought to define a common Franco-German position on arms control, as demonstrated by the Dumas-Genscher "duet" in Stockholm in early 1986 and the Kohl-Mitterrand-Chirac discussions in Paris in May 1987.

The growing appeal of antinuclear, and sometimes neutralist, themes among large segments of Western public opinion has been the other most significant factor behind the new French awareness. The apparent breakdown of the defense consensus among France's neighbors—here again, especially West Germany—shocked French policymakers into recognizing the need for their direct involvement in the European arms control debate.

The main objective, then, is to win European backing for France's nuclear posture. First, this requires a European commitment to the principle of nuclear deterrence and a joint effort to ensure that arms control talks do not lead to the progressive denuclearization of Europe. Second, and perhaps more important, France would like the Europeans, particularly the West Germans, to recognize the contribution of France's independent nuclear forces to the present and future security of Europe. As the only European nuclear force outside the integrated NATO structure, the force de frappe becomes an even greater asset as the perceived value of the U.S. nuclear guarantee declines. Moreover, preservation and modernization of the French strategic nuclear deterrent keeps all of Europe's options open as it contemplates its military future.

France's higher profile in arms control diplomacy has necessarily involved some discussion of its ambiguous commitment to the defense of Europe and of the concept of "sanctuarization." A growing number of politicians (as well as technocrats) are suggesting that in exchange for European endorsement of its nuclear posture, France should make an explicit commitment to participate in the conventional forward defense of Germany. At the same time it is no longer taboo to discuss France's nuclear deterrent. French and British defense officials have been exploring new avenues of nuclear cooperation as well as joint production of weapons systems. The polls show that public opinion, though it is not an active player in the decision-making process, is increasingly favorable to the idea of closer European defense cooperation, including a European role for the French deterrent force.

Finally, a more active involvement in arms control issues allows France to pursue another long-standing policy objective: that of fostering a "European identity." France has consistently opposed the Vienna MBFR talks, rejecting the bloc-to-bloc approach. It has proposed an alternative forum for conventional disarmament negotiations, covering the area between the Atlantic and the Urals and closely linked to the Conference on Security and Cooperation in Europe. Some analysts believe that this position is primarily designed to prevent progress in a set of negotiations that worry the French (although they suggested the negotiations). French officials, however, maintain that their insistence on the broader framework is part of a long-term policy to enhance the freedom of action of the smaller central and Eastern European nations and gradually to overcome the division of Europe.

France's basic attitude on arms control negotiations has not changed. Skepticism about the military benefit of arms control agreements remains widespread, but French policymakers increasingly recognize that they can no longer ignore disarmament issues. They will become more active players and whenever possible, major interlocutors. They will strive to win European, particularly West German, backing for France's positions on arms control issues.

Officials are increasingly compelled to face, and try to prevent, a contradiction between France's diplomatic and security needs. On the one hand, France continues to use security policy primarily for political ends. It derives international prestige and influence from its nuclear status. It seeks to use its possession of Western Europe's only independent nuclear deterrent as a bargaining chip with which to gain not only a voice in security issues but also some industrial and political benefits within Europe. On the other hand, France is increasingly worried that actual policy moves by other players, including the United States, are going to provoke new security dilemmas. Since the early 1980s, especially since President Reagan launched the idea of SDI and the Reykjavík summit, French dismay over apparent U.S. moves away from reliance on nuclear weapons has increased. More important, the perception of a gradual U.S. retreat from Western Europe is forcing France to rethink its security options and take a harder look at the credibility of its position on the defense of its territory—and of Europe.

French strategists are skeptical about the ultimate intent and potential of radical military reform and a new social and economic policy in the Soviet Union. On the contrary, many see recent Soviet arms control proposals, both nuclear and conventional, as extensions of the traditional Soviet objective of denuclearizing Europe. These could nonetheless create a climate in which France will have to devote more effort to preempting the possibility of political isolation in the West.

To a large extent the object of French disarmament policy is less the Soviet Union than West Germany. Stabilizing the West German "glacis" seems to be an ever more important and permanent feature of French security policy. France must increasingly take West German attitudes into account in defining its own positions on arms control and security issues.

France will only accept inclusion of its strategic nuclear force in any ongoing arms control negotiations, be they START or INF, on the three conditions outlined by President Mitterrand to the U.N. General Assembly in September 1983. They are, first and foremost, a substantial reduction of the arsenals of the two superpowers, each of which represents fifty times the striking power of the force de frappe; second, a reduction in the conventional weapons imbalance and the elimination of chemical weapons; third, a halt to the arms race in antimissile, antisubmarine, and antisatellite systems.

Many officials seem to view this package of preconditions as a magic formula that will protect France's forces from inclusion for the foreseeable future; that somehow legitimizes the French nuclear modernization program. They reject the view that France is in an increasingly uncomfortable situation, because it has set conditions that are gradually being fulfilled. These are set conditions that, even if based on the most optimistic hypothesis of arms cuts, will take years, if not decades, to materialize—and would still leave the Soviet strategic arsenal vastly greater than the French arsenal.

French officials also do not want a repeat of the deal contemplated briefly by NATO in 1975 (Option III) in the framework of the MBFR talks, which offered to reduce the number of American nuclear launchers and warheads in Europe in exchange for a reduction in the volume of East bloc army and air force personnel. One diplomat called this a "diabolical scheme" that could unfortunately once again be "just around the corner."

A growing number of analysts, and even diplomats, agree that France's attempt to galvanize Europe into doing more for its own defense, if only to encourage the United States to stay, will force it to face up to the contradictions in its security policies, including the need to take an active interest in arms control. "In the long run, it will be difficult to reconcile France's traditional posture with a truly European position," says a defense expert. "We can't hold out forever, but we still have some time left," a diplomat agrees.

But the French remain skeptical about the degree to which European disarmament notions affect seriously the security climate. France's allies will therefore face complicated problems in dealing with France. Even when it wishes to play a constructive role, France may be able to do so only at the price of political contortions that safeguard its doctrinal integrity while causing delays and irritation to the Allies.

4

Italian Arms Control Policy

Michael Harrison

Introduction

Until the current decade, the notion of analyzing Italian security and defense policies in depth was indeed a curious one. No independent national interest had been noted by domestic or foreign observers; Italian foreign policy was essentially that of a subordinate state accommodating itself to the views and preferences of stronger partners. For the United States, this situation meant that Italy was an unusually reliable, even subservient, ally willing to follow the American lead on most security and defense matters. In the context of Italy's membership in NATO, the American-Italian defense relationship was satisfactory for Washington, because the United States probably had a freer and less fettered use of facilities on Italian soil and the adjoining Mediterranean than was the case with any other ally. Similarly, in the realm of diplomacy Washington generally was able to count on Italian support for most security initiatives in the European and East-West contexts. At the very least Italy was unwilling to oppose American initiatives openly or unilaterally and might express strong reservations only as part of a clear West European consensus. Italy, then, has been as unconditional an ally as the United States could find in the postwar world.

There can be no sudden, dramatic changes in the politics or foreign policy of a country like Italy, so this description retains a certain validity. Nevertheless, it is clear to both Italian and foreign observers that the passive, unconcerned, ill-informed, and persistently subordinate Italy is undergoing a slow transformation into a more assertive and better-informed country with clearer ideas about its own defense and security interests. The international event that launched Italy on this unfamiliar path was the 1979 intermediate nuclear force (INF) decision, which prompted an unusual debate on the part of both experts and the general public, while the foreign policy activism that has been a hallmark of the government of Bettino Craxi (1983–87) confirms that this new awareness of defense and security affairs can be the foundation for a more assertive Italian foreign policy.

This unfamiliar attention to foreign and security policy matters has been unsettling for both Italians and their American interlocutors as they struggle to redefine the terms of what had been a rather facile relationship. The new situation presents a certain inconvenience for both partners: Italians have to define their own interests and fit them into the NATO and Atlantic contexts, while the United States has to take into account the attitudes of what has become a much less subservient as well as less predictable ally. There are, however, many positive aspects to the situation, including Italy's recent willingness to upgrade its military capabilities and undertake new responsibilities on behalf of the West in the Mediterranean region. Despite Italy's difficulties in defining a national security policy for the first time in the country's postwar history, and despite inherent tensions over mutual adjustments that have to be made in an Italian-American relationship that is now sometimes conflictual, the new situation is healthier for both Italy and an Atlantic alliance that can benefit from the contributions of more self-reliant but still cooperative allies.

The Security Legacy: A Passive and Accommodating Italy

There are several reasons for Italy's former passive approach to foreign policy and security affairs. One is the country's reaction against the activism and military adventurism of the fascist era, when Mussolini attempted to transform Italy into a great power but instead brought defeat, occupation, and a painful subordination within the European and international systems. All of Italy's elites in the early postwar years rejected an ambitious foreign policy, embracing instead an introspective and exclusively defensive military design. A very limited and circumscribed revival of Italy as a military power took place in 1949 with the country's admission to the North Atlantic alliance.[1] Since that time, Italy's military and security affairs have been closely tied to the North Atlantic Treaty Organization (NATO) and the bilateral Italian-American relationship. With the exception of the Italian Communist party (PCI) and its onetime ally, the Italian Socialist party (PCI), these events established a postwar political consensus supporting a security policy based on Italy's firm commitment to the Atlantic alliance which, along with membership in the European Economic Community (EEC), became one of the two pillars of the country's foreign policy, to the exclusion of any autonomous national considerations.

Once these fundamental choices were made, Italian foreign policy was largely set; it was used primarily as a tool in domestic political struggles that were so complex and all-consuming that parties and politicians were compelled to devote nearly all of their attention to the national political game. In this kind of political system, securing and maintaining power was (and remains) the primary goal of the players, while a tendency toward immobilism precluded the emergence of new policies from the political process. Whereas economic and social crisis might sometimes force the dominant political party, the Christian Democrats (DC), to shift domestic priorities and policies slowly over time, there was no compelling reason to alter a "passive Atlanticist" security orientation. Indeed, after 1948 the DC was able to present itself as the guarantor of Italy's Western and Atlantic orientation against the pro-Soviet or pseudo-neutralist designs of the PCI and its friends. In short, Italy's foreign policy served as a barrier to undesirable leftist shifts in government while its Atlanticism (and "Europeanism") became prerequisites for consideration as a partner. The Christian Democrats used this technique to bar the PCI from governing coalitions—until the Socialists embraced NATO and the EEC and joined the government under the "opening to the left" in the early 1960s. The PCI continued to be excluded under the same doctrine until the mid-1970s, when the foreign policy veto of the DC (internally) and the United States (externally) weakened considerably, while the Communists made some superficial accommodations with NATO and the Atlantic connection but nevertheless did not enter the government.

The Atlantic and NATO orientation of Italian security policy through the 1970s did not exclude certain other options from surfacing from time to time within the government, although their effect was minimal and transitory.[2] At the time of Italy's original alignment with the West, for example, there were neutralist currents within the DC. Figures such as Antonio Gronchi and factions such as the Malvesti and Dossetti groups were non-Atlanticist and tended to support neutralism and "third force" European ideas. Later, when Gronchi was serving as president of Italy in the late 1950s, figures such as Amintore Fanfani experimented with more flexible and independent Italian policies, under the umbrella of Atlanticism, in the Third World and especially the Mediterranean. For the most part, however, Italy remained firmly bound to European and Atlanticist options, eschewing the kind of dangerous exposure involved in pursuing experimental foreign policies.

One factor that helped sustain this situation was the pervasive apathy of the general public and elites toward foreign policy and defense issues that prevailed in Italy until the end of the 1970s. Once the basic Atlantic choice was made in 1948–49 and the Christian Democrats established their hegemony over the political system, external issues ceased to concern a political system preoccupied first with creating and sustaining the "economic miracle," and then with coping with the sociopolitical problems raised by economic transformation. Any sustained debate over the country's security policy was undermined and easily diverted by the fact that the only potential instigator of a reconsideration was the PCI, whose political legitimacy was tainted by its attachment to Marxism-Leninism and its residual loyalty to the Soviet Union. Mainly concerned with domestic politics, politicians in this party-dominated system (or "partocracy") paid scarce attention to foreign and defense issues, which in any case counted for little in the minds of the public. This preoccupation with the domestic political game meant that key politicians, including foreign and defense ministers, devoted minimal attention to the work of their departments and avoided any innovations or controversial delving into policy details. The situation was perhaps not so serious in diplomacy, especially in European affairs, where individuals such as Altiero Spinelli could play a major role and compensate for the poor quality of most Italian diplomats and top civil servants, who advanced as much through a political spoils system as through merit. In defense and security affairs, however, all these factors seemed to conspire to create a culture that ignored and even dismissed such issues as not worthy of serious attention.

The prime minister usually had little influence over foreign and security policy because his office had no clear authority in this area, while the Defense Ministry, with its large budget and quota of personnel, was essentially a Christian Democratic clientelistic fiefdom run in accordance with the national spoils system. Italian defense budgets have been labeled "obscure and indecipherable" by critics,[3] and even after the short-lived introduction of the policy, program, budgeting (PPBS) system in the mid-1970s it has been difficult to comprehend defense expenditures, much less control them and hold authorities accountable.[4] Thus the operations of the Defense Ministry were excluded from meaningful parliamentary and public inquiry, while the majority-run defense committees in the Chamber of Deputies and the Senate assiduously avoided shedding light on important decisions. Although the president of Italy is constitutionally responsible for the armed forces and is head of the highest defense organ, the Supreme Defense Council, the latter is only a consultative body, and the president's figurehead status, along with generally weak defense ministers, has meant that power was relegated to the bureaucracy and the military services themselves. Specifically, the General Staff and the General Directorate of the Defense Ministry were the locations from which most of the important decisions emanated.

It should also be noted that well into the 1970s there were no important defense-oriented private think tanks in Italy to provide outside expertise and criticism of national policy. The country's principal foreign policy institute, the International Affairs Institute (IAI) in Rome, was a generalist body, and, when pressed, most observers could readily identify only one or two nationally noted defense experts. Given the apathy of nearly all politicians and the public, and the secrecy that has surrounded military and security affairs, it is no wonder that Italian authorities concluded that their country lacked any significant attention to or understanding of security issues before the late 1970s, and that they consequently engaged in only sporadic and weak attempts to influence the security policies of the Western alliance. The feebleness of Italy's postwar security "culture" has been such that it is no exaggeration to state that the Italians have made no notable contributions to military affairs and thinking since General Guilio Douhet developed the theory of air superiority some sixty years ago.

In diplomacy Italy's passivity meant that its governments tended to let the Atlantic alliance Council of Ministers, the EEC, or the United States set a lead that Rome would follow. This self-generated dependency status has been especially marked in security and defense affairs, where domestic unaccountability and secrecy were reinforced by Italy's integration in NATO military institutions. Since 1949 Italy's defense strategy, the general structure and orientation of its armed forces, and the location and functioning of its key military installations have been determined, or at least "conditioned," by defense plans set up under the cover of secret bilateral agreements between NATO authorities and the Italian armed forces. NATO has scarcely been able to dictate policies to a national military establishment that purposely remains rather obscure and unfathomable to any outsiders, Italian or foreign. Nevertheless, the tendency to escape domestic accountability and controversy under the cover of international alliance obligations means that NATO and especially American defense activities on the peninsula are inevitably drawn into any effort to enhance civilian political control over national defense activities. One major consequence of this situation is that much of the new security and arms control debate in Italy is concerned with clarifying the extent of NATO and American military activities in the country and asserting more open civilian scrutiny and perhaps control over these activities. Indeed, because Italy is not involved directly in the most important East-West arms control issues, for many domestic political forces the arms control debate is primarily aimed at gaining leverage over national and alliance military activities, both conventional and nuclear, and is only secondarily concerned with interbloc problems.

Both NATO and the United States have profited from Italian disinterest in defense affairs and the relative autonomy accorded Allied military activities in Italy by setting up a large and only loosely controlled network of bases on the peninsula. Italy's strategic location in the center of the Mediterranean and its position as a way station for the Middle East supercede the country's importance as the focus of southern-flank NATO defense along the Yugoslav-Austrian borders. All of the south European NATO commands are located in Italy: the naval command was transferred to Naples from Malta after 1971, and has been under the command of an Italian admiral since 1967; the regional air-land command center is located at Verona, under an Italian general. In addition to housing the allied forces south headquarters, Naples is the home port of the U.S. Sixth Fleet. The United States has about fifty-three military installations in Italy with approximately 13,000 duty personnel. American bases tied to NATO include important submarine facilities, antisubmarine warfare installations, eleven NATO early-warning sites, and U.S. Air Force forward strike facilities.[5]

In general, Italy fulfills three missions in the U.S.-NATO security design. It is the focus of the southern air-land defense effort—clearly a secondary function in light of the more important central front, and one which recently has been downgraded further by shifts in the focus of Italian defense efforts (discussed below). Second, Italy is the center of crucial air-naval security operations in the Mediterranean, an effort that has grown in significance along with the size of the Soviet fleet and the escalation of tensions throughout the area. For U.S. air and naval operations, Italy's importance extends beyond the NATO treaty zone and includes the extension of American power into the eastern Mediterranean and the Middle East. Finally, Italy has served as a forward base for U.S. nuclear forces because American aircraft can reach the Soviet Union from the air base at Aviano (and two other bases) and from the aircraft carriers of the Sixth Fleet. The recent location of a cruise missile depot near Comiso, Sicily, from which weapons could be dispersed during a crisis, greatly enhances Italy's role in the fundamental East-West nuclear balance.

A notable feature of Italy's role as a center of NATO (essentially American) military activities has been the relative laxness and ambiguity of the authority exerted over the U.S. forces and weapons deployed in the country. Although agreements signed in 1952 and 1954 regulate American military movements in Italy, the United States has had unusual freedom to operate inside and from Italian territory. In a major public crisis involving non-NATO activities, such as the 1973 war in the Middle East, Italy may restrict American access, but in general this has not been the case. The incident at Sigonella in 1985 has focused greater attention on the uses made of American bases, however, and the question of closer control over U.S. facilities and movements is now debated even outside the usual left-wing circles.

A related issue concerns the nuclear weapons stored in Italy under NATO and American authority. It is not clear from public sources how many warheads the United States stores in Italy, and the number doubtless changes due to the drawdown of tactical weapons deployed in Europe, as well as shifts in location. The Sixth Fleet may have some 600 warheads in addition to those carried by missile-launching submarines stationed in the Mediterranean.[6] At one time there may have been as many as 1,500 warheads in depots on land, but recent estimates run from a high of 810, in a study by an Italian peace organization, to a low of 426 estimated by an Italian defense expert.[7] This is a relatively low percentage of the 1983 estimated total of 5,845 American tactical nuclear weapons in Europe.

The precise number of nuclear weapons in Italy is not particularly worrisome to Italian experts.[8] What has, however, grated on critics of Italy's status in NATO has been the uncertainty surrounding control of these weapons. Italians have been sensitive to the issue of whether or not they have a "second key" that could prevent the launching of nuclear weapons by American troops during a crisis. The problem has been exacerbated by unclear and perhaps incorrect statements by Italian political leaders, demonstrating their own uncertainty about the situation. In the late 1950s, for example, Prime Minister Antonio Segni asserted that Italy could veto the launching of the thirty Jupiter intermediate range ballistic missiles (IRBMs) on its soil, although that apparently was not true. More recently, with the installation of cruise missiles, the legacy of a muddle-through approach to the issue has been sustained. On April 11, 1984, Defense Minister Giovanni Spadolini asserted that no nuclear weapon could be launched from Italian territory without government authorization.[9] This is probably not the case, however, because the supreme Allied Commander of Europe (SACEUR) can almost certainly authorize (after receiving authority from the U.S. president) the use of such weapons for American troops under his direct command; no Italian official would necessarily be involved when both warheads and launch systems are in U.S. hands (apparently the case at the La Maddalena base). In the case of the cruise missiles, since plans call for a dispersion of launchers and weapons during a crisis, Italian troops could perhaps prevent such actions if the government reached a quick decision, but they could not prevent a launching from the home base without an open conflict. There are doubtless secret arrangements that attempt to regulate this situation, but the formal rules are less important than the existence of a fairly extensive debate in Italy over the question. The growing interest of politicians, experts, and even the general public in such matters is only one indication that Italy's passive role in Western security arrangements is coming to an end while a more self-conscious and assertive Italy is emerging.

A New Italian Approach to Security

Italy's new attentiveness to defense and security affairs dates from NATO's December 1979 decision to deploy American intermediate-range missiles in Europe in response to the Soviet installation of SS-20 missiles west of the Urals. Italy's agreement to take 112 cruise missiles and house them at a site in Sicily launched the first major domestic debate over defense issues since the late 1940s. It galvanized public opinion, forced the parties and politicians to develop an unaccustomed expertise on issues of deterrence and arms control, and prompted a small coterie of private commentators and experts to emerge and contribute to the debate. The Italian parliamentary debates on INF deployment, held in October and December of 1979, were the first important security policy discussions conducted in that forum since NATO was ratified in 1949, and the first in which a public choice had to be made concerning a key alliance decision. As one parliamentarian asserted, the incident effectively marked Italy's emergence from under the debilitating hand of NATO's "tutelege."[10] For Italy's politicians, according to the same source, the event was important because it demonstrated that some defense expertise was necessary and could even be politically rewarding—this had never been the case previously.

The decision also resulted in the first important foreign policy discord between the governing majority and the PCI since the 1960s, and all parties had to engage in an extended debate, explaining their positions on complicated strategic and arms control questions to each other and to the general public. Political elites began attending seminars on defense and security matters organized by the study institutes that began to proliferate and to concentrate on military affairs. The political parties themselves began studying these issues in greater depth in order to justify their positions and to provide their officials with more information. The Italian press did not only expand its coverage of security questions; papers such as *Corriere della Sera* and the financial daily *Il Sole 24 Ore* put defense experts on their payroll as regular contributors. The fuel that fired this new interest was public concern over the risks involved in the INF deployment, which focused unprecedented attention on such issues as nuclear strategy, Italy's role in NATO, the nature of the Soviet threat, and arms control negotiations. The opposition to the deployment included the PCI, which took a moderate and self-consciously "responsible" position, and a mass-based pacifist antinuclear movement that was independent of any political party but was able to organize such massive public demonstrations that all of Italy's political class was put on alert. Italy had previously had no large, organized antinuclear movement, and in a country where politics are generally well controlled by the established parties this development unsettled the ruling elites and reinforced a conviction of the necessity to undermine antinuclear, anti-NATO sentiments by meeting the issues head on.

The Euromissile question effectively ended Italy's long-standing parochialism on security affairs. For the first time the country became a key actor in East-West politics, and elites had to cope with both domestic and external policy pressures. Other developments in Italian defense policy and foreign affairs during this period reinforced the new attention accorded to security issues. After decades of a somewhat stultified armed forces policy, toward the end of the 1970s Italy adopted a series of ten-year modernization plans for each service, scheduled to run through 1990, which led to an increase in defense spending from an annual average of 2.5 percent of GNP between 1970 and 1981, one of the lowest in NATO, to over 4 percent (after 1983) by some calculations, now one of the highest.[11] As a result, there was more public and political scrutiny on military policy in a country with a public deficit that was already out of control. Linked to the modernization program was a redirection of defense strategy away from a focus on the northeast sector and toward the Mediterranean, in order to counter growing security risks in the area. This "new model of defense" was controversial because of its costs and because it was perceived as a step toward a more activist and risky military policy in the region. In general this shift in military policy focused attention on the structure and strategic orientation of Italy's own armed forces, reinforcing the debate over NATO affairs.

During this same period Italy engaged in a number of international military activities which not only reflected the country's new activism in such matters but also intensified national awareness of the importance of security policy and the necessity of carefully considering policy choices. In July 1979 Italian troops replaced the Norwegian contingent as part of the United Nations force in southern Lebanon. Later, the 1982 Beirut peacekeeping mission of the Italian armed forces was Italy's most significant extraterritorial military action since World War II; it created a great sense of national pride as well as some trepidation at the risks involved. In September 1980 Italy committed itself to guaranteeing Malta's neutrality and providing economic, technical, and military assistance. In March 1982 Rome agreed to contribute to the multinational force created to guarantee the full application of the Israeli-Egyptian peace treaty, eventually sending a naval group to patrol the Gulf of Aqaba and the Tiran Strait. Most recently, in August 1984, Italy met a request of the Egyptian government to send a small force of minesweepers to help clear the Gulf of Suez of mines that had been impairing navigation. With the exception of the Beirut mission, these actions were fairly small in scale and involved minimal risks; all took place in the context of internationally sanctioned, multilateral peacekeeping efforts. In the context of the Euromissile debate, which remained significant through 1985, however, the proliferation of Italian defense commitments ensured that public and political attention in such issues would not lag.[12]

In the Italian political system, foreign policy traditionally has been wielded primarily for domestic political leverage. In the new Italian context of the early 1980s, a national security policy began to take on its own dimension, as elites grappled for the first time with the unsettling idea of identifying specific Italian interests within the predominantly Atlantic framework. It was still primarily the political gains to be made from manipulating foreign and security policy that created such intense interest in these issues. The new situation, however, was markedly different from previous decades, when a kind of intransigent, unimaginative, passive, and usually ill-informed Atlanticism was manipulated by the Christian Democrats both as a way of staying in power and as a gatekeeping device for limiting political coalitions, especially excluding the Communists. Since 1979 the formulation of more concrete and assertive foreign policy and defense ideas has served as a tool for claiming and finally wielding national power in a way that has transformed the political utility of external issues in Italy.

The Italian Socialist party and its leader, Bettino Craxi, were primarily responsible for this development after 1979. During the 1970s

Italian politics (and foreign policy) had been paralyzed by an acute
domestic economic and social crisis marked by major acts of terrorism
and a preoccupation with possibly radical solutions, such as PCI
participation in national government. The end of this immobilist
phase coincided with the new salience of security issues for Italy.
Although the small Republican party led by Spadolini used a new
foreign policy image to bolster claims to national authority, it was
Craxi and the PSI who most adroitly wielded a more assertive foreign
policy line in the quest for national power; they found that pro-
Americanism, anti-Sovietism, and restrained nationalism could bolster their political fortunes. This tactic enabled Craxi to embarrass
and isolate the PCI within Italian politics, to establish the PSI as a force
associated with a reinvigorated Italy both at home and abroad, and
to convince Italians as well as Americans that a Craxi-led government
would be a desirable formula for protecting and enhancing Western,
including American, security interests in Europe and the Mediterranean.[13] One device the Socialists used to establish their competence
in security affairs was their control of the Ministry of Defense from
1980 until mid-1983, a period when a party ally of Craxi's, Lelio
Lagorio, headed the ministry and was responsible for both an accelerated modernization program and the implementation of the new shift
in emphasis away from the northeast and toward the Mediterranean.
Among his accomplishments was the publication of a white book on
defense policy for the defense committee of the Chamber of Deputies
and Senate, an impressive document compared to Italy's very first
rudimentary one issued in 1977.[14]

After Craxi's accession to power as Italy's second prime minister
from outside the Christian Democratic party in August 1983, he managed to remain in office through a scheduled departure in March
1987, thereby setting a postwar Italian record for longevity. One of
the most interesting and novel features of this period was the way in
which foreign and security policy matters could be manipulated by
the prime minister in order to convey the impression of assertiveness
and activism and thereby secure greater prestige both abroad and,
especially, at home. With still quite intractable domestic problems,
foreign policy became a hallmark of the Craxi prime ministership as
a way of mustering and exerting authority.

To accomplish this the PSI leader upgraded the quality and influence of the four-man foreign policy team assigned to the Palazzo

Chigi (the prime minister's office) and instructed its members to identify policy areas (the Mediterranean, the Middle East, Central America, arms control) where he could innovate with a certain domestic and foreign impact. During Craxi's tenure the split between the secretive, independent, and pro-Arab foreign minister (Giulio Andreotti) and the very pro-American, pro-Israeli defense minister (Spadolini) helped the prime minister assert himself even more. In this context it should be noted that the Defense Ministry is a legitimate player in the broad arena of security policy only when military questions are directly involved. Otherwise, the minister of defense may not be consulted even on important decisions. In arms control policy the Foreign Ministry plays the preponderant role, while (under Craxi) the prime minister's office may choose to intervene; the Defense Ministry, however, usually keeps out of policy matters and has only a small staff to furnish technical advice.

In terms of substance Craxi focused on a strong Atlanticist and prodefense approach by implementing the Euromissile deployment in the face of widespread public opposition. He also reinforced the new Mediterranean security orientation of Italian security policy and, along with his DC foreign minister, adopted a more overtly pro-Palestinian approach to Middle East problems. Although generally pro-American in the Italian tradition, Craxi sensed an incipient Italian appreciation of greater independence to the point where he was willing to distinguish himself from U.S. policies on a number of issues. This was true of Central American policy for a time; even on the cruise missile issue he indicated in Lisbon in May 1984 that he might be willing to consider suspending deployment to encourage an arms control agreement—going beyond NATO and U.S. policy at the time.

Contemporary Italian judgment on the long-term effects of the Craxi experiment is divided. Most political leaders and foreign policy experts agree that the taste for activism and a certain independence in the face of the United States is now ingrained in the political system because Italians have discovered an unaccustomed pride in acquiring international attention and respect. One of the prime minister's closest associates in the PSI concludes that Craxi has "deprovincialized" Italy in this respect, and by creating a new foreign policy culture he had "invested" rather than "consumed" during his term in office.[15] It does seem that the Craxi government has been a decisive turning point in this respect. Italy is unlikely to return to the former passive, introspective pattern of behavior. On the other hand, in this politically fragmented country the content of any assertive policy creates tensions and disagreements that can jeopardize the stability of cabinets.

One consequence of Craxi's new independence and assertiveness was a strong dissent by the Republican party (PRI) led by Defense Minister Spadolini, which has opposed both the pro-Arab inclinations of most other parties and any overt conflict with the United States. Such friction, fueled by personal antagonisms and rivalries, led to a temporary collapse of the government in October 1985 over the handling of the *Achille Lauro* affair—the first government crisis over a foreign policy issue since 1948.[16] This incident confirmed that the PRI remains the principal opponent of the trend toward a more assertive and distinctive Italian foreign policy, partly on tactical grounds and partly because the Republicans are the last bastion of an almost subserviently pro-American outlook that deliberately eschews any incipient Italian nationalism. In the governments that follow Craxi's, new political circumstances and different personalities in key ministries may lead to a deemphasis of foreign policy innovation for a time. In the long run, however, the new awareness of the early 1980s seems likely to remain alive and even expand because of the precedents set under Craxi, and because Italy's key political institutions, especially the parties, have acquired vested interests in foreign policy expertise.

Security and Defense Issues in the Italian Debate

Some of the general themes and most controversial issues in Italy during the 1980s have already been mentioned above. In addition to the new general approach to foreign and security policy, a number of specific problems have become especially important in the Italian security debate in recent years. The principal issues are: (1) the nature of the Soviet threat—and Italy's role in the East-West competition; (2) Italy's position in NATO; (3) the "new model" of Italy's defense orientation and the Mediterranean focus; and (4) arms control issues.

Détente and the Soviet Threat

Probably the most important development in Italian thinking on foreign policy issues during the 1980s was the discovery that Italy could have independent positions on security issues that involved carefully nuanced differences with the United States. As one authority wrote, "the country is slowly acquiring a large national consciousness and sense of the state" that involves the "recovery of nationality and not of nationalism."[17] For many this meant that "the basis of Italian foreign policy, the absolute coincidence of American and Western European interests, could no longer be defended with the same credibility as before."[18] For Craxi and Andreotti, this sense of a separate national interest extended to East-West affairs, and they began exploring a distinctive role that carried its own Eastern policy. As one Socialist party official put it, this amounted to the creation of a modest Italian Ostpolitik ("piccola Ostpolitik Italiana")[19] and the creation of a network of ties to Hungary, Romania, Yugoslavia, and even East Germany. For Craxi himself, this policy was based on the conviction that Italian and West European security interests should not be hostage to an exclusively U.S.-USSR bilateral relationship. He saw Italy's independence dialogue with the East as an attempt to influence the superpower dialogue.

In particular, Craxi was unhappy with the confrontational approach of the Reagan administration in 1983–84 and wanted to demonstrate that Italy's agreement with INF deployments did not also imply a hostile stance toward the East. What this amounts to for Italy's political class as a whole is a growing conviction that Italy can now disagree with some aspects of American East-West policies without jeopardizing the sense of attachment to either the United States or the Atlantic alliance. In this sense, Italy sometimes attempts to act as a kind of third force, or "cushion"—a moderating influence—in the confrontation between the superpowers. This approach seems to coincide with the attitudes of the Italian public, which remains pro-American and favors strong American leadership in the world but also prefers more maneuvering freedom for Italian foreign policy.[20]

Like the general public, most experts and politicians from the right through the center-left allocate the primary responsibility for increased international tensions to the Soviet Union, especially because of its military buildup in recent years and the deployment of the ss-20 missiles. Although there are varying views about American defense and arms control policies among experts and establishment politicians, they are not out of line with the diversity found in the rest of Western Europe and the United States itself. The Italian Left, however, has distinctive perspectives worth noting because many elements allocate equal and sometimes primary responsibility for East-West conflicts and the arms race to the United States. Probably the most notable feature of conflict and arms control literature produced by the Italian Left is its focus on Western, and especially American, policies; by implication, if not design, the United States and NATO appear to bear the brunt of responsibility for European insecurity.

For some on the left, responsibility for the arms race is shared equally by the United States and the Soviet Union, both of which are seeking to maintain global hegemony. The Soviet Union is attempting to enhance tensions in Europe in order to keep the East bloc under control, while the United States diverts attention from its leaky nuclear umbrella by having the Europeans accept a largely useless, if not dangerous, INF deployment.[21] The subtly different view of disarmament activist Fabrizio Battistelli is that the superpowers share responsibility for a dangerous arms race. The Soviet Union is less at fault because it does not have an independent military-industrial complex that influences government policy; also, U.S. officials support a dialectic based on deterrence and balanced forces, while the Soviet Union preaches a discourse of peace "which one cannot underestimate."[22] For the Left, the Reagan administration's emphasis on an arms buildup is a particularly deplorable development, as is the unreasonable view that the arms race cannot be ended "except at the price of a radical change in the politics (domestic and international) and in the economic system" of the Soviet Union.[23] Finally, whereas the USSR is said to seek only strategic parity, some of the Italian Left agree that the United States is now destabilizing international security by attempting to reestablish a position of clear superiority.[24]

Of all the major political forces, the Communist party has the most difficulty in arriving at an independent and broadly defensible view of the nature of the Soviet political-military menace to Italy and Western Europe. Despite the party's achievement of autonomy from Moscow by the early 1970s and its formal acceptance of Italian membership in NATO by 1975, the PCI has never had a clear perspective on whether or not the Soviets present an actual threat to Western interests. Instead, it vaguely supports a continued balance of forces between the two blocs as the basis for an expansion of détente and new arms control and disarmament measures, eventually leading to the dismantling of both military blocs. When confronted with particular policy problems, the PCI tends to respond with ad hoc approaches that it feels may balance off its new, partial commitment to the West with its aversion to any overt antagonism toward the USSR. Despite significant disagreements with the Soviets over events such as the 1979 invasion of Afghanistan and the 1981 coup in Poland, most of the PCI still seems unable to identify an overt Soviet menace in the world. The PCI is, of course, divided into factions with leaders who take fairly distinctive positions: Giorgio Napolitano is a leading moderate whose views are close to those of the German SPD and who can support certain Western military responses to Soviet moves. Other moderates of this kind include Alberto Reichlin and Luciano Lama. The party Left, however, led by figures such as Pietro Ingrao, tends to be very anti–United States, and although few of its members are actually pro-Soviet (like Armando Cossutta), they downplay the Soviet threat and see American global economic and military imperialism as the main threat to peace.

The PCI often takes arms control positions that coincide with Soviet proposals, partly out of habit, partly because its leaders are unsophisticated in the nuances of defense and strategic issues, and partly because they discount the danger associated with Soviet political-military advantages in Europe. Thus, for example, a leading figure in the PCI Foreign Affairs Department asserts that the Soviet Union represents an extremely weak threat to Europe because it is pressed by so many intractable internal problems. In his view, elements within the Soviet Union and the East bloc can readily be convinced to deescalate the arms race in order to spare their economies further strain.[25] On the other hand, the PCI's leading technical expert in defense and arms control policy tends to take a more balanced position that allocates arms race responsibility between the superpowers, noting that each side has hawks and doves that compete for influence over policy. Gianluca de Voto adds, however, that the American preoccupation with nuclear deterrence is not necessarily shared by the Soviets, to whom "atomic war has never been seen as wholly improbable," while in the USSR "the nuclear forces, more than in the West, have been integrated with the others."[26] Some elements of the PCI must frequently be exasperated with the ideas of the party's own experts, particularly when the director of the Communist Foreign Affairs Research Institute can publish an article that ascribes to the Soviets primary responsibility for East-West tensions and labels the ss-20 a major threat to Western security.[27]

Italy's NATO Connection

In a country with a large and vociferous left wing, it is not surprising that the United States and the American alliance system should be the objects of much criticism. What is unusual today, however, is that the Italian role in the alliance and NATO's relative disinterest in Italy's specific security problems have become the subjects of widespread discussion and debate well beyond leftist circles. Part of this reflects a long-standing dissatisfaction with the Western tendency to take Italy for granted; the new mood of assertiveness in the country finds many willing to insist that both Italy and her partners pay more attention to specifically Italian security interests. This, for example, is the source of complaints that Italy had benefited little from NATO's focus on the central front because the southern flank had been left out of major program developments. Although Italy may have been lax in not sending the most capable military officers to the integrated commands, Rome in recent years had been upgrading its military efforts but had received little recognition or enhanced status as a result.[28] On the official level the criticism is muted in most instances, and the practical consequence has been for Italy to redirect its defense efforts away from NATO's favored northeast sector and toward the Mediterranean.

The NATO-related issue that has most interested the Left, and in 1985–86 drew the attention of other political forces, has been the issue of American military bases operated under NATO auspices in Italy. For a long time the PCI has attempted to delve into the secret agreement covering the NATO/U.S. military presence and has insisted that under Article 80 of the Constitution (dealing with parliamentary oversight of international agreements), the legislature should have the right to examine and approve such agreements. The avowed aim of the PCI is to create a juridical and organizational framework that will regulate and control the bases—hence the activities of American armed forces—and assert authority over the NATO-related activities of the Italian armed forces as well.[29] One specific goal has been to recover control of the facilities for air defense of Italian territory from the NATO commands, where it is now assigned even in peacetime.

The view of Eliseo Milani, an independent-left senator, is identical with that of the PCI: "[it] . . . is intolerable that the NATO and U.S. bases on national territory are utilized in an uncontrolled way outside of the strict competence and limits of the Alliance."[30] The October 1985 incident at the Sigonella base, where American and Italian troops engaged in an armed standoff over the disposition of the *Achille Lauro* hijackers, furnished critics with ammunition against unfettered American use of bases. Some PCI officials found this incident to be confirmation that NATO serves as an instrument of U.S. imperialism, or at least treats Italy with intolerable arrogance. The official PCI and leftist position has been to try and subject base operations to parliamentary and other controls, both Italian and multilateral, to ensure that these facilities are used only for approved defensive purposes. It seems clear that if the Left were to have its way, the usefulness of Italian territory to U.S. security interests would be drastically reduced and, more generally, a wide range of Italian commitments to NATO would be subject to open reexamination.

Such views on the part of the Italian Left are not surprising. What is remarkable is that for a time following the Sigonella incident resentment over the American free hand in Italy spread to other political groups, and the urge to implement closer surveillance of the bases was deeply felt. It seems unlikely that such bad feelings will dissipate entirely, and they may instead lead to some tightening up of controls over American and NATO bases. Indeed, the question had already been discussed within the Defense Ministry before October 1985; informal studies had been done on ways to reinforce Italian sovereignty without damaging Italian-American relations or mutually beneficial security operations in Europe and the Mediterranean.[31] At the time of the *Achille Lauro* crisis, Craxi apparently was willing to go further; in a draft platform submitted to the five parties that made up the reconstituted government, he proposed an agreement that NATO bases in Italy could be used by allies "only for ends specific to the Atlantic Alliance as laid down in the agreements."[32] The pro-American Republicans, backed by the Liberals and Social Democrats, vetoed this clause, but Craxi's sentiments were shared by many at the time. One idea discussed in 1986, which may eventually be implemented, was to create an international crisis group in the prime minister's office to ensure interministerial coordination and effective Italian management of crises of the *Achille Lauro* type. Such an arrangement, presumably, would have to be closely linked to the NATO and American commands in Italy and might affect some of their independence.

In the meantime Italy has acted to restrict American access to its national territory when military actions unrelated to NATO are involved and has recovered control of some minor installations from U.S. hands. Like other European NATO members except Britain, Italy refused to lend direct aid to the April 15, 1986, U.S. air strike against Libya. This stand was based on the refusal of the Roman government to back Washington's bellicose reaction to Libyan support of international terrorism. Despite a range of views within the coalition cabinet, the prevailing inclination was to avoid military confrontations with Libya and instead use diplomatic resources to induce better behavior from Muammar Qaddafi. Foreign Minister Andreotti, especially, attempted to mediate between Washington and Tripoli well into 1986, although Italy's growing suffering as a target area for Middle East–based terrorist activities has gradually produced a firmer attitude toward Libya and other radical Arab groups. The immediate result of the U.S. raid on Libya was a failed, semicomical Libyan shelling of the Italian southern Mediterranean island of Lampadusa, where there is a loran station managed by the U.S. Coast Guard. The reaction in Rome was to recover control of this and a similar facility in Calabria on June 1, 1986, some two years before the existing agreement was due to lapse. Although this incident was clearly not a precursor of later moves to recover national control over foreign military or semimilitary installations, it did confirm a new Italian willingness to reduce certain regional Mediterranean tensions by restricting a minor, but visible, link to the United States.

Italy's New Defense Policy

During the 1980s the principal development in Italian military policy has been a shift of emphasis from the northeast sector toward the Mediterranean. This has affected the budgeting and modernization plans of the armed forces and has led to the modest assertion of a distinct Italian national security interest within NATO. Although the new Italian approach complements American security interests in the Mediterranean and should reinforce bilateral cooperation in the region, Italy has a new sense of self-assertion in the area that may create some difficulties with both the United States and NATO. As noted, this has already occurred in terms of regional diplomacy, where Italian interests have clashed with those of the United States and produced serious foreign policy confrontations between the two countries and within Italy itself.

Italy's new Mediterranean defense orientation dates from 1980, although the idea of a special mission in this region goes back to the Mussolini era and subsequent notions of Italy serving as a bridge between Europe and the Third World to the south. According to Army Chief of Staff General Umberto Capuzzo, the recent shift of emphasis was based on the conviction that "the center of crisis in Europe has shifted notably southward, and above all to the Mediterranean, the crossroads of both East-West and North-South tensions." Because of the dual nature of this instability the Mediterranean was supplanting the German central front as the "epicenter" of crisis.[33] Italian defense officials felt that NATO, with its central-front fixation and defined geographical limitations, was not attentive enough to Italian security needs on the southern front. According to Capuzzo, then, Italy decided to "enhance its potential and capabilities in the region and to consider a new set of direct Italian commitments outside of NATO's area of jurisdiction in the interests of peace and progress."[34] Defense Minister Lagorio, the architect of the new southern defense orientation, was even more candid about Italy's decision to redirect its military activities away from strictly NATO goals: "The Atlantic Alliance, however, does not and cannot exhaust the Italian policy. Our country follows its 'own' policy which, even though largely coinciding with the Atlantic one, does not fully mirror it in all its actions and, above all, is independent and autonomous regarding all territories not covered by the North Atlantic Treaty. Unlike in the mid-70s, the Alliance does not offer anymore a total defense guarantee to our country."[35]

In line with this new military policy, the Defense Ministry has redirected some resources away from the northeast and drawn up a program for integrating the armed services according to various missions: northeast defense, southern and maritime defense, air defense, operational land defense, and peacekeeping and civil protection.[36] The new plans call for Italy to count on mounting only short-term holding actions in the northeast, pending the arrival of NATO reinforcements or the resolution of a conflict due to the main confron-

tation on the German central front.[37] The broad changes in the structure and equipment of the Italian armed forces are too complicated
to discuss here, but this new focus on the Mediterranean involves
an upgrading of aero-naval capabilities in the south, including the
creation of naval air intervention capabilities centered on the helicopter carrier *Garibaldi,* which is scheduled to be armed with s/VTOL
aircraft (Harriers) in addition to existing heavy antisubmarine heli-
copters. The Italian air force also has acquired an enhanced ability
to operate at some distance over the Mediterranean with its acquisi-
tion of Tornado fighter aircraft and its replacement of light fighter-
bombers with the AMX. Finally, Italy has created its own version of
the rapid intervention force (Forza di Intervento Rapido, or FOIR), a
unit of ten thousand men that would be able to move on twenty-four
hours notice. There has been much political and service wrangling
over the kinds of mission capability the force should have. Although
many foresee some sort of external regional action in the future, for
now the force is limited officially to "reaching in the briefest time
any area of the national territory subject to external attack."[38]

   Italy has been in the midst of an intense debate over this new
southern military dimension of national security policy; the propo-
nents of activism support the development of external intervention
forces, while the minimalists prefer to focus on an exclusively territorial defense. Many also believe that security problems in the Mediterranean (such as terrorism emanating from Arab countries) are primarily political-diplomatic and thus not very susceptible to ordinary
military force. Although force development plans continue to redirect
efforts toward the south, while Spadolini was defense minister
(1983–87) the policy was to tone down the Mediterranean bias of
defense planning and explicitly reject any independent Italian security vocation in the region outside of actions in complete coordination
with NATO and the United States. Spadolini's view has been that Italy
is too weak politically and economically to contemplate independent
initiatives or even conceive of a security policy that is not rigidly tied
to the prevailing East-West confrontation and subordinate to NATO
and American plans and strategy. In the defense minister's November
1983 statement to Parliament, he noted: "We must resist the tempta-
tion to theorize 'Mediterranean vocations' or autonomous East-West
mediation roles. In the tight East-West competition, which more and
more expands in Third World areas, there is no place for medium

powers' spontaneous initiatives, especially if they have, like our country, serious economic problems. Italy can and must give its contribution to the stability of international security only in close connection with the Western strategic design."[39]

On this issue, however, there is no consensus in Italy, and the governing parties have been very divided about the implications for foreign policy as well as for defense of Italy's flirtation with a more autonomous regional role. The principal advocates of Italy's self-assertion have been the Socialists, who focused on the Middle East crisis and developed close ties to moderate Arabs and the Arafat faction of the Palestine Liberation Organization. The Christian Democrats actually pioneered this approach, and it reputedly was Andreotti who created the mid-1970s bargain under which Italy would be spared Arab-instigated terrorism in return for supporting the Palestine cause. After 1983, Craxi and Andreotti expanded Italy's network of relations in the Arab world and were attempting to deal with it on behalf of the West and the United States, whose position in the area, in their view, was deteriorating. This was recognized as a risky policy. It was strongly opposed within the government by the Republicans, who are the only important pro-Israeli political force in Italy and have therefore sought to minimize the expanded Arab connection. More generally, the Republicans prefer to leave Middle East and Mediterranean politics in the hands of the United States, believing that Italy can only become tangled up in a situation it cannot handle. In their view, Italy would only become the hostage of one or another faction in the Arab-Israeli struggle.

This ongoing debate over Italy's foreign policy and security interests in the Mediterranean region is unlikely to be settled in the foreseeable future. It will remain controversial not only because of the kind of activist/pragmatist cleavage just discussed but also because there are overlapping and contradictory views that confuse the situation. For example, the PCI and independent-left groups favor a pro-Palestinian approach and a deemphasis of the East-West conflict in the region but strongly oppose the development of an interventionary defense capability for use outside Italian territory. For such critics, the militarization of Italian foreign policy fits in with American plans for extending its influence and offsetting the ostensible growth of Soviet influence along the Mediterranean. Many in Italy are therefore uncomfortable with a stronger political-military profile in general, while others feel that the trend toward a more assertive foreign policy requires the country to take independent and inherently risky positions on issues that affect national security. After Craxi relinquishes the post of prime minister, recent tendencies toward adventuresome risk taking may abate somewhat, depending on the personality and inclinations of the successor prime minister and others in key security policy positions.

Policies and Perspectives on Arms Control

Italians do not consider their country a major influence on the most significant East-West arms control and disarmament questions, and they seldom develop significant, detailed, well-thought-out policies on most arms control questions. Because Italian influence over superpower decisions is felt to be minimal, and because Italy is not involved directly in the most important decision-making forums, arms control policy tends to follow the lead of the United States and NATO, with only minor variations produced by ad hoc decisions within heterogeneous and conflict-ridden Italian governments. This tends to be true even when Italy might be strongly affected by arms control negotiations, such as the INF talks.

Despite this lack of a consistent and assertive arms control policy, there is a strong Italian cultural-political bias in favor of arms control and disarmament, so that all political parties are under constant pressure to favor, and even to advocate, negotiations and specific measures, even though such positions may be untimely or irresponsible. The Catholic peace tradition pushes the DC in this direction, while the socialist peace tradition influences the PSI in much the same way. The PCI is intrinsically favorable to most arms control proposals, especially Soviet ones, and other parties are reluctant to be outflanked on the left on this issue. The large and vociferous peace movement in Italy further encourages political leaders to establish themselves as pro–arms control in the domestic debate. Thus, the knowledge that Italy will probably have little effect on major international decisions in this arena, combined with an awareness that prodisarmament posturing has a domestic political payoff, often produces ill-considered opinions and a general confusion in terms of policy. There is, paradoxically, a general skepticism about the likelihood that international arms negotiations will ever accomplish very much, which further reduces serious Italian interest in the whole subject.

The arms control policies of Italian governments are more or less the exclusive domain of the Foreign Ministry, where the director general for political affairs advises the foreign minister on the development of national positions. In the Craxi government Foreign Minister Andreotti was the principal architect of Italy's approach to arms control matters. Defense Minister Spadolini reportedly had only a rudimentary understanding of and interest in such issues aside from their domestic political impact. Andreotti's general approach was not to let Italy get out in front on these issues but to follow the lead of others, especially the United States, while sometimes working behind the scenes in order to adjust American policy (or its image) to make it more suitable to Italian domestic exigencies.[40] The Foreign Ministry lacks technical expertise on arms control questions; hence, it focuses on general matters of principle, which have more political importance in Italy.[41] Recently, however, Italy did take an active interest in the Stockholm conference and worked closely with West European partners to develop confidence-building measures such as exchanges of military information, prenotification of maneuvers, and verification.[42]

Italy's close cooperation with other West European governments before and during the Stockholm conference is an example of the national preference for developing common positions with allies and then working jointly with them, making whatever policy adjustments are necessary as part of a common effort. The preference of officials at the Foreign Ministry for broad multilateral settings and a low national profile often keeps Italy from participating in some forums and was one of several motives for taking only observer status at the Vienna MBFR talks. On the recent INF issue, the Foreign Ministry vetoed the suggestion of an outside expert that it propose the creation of a privileged tripartite group of future host countries (Germany, Britain, and Italy) to influence American positions at the Geneva negotiations. Instead, the Ministry of Foreign Affairs preferred to work through the Nuclear Planning Group, the special consultative group, and the broader NATO setting.[43] This was consistent with a pattern of developing arms control positions only with as broad a group of allies as possible, taking great pains to avoid a national stand that might damage Western cohesion.

Between 1983 and 1986 the normal Italian low profile, even passivity, on arms control issues was challenged to a certain extend as Prime Minister Craxi and his advisers tried to be more innovative. This was partly for domestic political reasons but also because of the conviction that Italy should be more assertive in this arena as well as on other foreign affairs matters. Craxi was apparently dissatisfied with the work of the INF special consultative group at NATO and was concerned that the Soviet Union seemed to be taking all of the initiatives while the West appeared obstructionist. Craxi was also unhappy with the slow, bureaucratic approach of the arms control officials at the Italian Ministry of Foreign Affairs, who seemed often to make their own policy with little reference to other ministers. Thus, some of Craxi's unusual forthrightness and attempts to suggest ways out of the Geneva bottleneck and other unproductive negotiations were part of a general strategy aimed at pushing both the West and Italian officials out of the doldrums.[44] Finally, the prime minister felt that arms control questions were of growing political importance to the Italian public, and he was unwilling to leave an important policy arena in the hands of diplomats, most of whom are Christian Democrats. Although Craxi's initiatives had little practical effect, the political motivations that lay behind them seem likely to remain valid for future prime ministers.

Apart from some occasional ad hoc statements and positions, distinctive arms control positions are unlikely to emerge from officials and the governing parties in Italy. On the left of the political spectrum, however, there are fewer conformist ideas that condition the nature of the debate in Italy, even though they do not have much impact on policy. The most important agent in this regard is the PCI. The Communists do not have a comprehensive arms control policy and consciously avoid detailed discussions, but they do have a general, very pro–arms control position. The PCI claims it favors balanced arms control agreements and hopes the great powers can move from mere control to actual disarmament in the near future. Many of the party's "arms control" positions seem to deal more with restricting NATO bases and armaments within the West and are especially aimed at reducing or eliminating the various nuclear weapons on Italian and European soil.

One specific measure with a PCI sanction interests much of the Italian Left—the creation of a denuclearized zone in central Europe that would extend 150 kilometers on either side of the bloc's frontier. The PCI adds that Italy could make part of its northeastern area into a denuclearized zone as well, with equal compensation from the East bloc.[45] The PCI also dismisses the West's preoccupation with on-site verification of eventual agreements with the Soviets, contending that modern technology has largely solved these problems. The left wing of the party has been antagonistic toward all nuclear weapons and tends to take unrealistic positions based on this emotional perspective. Moderates in the party attempt to be more pragmatic and envisage gradual mutual arms reductions that they hope will reduce the numbers of nuclear weapons in Europe and raise the nuclear threshold considerably.

The Centro Studi di Politica Internazionale's (CESPI) leading arms expert, Gianluca de Voto, has developed a comprehensive approach that does not necessarily reflect PCI policy but is indicative of measures that the party might support. He favors umbrella negotiations that would cover all of the weapons systems of the two blocs, especially the nuclear ones, and he wants to bring the British and French forces into the talks eventually. The aim of such negotiations would be to limit or reduce opposing strategic arms, abolish Eurostrategic nuclear weapons everywhere on the European continent (including European Russia), and commit the powers to renounce all strategic defense systems, including those based in space.[46] In Europe, de Voto has favored the gradual renunciation of the concept of "extended deterrence" and would eliminate tactical nuclear weapons from the European theater via denuclearized zones. He hopes that the opposing blocs will eventually rely more on conventional forces for both deterrence and defense.[47] During 1986 the PCI aligned itself with these views by publicly and specifically supporting measures such as the dismantling of all Euromissiles and banning every form of nuclear testing.

It should be noted that for the PCI as a whole, the United States is not an unmitigated villain in the arms control field, although the U.S. government is seen as particularly intransigent and unwilling even to consider some interesting Soviet proposals. However, the PCI is constantly on the lookout for possible "allies," or at least sympathetic attitudes, in the United States. The nuclear freeze movement was identified as one of these in 1982, along with figures such as Senator Kennedy and Senator Hatfield. The "gang of four" responsible for the spring 1982 *Foreign Affairs* proposal for a "no early first use" NATO nuclear weapons doctrine were also viewed favorably because they were "proposing an important change in strategic thought on the part of the West."[48] In general, "no first use" proposals emanating from the United States and Europe have met with approval from the PCI and large sectors of the Italian Left as a first step toward more concrete arms control achievements. On the other hand, Italian government and establishment opinion has been negative because "no first use" is seen as giving the Soviets a unilateral advantage in the European theater, where its conventional forces are stronger than those of the West. Defense experts in Italy have, however, viewed the Rogers Plan for shoring up conventional defenses and raising the nuclear threshold favorably, partly on the grounds that it might undermine support for irresponsible "no first use" proposals.[49] The Foreign Ministry, especially Andreotti, have also favored a Western "no first use of force" doctrine, partly on the grounds that it would invalidate the Brezhnev doctrine. During 1986, growing Italian opposition to civilian as well as military uses of nuclear energy was beginning to influence the perspectives of left-wing political leaders in both the Communist and Socialist parties.

Outside of the mainstream Left in Italy, more radical elements and pacifists do not take much trouble to provide nuanced criticism of Western arms control efforts or to make serious policy suggestions of their own. Their attitude is that existing arms control efforts between the superpowers or under United Nations auspices are hopeless. They tend to put their faith in the long-term effects of the mass-based antinuclear and antiwar movements in Europe and the United States, which, according to one source, represent "the only really new factor in terms of disarmament in the eighties."[50] Another extremist spokesman simply opposes allowing governments to negotiate on matters of such significance, because it robs people of the right of self-determination when power is delegated "to negotiate about our life, our future, the use of our resources."[51] This perspective, which is not supported by any major political party in Italy, is part of the Third World radical perspective present in so much of the European peace movement and is simply a variety of anarchism that has minimal influence on national policy.

One specific arms control issue that receives some attention in Italy and produces detailed analyses and proposals is the matter of chemical weapons. Italy is a signatory of the Geneva Convention (ratified in 1928); in 1975 Italy ratified another agreement prohibiting the development, production, and storage of biological or toxic weapons. Experts, however, have noted that all of Western Europe is threatened by the large Soviet and Warsaw Pact stocks of chemical weapons. The Soviets have about 300,000 tons of them, while the United States has about 42,000 tons, 4,000 of which are stored at a facility in West Germany.[52] Italian experts feel that the Soviets may be tempted to employ these weapons in a war in Europe, and even on the southern flank. Enrico Jacchia (head of the Centro de Studi Strategici) has criticized proposed solutions to the problem, such as the 1982 Palme Commission suggestion to create a chemical-free zone in Europe, on the grounds that the Soviets could still store materials in Asia. He has favored a global ban on the weapons, with as many states adhering to the agreement as possible.[53] Jacchia also has supported the U.S. draft treaty tabled in April 1984 at the Geneva Disarmament Conference and has criticized Soviet reluctance to accept it. He argues that full and reliable direct on-site inspection is required for the proper monitoring of the production and commercial movement of primary materials. This should involve "physical inspection, carried out by regularly designated inspectors, granted effective powers which guarantee their access, at any time, to any place and any person who handles materials or facilities subject to control."[54] At Geneva, the Italian Foreign Ministry has generally taken a similar position supportive of U.S. policy but has suggested some flexibility in verification procedures.

A final arms control issue that is as much the subject of current debate in Italy as elsewhere is the U.S. Strategic Defense Initiative (SDI). Through 1986, arms control discussion in Italy did not have much of a distinctive Italian flavor; instead, it mirrored the same uncertainties and controversies that accompany the notion in the United States and Western Europe. Although most Italians are, in private, skeptical of the long-term possibilities of providing a workable multilayered defense shield for the United States, much less Western Europe, the government has taken the position that the SDI program is currently a research program and not an irreversible strategic and political decision. Defense Minister Spadolini, strongly backed by Italian industrialists such as Giovanni Agnelli, has asserted that Italy should participate in the research stage as long as the other major West European countries, Germany and Britain, do the same. By October 1986 Rome and Washington had reached an agreement on SDI that would permit at least six major Italian firms to sign research contracts with the United States. This did not amount to blanket political approval of SDI, however, because Foreign Minister Andreotti has often expressed what most would consider ambivalent support for SDI, reflecting Foreign Ministry fears that the program may eventually destabilize East-West relations. He has, for example, insisted that the superpowers should "avoid an uncontrolled and competitive militarization of space which would have very serious destabilizing implications."[55] In the meantime, however, Italy has been unwilling to antagonize the Reagan administration over the issue. At an important speech before the West European Union on December 4, 1985, Andreotti said that imperfect defense systems would nevertheless reinforce the sense of uncertainty that underlies deterrence, so that an eventual SDI system would perhaps "complement, rather than substitute for, nuclear deterrence." He also criticized the Soviet Union for using SDI as a pretext for refusing to negotiate on offensive systems, which he identified as the main problem now.[56]

The views of Italian defense experts are based primarily on information from the extensive American debate over SDI, and they have little independent information or criticism to offer. Most authorities seem to be skeptical of the possibility that SDI will provide substantial protection, even in the distant future, and tend to reject the argument that it is an alternative to the arms race or dependence on nuclear weapons for security. Like some American analysts, Italians may argue that a partially effective defense network would reinforce deterrence because decisive advantage could not be gained from a first strike, while the threat of accidental nuclear war probably would be eliminated. A principal problem with SDI for Europeans is that the viability of British and French forces might be reduced by a Soviet program. Italians, however, have never been drawn to Gaullist notions of an independent European defense, so this objection does not preoccupy them very much. They are, however, concerned that a deployed strategic defense system would greatly increase Europe's dependence on the United States and might leave Europe excessively vulnerable to military crisis and even attack, while the United States could be tempted to withdraw behind its shield. For this reason experts such as Luigi Caligaris favor either the development of a complementary European system or, preferably, a joint U.S.-European defensive program and system.[57]

Italy's political parties began to devote much attention to the SDI issue only in 1985–86, and the initial response has not been favorable. Perhaps because Craxi himself was not well disposed toward the program, PSI spokesmen like Valdo Spini and Pablo Vittorelli have been critical of the destabilizing effect SDI may have on East-West détente and the arms control process. Vittorelli has proposed that the Europeans pressure the United States into accepting a new space treaty to ensure that the research phase of SDI goes no further than that, while he has denounced "the destabilizing character of a unilateral [arms] race into space."[58] As might be expected, the PCI has taken the most negative position on SDI of any Italian party. Communist officials state that the American program will be responsible for relaunching an offensive arms race on the part of both superpowers, thereby destabilizing East-West relations and decreasing the security of all states concerned. Indeed, a principal concern of most Italian political actors is that the SDI program will further erode the détente process, which has been the source of minimal foreign policy consensus within the country and the foundation for the slow emergence of a more independent, unified, and assertive Italy.

Conclusion

This analysis has depicted Italian foreign and security policy at a stage of transition from a passive, introspective, generally accommodating Atlantic partner to a relatively more assertive ally now willing to take independent positions on issues of significance to the national interest. Although there has been a clear trend toward greater Italian activism and self-assurance during the 1980s, it should not be exaggerated or interpreted as an Italian version of Gaullism or an emergence of some brand of anti-Americanism that may threaten Italy's basic ties to NATO and the Western alliance. Instead, the situation in the mid-1980s is that Italy is now more like other West European partners of the United States—willing to express its own views and to occasionally disagree with Washington when key Italian interests are perceived to be at stake. The principal conclusion to be drawn from the emergence of a more independent-minded Italian ally is that the United States should no longer take Italian loyalty—much less subservience—for granted and, at a minimum, should take the normal precautions in terms of prior consultation and respect for national views that for decades have been applied to senior partners in northern Europe.

This injunction to treat Italy as a mature Atlantic ally and to work for a more overt, carefully prepared reconciliation of potentially divergent U.S.-Italian views and policies is valid regardless of the posture of a particular government in Rome. Although the "Craxi effect" described above is likely to remain a recurrent and even notable feature of Italian foreign policy, the trend will be sporadic and subject to periods of quiescence. Indeed, since the spring of 1986 Italy has been less assertive in foreign affairs, and there have been no major conflicts between the United States and Italy. One reason is that the Italian political system has been increasingly preoccupied with domestic wrangling as party leaders maneuver for advantage in the governments that are expected to succeed Craxi's tenure as prime minister. In the absence of a major international crisis, Italy will probably continue to focus on domestic developments until a stable post-Craxi political formula emerges. Despite the recent priority accorded domestic politics, any escalation of existing security risks in the Mediterranean or another U.S.-Italian confrontation like the *Achille Lauro* affair would almost certainly become an issue in the internal political struggle, which would further intensify Atlantic tensions. From this perspective, a principal goal of the United States should be to avoid overt conflicts with Rome that subsequently become entangled in this country's complicated internal political maneuvers.

How might changes in the composition of Italy's cabinets affect the country's more assertive style in international diplomacy? The new activism was to a certain extent tied to Craxi's own style, personality, and sense of tactics, and future governments in Italy may be less overtly independent in both rhetoric and behavior. On the other hand, the successors to Craxi in the prime minister's office will probably find it advantageous to avoid reverting to the passive approach that once prevailed in the conduct of foreign affairs. As has been discussed above, changes in public and elite expectations and the greater significance of security issues in domestic politics seem to guarantee that Italian assertiveness will continue, even if on a somewhat more subdued level than before.

Mediterranean issues, including terrorism and the Arab-Israeli dispute, have been the major causes of bilateral tension between Rome and Washington. Despite a recent convergence of policies in these areas, Italy's perspectives and interests remain distinctive, and clashes with the United States will doubtless recur. A major source of disagreement has been Rome's preference for discussion, negotiation, and mediation when faced with security risks in this region, while the United States under Ronald Reagan has been willing to resort to threats and actual use of military force. The Bush administration in Washington may be more or less inclined to substitute diplomacy for force, but Italy's ingrained preference for negotiation over action is unlikely to change significantly, or will do so only slowly. Because the Mediterranean is an area of crucial security interest to both countries, this is one aspect of foreign policy where well-prepared bilateral coordination and cooperation may avoid public misunderstandings and disagreements.

Italy is less activist and has less clearly defined national interests in East-West affairs; Rome has more often been content to let the United States and north European allies play the major roles. Nevertheless, Italy's public and elites have acquired a measurable stake in the continuation of East-West détente. It stabilizes the country's domestic politics by serving as an element of consensus uniting all major parties and, in particular, it helps legitimize the PCI's role as an acceptable player in national politics without actually opening up the government to Communists. An erosion of détente inevitably threatens this fragile arrangement in a generally chaotic political setting, so every Italian party is disconcerted when U.S.-Soviet relations take a turn for the worse and threaten to destabilize both East-West relations in Europe and the Italian political scene. The emergence of a large public constituency favoring progress in détente and actively promoting progress in arms control encourages the inclinations of Italian politicians to support détente and its major concrete achievements in the realm of arms control.

For the United States, this means that Italy has acquired a psychological and political stake in the continuation of arms control discussions and reacts negatively to real or potential breakdowns in the dialogue. As in Italy's own political culture, it is probably the continued existence of dialogue that is important rather than any particular concrete results.

Conclusion

Arms control has become an increasingly significant component of effective alliance management. Arms control is concerned not only with stabilizing the East-West military competition; it also relates to ways in which the alliance can hold together on political-military issues. While American analysts are quite familiar with the processes of alliance management at the NATO institutional level, they still may be confronted with the problem of assessing the dynamic and divergent set of arms control policy processes extant in the political systems of their key West European allies. This book has assessed those dynamics and tries to provide the reader with some insights into the idiosyncratic and comparative dynamics of arms control policy in Great Britain, West Germany, France, and Italy.

The book makes it abundantly clear that there is no single West European arms control policy process or outcome to that process. Although the book documents the gradually increasing efforts made by the key countries to coordinate positions wherever possible, the differences in policy-making styles, national political cultures, and in the degree of political conflict over security policy across the four countries are often more prevalent than the similarities. Nevertheless, there are important similarities among the countries examined in this book. All of them are dominated by the executive arm of government in the shaping of arms control policy, and they have much greater latitude in the formulation of arms control policy than does the American executive. This is largely due to the domination of European executives over their respective legislatures as compared to the

American situation with Congress but it is partly due to the relative lack of expertise outside those governments as well.

In order to be in a better position to influence the Americans and to protect their interests, European leaders have sought to develop and then to enhance European arms control expertise. Because of the political-diplomatic nature of the European arms control orientation, the arms control units have been located almost entirely within the various foreign ministries. These units have been small but are growing in size as the arms control process has developed over the past ten years. The experts in these units have learned the technical language of arms control as a means of influencing the arms control process and, especially, the Americans. It should be realized that the body of technical expertise in Western Europe on arms control issues is very small, however, and that it is limited in its impact on security policy decision making within the governments. For example, the European militaries are the critical shapers of operational military policy. Historically, European forces have been involved only in a limited way in the arms control process. This could change, however, if the conventional arms control talks become more significant and dynamic than they have been in the past.

The Americans have affected the European arms control process not only directly through the generation of arms control proposals but by creating innovations in alliance strategy as well. Coping with American innovations in technology and strategy is a major European problem. European governments' responses to American initiatives entail the problem of determining how to deal with the American-Soviet rivalry. Among the most significant challenges American policy has faced in the alliance are the perception of changing Soviet capabilities and strategies and the need to gain European support for American "responses." Because the United States is often the innovator in the alliance military posture, Europeans are placed in the position of reacting to American initiatives. Europeans more likely than not tend to focus on American actions rather than on the Soviet initiatives that spawned American rethinking of its military posture. The Americans think they are responding to the Soviets, the Europeans think they are responding to American initiatives, and the Europeans and Americans end up frustrated with one another.

For example, the shift in Soviet strategy to a more effective conventional war-fighting posture has led the American army and air force to alter their doctrines for waging war. With the implementation of the Counter-Air 90 and Airland Battle doctrines, American forces in Europe hope to be able to conduct deep-interdiction campaigns against Soviet forces operating throughout the entire European theater. The Americans do not wish the Soviets to be able to operate using Warsaw Pact territory as a sanctuary. The Counter-Air 90, Airland Battle, and Follow-on Forces Attack initiatives have been conceived in large part in order to counter Soviet forces and strategy. Nonetheless, the debate within the alliance over American "initiatives" tends to focus on American actions rather than on the Soviet capabilities that prompted the American actions.

A second example is the development of PD-59 and the Single Integrated Operations Plan (SIOP) implementing it. Both were designed largely in response to the development of Soviet strategic forces and the war-fighting doctrines perceived to guide those forces. Again, the visible discussion in Europe of changing American doctrine and capabilities has focused primarily on American actions, not Soviet ones. Put bluntly, many American analysts of the Soviet Union and various government initiatives in the security area are acting under the assumption that Soviet capabilities and strategies have been changing; conversely, many European analysts and governments are not.

American arms control policy has obviously been crafted to protect American initiatives in the development of strategic and conventional forces. The debate within the alliance about changes in strategy has been an important component of intraalliance tensions over arms control policy as well.

The impact of executive predominance on security policy decisions in Western Europe may have an important consequence for American-European tensions as well. In Western Europe there tends to be a high positive correlation between governmental declaratory and actual policy in the detailed making of policy. Europeans tend not to understand that American declaratory policy is often part of the struggle between the U.S. executive branch and Congress. Europeans tend to believe that the U.S. policy process is a mirror image of their own; they thereby assume greater executive predominance than is often the case. Conversely, when an American executive policymaker issues a public statement designed primarily for domestic consideration, often European policymakers read much more into the statement with regard to actual U.S. policy than may be the case.

For example, when former president Reagan made his famous "Star Wars" speech in 1983, many European policymakers assumed that the speech reflected the outcome of a deliberate process of decision making in the U.S. government with regard to the future of nuclear deterrence. Of course, it was simply the opening salvo in the making not only of administration policy (which had to backfill the policy process) but of U.S. policy more generally. The Europeans often proceeded as if the Americans had already made up their minds to move ahead on the subject.

This general problem of mirror imaging is often exacerbated by the lack of genuine expertise in dealing with the Americans. The European governments tend to rely heavily on their embassies to report on U.S. developments, which means that the quality of embassy reporting is especially significant. The British embassy in Washington is unusual in the quality of its analysis of the U.S. policy process; it is aided to a large extent by the special access the British have with the Americans. Also, civil servants who have previously been posted to Washington form an alumni group of experts for interpreting American developments, although the European governments vary widely in the extent to which they allow civil servants to continue to work in areas which further or require their American expertise. Nonetheless, the expertise on the United States that does exist in the European governments is tempered by a general lack of understanding among high-ranking politicians in Western Europe. The European think tanks and universities, as well, have a very thin capability to analyze American developments.

There are, however, important differences among these countries— for instance, in the degree of centralization in the executive branches dominating the arms control policy processes. The British, for example, have the most centralized policy process of any European executive branch, which means that it is highly unlikely that one would see differences among departments affecting the public presentation of policy. The prime minister can, of course, take initiatives which surprise the bureaucracy, such as when Thatcher embraced the double zero option prior to calling the election in May 1987. When differences emerge, such as the one over the question of British participation in the American SDI program, they are bargained out at the cabinet level. It is useful for an American administration to remember that compromise has been required on such an issue, because differences among departments can reemerge, but are unlikely to surface publicly.

At the other end of the centralization continuum is the policy process in the West German government. Not only are the Germans governed by a coalition of parties, but the division directors in the MOD and the Foreign Office have much greater power than in the British civil service. This means that differences here are more difficult to resolve and are more likely to be reflected in public debate than in Britain. The West German response to the double zero option is a useful reminder of the relative diffusion of power and its effects on German policy in the arms control area. In addition, it has not been considered a legitimate province of persons outside of government to examine the details of that government's foreign and security policy, including arms control (as opposed to disarmament). Information flows have been tightly circumscribed, and often the control of information has been more important than the generation of qualitatively better information. The West European governments have a much more insulated decision-making process than does the American government on the details of arms control policy.

The information that generates the arms control discourse both inside and outside governments in Western Europe often comes from the other side of the Atlantic. A key question which emerges is how the debate in the United States shapes the European debate, given the paucity of information the West European governments provide for their publics. Even with the formation of new or upgraded research institutes in all of the countries examined, the key specialists have either been trained in the United States or rely heavily on American specialists and information to participate in the more technical aspects of the debate about arms control.

There is an interesting parallel between Western Europe and the Soviet Union. Soviet specialists who are accessible to the West (as well as Soviet negotiators on arms control) largely use American information as well. Westerners often are concerned that these Soviet specialists are purveyors of disinformation or are simply trained in the care and handling of Americans. The situation, however, is analogous to the West Europeans'. The specialists accessible to Americans through the research institutes are rarely well plugged in to their governments, but because they are accessible Americans consider them to be important. Getting access to West European elites who are affected by arms control matters, as opposed to those in the government charged with handling Americans, is a related problem.

Because the thrust of arms control agreements (as opposed to talks) has been upon U.S. and Soviet nuclear weapons, European involvement has focused on the diplomatic game of alliance management, or, basically on managing the Americans in such a way that European interests are not neglected. The Europeans have varied significantly, however, in the way they have handled the question of influencing the Americans in the arms control process. The British have pursued a process of direct influence over the Americans through the "special relationship." This has included considerable interaction at all governmental levels and has been encouraged by frequent British-American summits. The Germans have pursued a similar policy, the effectiveness of which has been limited by the much lower degree of German centralization and by the presence of a chancellor more capable of being a domestic power broker than a foreign policy statesman. The French have sought to influence the Americans by pursuing a European-oriented policy, particularly through their relationship with the Germans. The Italians also have primarily used the multinational institutions, especially NATO, although they have begun to use bilateral European relations as well. Increasingly, the four European countries surveyed have pursued a European-oriented strategy to better influence Washington in an alliance management context. The revival of the WEU, for example, has involved an effort to enhance European coordination between the bilateral and NATO levels as a better means of influencing Washington.

This nascent Europeanization has been limited, however, by the growing propensity of the Europeans to pursue national interests in the arms control process. For example, the Germans have sought relief from domestic pressures in dealing with the nuclear challenge facing the alliance, and German governments have sought to ensure that their interests are as well served as possible by arms control agreements. The widely shared sentiment in West Germany—"the shorter the range of nuclear weapons, the more German the effect"— will have a decisive influence on how the Germans pursue arms control agreements in the years ahead.

Europeanization is thereby often reduced to its lowest common denominator; namely, the West European governments seek to protect national interests through European cooperation wherever possible. There is little effort to protect "European" interests in a give-and-take atmosphere in which British, French, German, and Italian interests are amalgamated into a larger European interest as a whole. As a result, the kind of Europeanization which has emerged complicates rather than resolves U.S.-European differences on arms control issues.

Europeanization may, however, serve an important political purpose by allowing the European governments to stand before their publics and take more responsibility for their actions. For example, tension between the Americans and Germans over what many Americans perceive as German unwillingness to take responsibility for their actions in the INF area (dating from the chancellor's speech in 1977) might be reduced to the extent that Europeanization allows the German government to be seen by its public as playing a more assertive role in defining its interests and not "sacrificing" them to American diktat. The image of being the United States' lackey is not a positive one for a European leader; Europeanization may well be a help in dealing with this problem.

Nonetheless, alliance management is only part of the challenge to the West European policy process. Dealing with the disarmament and strategy debate is critical as well, especially in terms of the future of the alliance. Clearly, the British and German governments have been the most affected of the four governments in terms of the need to pursue an arms control policy supportive of their strategy. Both conservative governments are facing serious challenges from the Left about the legitimacy of nuclear deterrence. Arms control agreements, or at least the propensity to pursue them, are important contributors to the disarmament debate they face. As a result, these governments present a political image of desiring to pursue arms control agreements, which may be at odds with the proclivities of arms control decision makers in those governments who deal with the technical details of such issues. This tension between political requirements and participation in the technical assessment process leads to contradictory impulses coming from Western Europe and is an irritant to European-American relations.

An important problem confronts an American analyzing the European arms control policy process. For Americans, arms control encompasses both technical details and political choices in dealing with the Soviet Union. For Europeans, arms control is limited to governments dealing with technical details, whereas the public debates involve political choices in strategy or disarmament. Arms control is, after all, an American term that has been grafted onto European political-military discourse. The Europeans are likely to think initially more in political than in military terms when dealing with arms control and disarmament issues, whereas the Americans are more likely to think in military terms first. In other words, there is an important gap between technical language and political language. Arms control discussions entail the use of technical language— mainly initiated, it should be remembered, by the U.S. government and private specialized research institutes. In large part the Europeans are following the American lead. In contrast, disarmament discussions entail the use of political language and an emphasis on security provided by political means. To many Europeans, for example, verification relates to the politics of trust in East-West relations, not the resolution of technical details for negotiations.

For Americans listening to the European debate, the people who use the technical language of arms control seem to be more serious and realistic, as opposed to the abstract and unrealistic analysts and ideologues involved in the disarmament debate. This perception has been, in fact, a major motivation for the West European governments who are seeking to develop technical expertise in order to influence the Americans. But it is the disarmament debate which matters most to the political future of the alliance, not debate over the technical details of arms control issues. The difficult challenge facing the U.S. government and the specialized research community is how to influence both the arms control and the disarmament debates—two related but not synonymous issues.

The Future

A central tension in the European arms control policy process exists between Europeanist and nationalist tendencies. The key West European countries are trying to pursue European cooperation where possible; a good example is the Anglo-French cooperation on nuclear arms control issues. Europeanization will clearly become a more significant factor affecting the American approach to alliance management, yet this European cooperation trend is limited by the enhanced national assertiveness on security and arms control issues of these same countries.

An additional trend overlays the European cooperation-nationalistic trend. The Europeans are increasingly concerned with ensuring a substantial American military presence in the years ahead, even if reductions have to be tolerated. They will seek to ensure that arms control agreements bind rather than free the Americans from their commitment to Europe, especially in the nuclear weapons area. Nonetheless, for Europeanization to be pursued it is clearly necessary to shift the balance of power and managerial relationships within the alliance. In other words, there is an additional tension between Europeanist and Atlanticist impulses that will shape the European arms control effort.

The result of these twin sets of tensions—Europeanist versus nationalist and Europeanist versus Atlanticist—will be the existence of shifting coalitions among the European powers and between selected European powers and the United States on security and arms control issues confronting the alliance. The French and the British, in particular, have every incentive to enhance their cooperation on nuclear arms control matters. The Germans may follow a European policy, but their goal will be to ensure continued presence of significant American conventional forces, which will create a natural coalition with the British, who will follow the same objective. The Germans will seek through the arms control process not only to anchor the American commitment to forward defense but to draw the French into a greater commitment to the conventional defense of Germany. The Italians will place increasing emphasis on the Mediterranean dimension of their security and seek cooperation with the French; this cooperation may create tensions with the Germans. The Italians and French will continue to try to ensure that no serious limits on naval forces in the Mediterranean are introduced into arms control talks and will be concerned that the Germans will allow the Soviets to lay down precedents for limits on naval forces in new conventional arms control talks.

Such cleavages will continue to provide the Americans with ample opportunities to exercise leadership, but the Europeans will increasingly seek European institutional settings in order to limit the scope of that leadership. The WEU, or some equivalent, will be necessary to provide an effective halfway house between simple bilateral cooperation and the NATO institutions.

European complaints about the lack of consultation will increase in the years ahead as the United States becomes more concerned with reducing its defense burden in Europe. American administrations will almost assuredly seek to reduce American forces in Europe through unilateral or negotiated measures. In contrast, the Europeans will seek to tie up the American forces in complex bargaining through multinational negotiating forums. Although the Europeans have a common interest in seeking Soviet reductions while maintaining a substantial U.S. presence, it is unlikely that they will be able to agree on a common set of negotiating goals. The inability of the Europeans to present a cohesive image will be very frustrating to future American administrations, however, and may well lead to the exacerbation of alliance tensions.

There is a movement under way in Europe to try to develop more realistic and positive proposals rather than just vetoing or "directing" the American effort. The European governments may well beef up their arms control units to develop a greater capability to generate proposals of their own that will shape the Atlantic debate. In other words, perhaps the INF debate will leave behind the legacy of a greater European effort to initiate rather than simply to react. The Europeans are rather limited in their ability to initiate, given the significance of the American nuclear deterrent to Western security. As far as the central strategic systems are concerned, the Europeans can only be observers, although they will clearly try to be more active in shaping American thinking on extended deterrence.

We can anticipate institutional changes in the European arms control process as well, in order for it to become more effective in the arms control area. The uniformed military and the civilian MODs are already becoming more involved in informing the policy process in the European governments. To become more active, the governments will almost assuredly have to provide greater opportunities for their militaries to play a role in assessing arms control options. Greater involvement in the alliance management of arms control issues contains within it, however, an important political challenge to the European governments. Increased involvement by the European governments will almost assuredly elevate public attention to security issues. The disarmament debate is unlikely to disappear, and the prospects for reestablishing a European consensus on the validity of any form of nuclear or conventional deterrence will remain slim.

The absence of consensus and the challenges the Left will pose in the evolution of American strategy will be constant irritants to the transatlantic relationship. In fact, the evolution of American strategy will itself continue to be the central bone of contention among the various political factions in the European politics. An arms control card has become a sine qua non of American security policy toward Western Europe, and this will undoubtedly continue to be the case in the future.

It is clear as well that the British and French nuclear forces are becoming far more important to the future of European nuclear deterrence than either of those countries would wish. It may well be difficult to avoid formulating an effective strategy including these forces in future arms control talks that will protect them from antinuclear pressures in Western Europe. Creating such a strategy will be immensely difficult and will require American support of an Anglo-French dialogue on this subject. A serious crisis in British and French relations with the United States will emerge if the United States does not handle this issue carefully. The Soviets will, of course, do nothing to help the United States in this score, having had for many years the objective of encouraging the United States to ignore its alliance responsibilities, for example in the technology and weapons transfer area. The Soviets have raised the Pershing I issue in the INF discussion for just this reason.

Soviet actions and public diplomacy have clearly been an additional factor affecting West European arms control policy, since they have influenced Western threat perceptions. Most significant has been the new flexibility evident under General Secretary Gorbachev and the "charm offensive" associated with it. The charm offensive, and with it the prospects of an agreement on the double zero, have had a significant effect on the disarmament debate in Western Europe. Gorbachev is trying to place the West, particularly the United States, in the position of appearing to escalate the arms race. For example, any Western discussions about modernizing nuclear weapons under 500 kms will be controversial among Western governments on their own merits, but the public debate will heat up that controversy because of Soviet efforts to appear willing to negotiate to lower levels in pursuit perhaps of a denuclearized European theater, if Europe is understood not to encompass Soviet territory. Defining the proper European role in the U.S.-Soviet competition has been a long-standing concern to European leaders. This concern has simply deepened with the emergence of the Gorbachev challenge.

In short, the need to assess developments within Western Europe in the years ahead will grow rather than diminish. The dynamics of the security debate, the processes of governmental management of arms control issues, and the European cooperation phenomenon will create a fluid environment within which the United States must exercise its alliance leadership. It will not be an easy task, and keeping an ear close to the ground will be critical to the effort.

Notes

1. British Arms Control Policy

1. *Financial Times*, February 17, 1986.
2. Government estimates place the cost at slightly more than £9 billion. See *The Defence Estimate* (London: HMSO, 1987).
3. *The Alternatives to Trident* (London: HMSO, 1987).
4. Phil Williams, "The British Perspective on Arms Control," unpublished paper, 1987.
5. For example, the leading role of the British in shaping the U.S. position on a nontransfer provision in SALT II was clearly identified by Cyrus Vance: "In bilateral consultations held during the summer and fall of 1978 with the British and Germans (the two allies most concerned about the non-circumvention provision), and later with the whole alliance, we worked out the wording." See Cyrus Vance, *Hard Choices* (New York: Simon and Schuster, 1983), p. 97.
6. "NATO Accepts Thatcher Prescription," *Guardian*, December 13, 1986.
7. Based on interviews with high-ranking British officials.
8. *Financial Times*, November 10, 1986.
9. Such a move was suggested, for example, by David Steel, leader of the Liberal party, in the *Guardian*, March 9, 1987.
10. *Daily Telegraph*, November 10, 11, 12, 15, 1986; *Guardian*, November 11, 1986; *Observer*, November 16, 1986; and *Sunday Times*, November 16, 1986.
11. *Daily Telegraph*, March 4, 1987.
12. George Younger, "Defence: A Sense of Balance," speech delivered to the Royal United Services Institute, October 1, 1986, pp. 9–10.
13. *Guardian*, March 12, 1987.
14. Younger, "Defence: A Sense of Balance," pp. 9–10.
15. *Financial Times*, and *Daily Telegraph*, July 16, 1986.
16. *The Times*, February 2, 1987.
17. Simon Jenkins and Anne Sloman, *With Respect Ambassador* (London: BBC, 1985), p. 115.
18. These two paragraphs were provided by Michael Clarke.

19. Anthony King, ed., *The British Prime Minister* (Durham: Duke University Press, 1985), pp. 122–23.

20. This paragraph was provided by Michael Clarke.

21. Peter Hennessy, *Cabinet* (Oxford: Basil Blackwell, 1986), p. 100.

22. In the 1985–86 period there were at least 160 groups within the span of the cabinet subcommittee system, although Mrs. Thatcher has admitted the existence of only four. See Hennessy, *Cabinet*, p. 26.

23. Peter Nailor, in *Developments in British Politics*, ed. Henry Drucker et al. (London: Macmillan, 1985), p. 181.

24. Hennessy, *Cabinet*, pp. 102–3.

25. As quoted by Peter Hennessy in *Thatcherism: Personality and Politics*, ed. Kenneth Minoque and Michael Biddiss (London: Macmillan, 1987), p. 65.

26. Sir Geoffrey Howe, "European Security," speech delivered to the Royal Institute of International Relations, Brussels, March 16, 1987, paragraphs 37–38.

27. For Heseltine's presentation of his disagreement with the prime minister, see the *Observer*, January 12, 1986.

28. George Younger, "Europe or America, A False Dilemma," presented at Wehrkunde Conference, 1987, p. 1.

29. Kevin Theakson, *Junior Ministers in British Government* (Oxford: Basil Blackwell, 1987).

30. The Nuclear Energy Department is also involved in its responsibility for nonproliferation issues.

31. William Wallace, *The Foreign Policy Process in Britain* (London: Allen and Unwin, 1977), p. 74. This book is quite dated but remains the only book in print on the British decision-making system.

32. Sir Julian Bullard, "European Defence Cooperation," unpublished speech, March 14, 1985.

33. *Trident and the Alternatives* (London: HMSO, 1987), p. 8.

34. Michael Clarke, "The Policy-making Process," unpublished paper, p. 6.

35. Paul Silk, *How Parliament Works* (London: Longman, 1987), p. 222.

36. Clarke, "The Policy-making Process," p. 7.

37. *Defence without the Bomb* (London: Taylor V. Francis, 1983).

38. This point was raised in the Commons, to the consternation of the Labour party leadership, by former prime minister Callaghan. See the *Guardian*, March 10, 1987.

39. The members of the commission were as follows: John Edmonds (chairman); John Roper (secretary); Paddy Ashdown, M.P.; General Sir Hugh Beach; John Cartwright, M.P. and the SDP defence spokesman; David Dunn; Lady Grimond; Richard Holme; Lord Mayhew; Edwina Moreton; William Rodgers; James Wallace, M.P. and Liberal party defence spokesman; James Wellbeloved; and Elizabeth Young.

40. *Guardian*, June 7, 1986.

41. *Guardian*, June 5, 1986.

42. *Daily Telegraph*, June 7, 1986.

43. *Financial Times*, June 18, 1986.

44. *Guardian*, June 10, 1986.

45. William Rodgers, "Keep the Defence Options Open," *The Times*, June 12, 1986.
46. *Guardian*, December 18, 1986.
47. *Britain United: The Time Has Come* (London: The SDP/Liberal Alliance, 1987).

2. West German Arms Control Policy

1. This is especially true in the condition of the coalition government, where Gen-scher is the critical linchpin to the coalition staying in power. His political position clearly reinforces his ability to arbitrate on arms control matters. The important role of the FDP as the linchpin is mentioned often by West German politicians in explaining Genscher's dominance over arms control issues.
2. Renata Mayntz and Fritz W. Scharpf, *Policy Making in the German Federal Bureaucracy* (Amsterdam: Elsevier, 1975), pp. 86–89.
3. Hans Günter Brauch, "Arms Control and Disarmament Decisionmaking in the Federal Republic of Germany: Past Experience and Options for Change," in *Decisionmaking for Arms Limitation: Assessment and Prospects*, ed. Hans Günter Brauch and Duncan L. Clarke (Cambridge, Mass.: Ballinger, 1983), pp. 144–49.
4. Helga Haftendorn, "Der Abrüstungsbeauftragte. Zur Organisation der Abrüstungs-politik in der Bundesrepublik Deutschland," *Politische Vierteljahresschrift* 13 (August 1972):34–35.
5. Brauch, "Arms Control and Disarmament Decisionmaking," p. 151.
6. Wolf-Dieter Karl and Joachim Krause, "Aussenpoltischer Strukturwandel und parlamentarischer Entscheidungsprozess," in *Verwaltete Aussenpolitik: Sicherheits und entspannungs-politische Entscheidungsprozesse in Bonn*, ed. Helga Haftendorn et al. (Cologne: Verlag Wissenschaft und Politik, 1978), pp. 71–75.
7. Simon Lunn, "Policy Preparation and Consultation within NATO Decisionmaking for SALT and LRTNF," in *Decisionmaking for Arms Limitation*, p. 262.
8. *Der Spiegel*, November 23, 1981, p. 57; Richard L. Merritt and Donald J. Puchala, eds., *Western European Perspectives on International Affairs* (New York: Praeger, 1968), p. 209.
9. For example, the Foreign Ministry was involved in the drafting of the Bundestag resolution on INF, which reflected the language used by the Germans in shaping the Reykjavík summit language in June 1987.
10. The party's position on this issue has been articulated by Ehmke and reflects the ongoing dialogue between the French PSF and the German SPD on security issues.
11. In June 1987 Dregger argued in a Bundestag speech that in light of the reduction in credibility of the American nuclear guarantee (given a prospective INF agreement), France should not provide Germany with an explicit nuclear guarantee. Typical of Kohl's leadership, the chancellor proposed the formation of a joint Franco-German brigade as a way of heading off CDU pressures on the Franco-German relationship in the aftermath of a potential INF agreement.
12. *Frankfurter Allgemaine Zeitung*, April 25, 1985; Paul Pucher, "Der Pfaelzer und der Bayer," *Der Spiegel*, August 26, 1985.
13. Interviews with virtually all members of the SPD delegation have revealed that the West German negotiators felt a tremendous sense of emotional pride in discussing

"their" security issues directly with their East German counterparts without super-power interference. It is also clear from interviews with German governmental officials that despite concerns about the precedent set by such negotiations, this sense of emotional pride was widely shared.

14. Genscher is clearly the prime mover for Europeanization in the German govern-ment and is perceived as such by French, British, and Italian officials. Based on interviews in Paris, London, and Rome.

3. French Arms Control Policy

1. Robbin F. Laird, ed., *French Security Policy: From Independence to Interdepen-dence* (Boulder, Colo.: Westview Press, 1986).
2. For an excellent French treatment of Franco-German security cooperation by a former player at the government level on this issue, see Pascal Boniface and François Heisbourg, *La Puce, Les Hommes et La Bombe* (Paris: Hachette, 1986), pp. 236–78.
3. See, for example, the argument made by General Georges Fricaud-Chagnaud, in *French Security Policy*, pp. 121–30.
4. This point is discussed in Edward Kolodziej, *Making and Marketing Arms: The French Experience and Its Implications for the International System* (Princeton, N.J.: Princeton University Press, 1989), pp. 107–19.
5. For two assessments of the range of alternatives bubbling under the "consensus," see Jolyon Howorth, "Consensus of Silence: The French Socialist Party and De-fence Policy under François Mitterrand," *International Affairs* 60, no. 4 (Autumn 1984):579–600; and Robbin Laird, "The French Strategic Dilemma," in *French Security Policy*, pp. 81–104.
6. Mancur Olson, *The Logic of Collective Action* (Cambridge, Mass.: Harvard Univer-sity Press, 1965).
7. For example, see Pierre Lellouche, ed., *Pacifisme et Dissuasion* (Paris: Economica, 1983).
8. *L'Express*, July 17, 1987, p. 8.
9. This comment appears in Laird, *French Security Policy*, p. 112.
10. For a relatively rare detailed article by a high-ranking arms control official assess-ing the nuclear arms control issue, see the article by French Foreign Ministry official Phillippe Boone (pseud.), "L'affaire des FNI et l'avenir des négociations stratégiques," *Défense Nationale* (May 1984):33–43.
11. François Gorand (pseud.), "Aprés Reykjavík," *Commentaire* (Spring 1987).
12. Typical of this position was the report of the special French commission on the future of space arms: *Rapport de Synthèse Presénté au Ministre de la Défense* (Paris: Commission d'études sur les armes spatiales, January 1986).
13. See the *Rapport a la Commission de la Défense Nationale et des Forces Armées sur le projet de loi de programme relatif à l'équipement militaire pour les années 1987–1991* (Paris: National Assembly, 1987).
14. The organizational impact of CDE involvement has been substantial in moving the French from declaratory to practical involvement.

15. Étienne Copel, *Vaincre la guerre* (Paris: Lieu Commun, 1984), chap. 4.
16. Extensive discussions with Copel and his former colleagues in the military have revealed that his emphasis on the chemical threat was strongly supported by high-ranking French officials.
17. *Intervention du Ministre devant la Conférence du Désarmement*, Geneva, February 19, 1987.
18. Samy Cohen is the leading French academic observer of the French policy process, and his two key books on this process are: *Les Conseillers du Président de Charles de Gaulle a Valéry Giscard d'Estaing* (Paris: Presses Universitaires de France, 1980); and *La Monarchie Nucléaire* (Paris: Hachette, 1986).
19. In Africa, for example, where French influence is still strong, both Giscard d'Estaing and Mitterrand have been able to make crucial decisions in a highly personal manner with a minimum of consultation. In November 1984 most members of the Socialist government woke up one morning to learn that Mitterrand was meeting in Crete with Colonel Qaddafi.
20. Cohen, *La Monarchie*, p. 20.
21. Ibid., p. 20.
22. Ibid., p. 59.
23. Ibid., p. 57.
24. Cohen, *Les Conseillers*, chap. 6.
25. Based on extensive discussions with a former secretary general.
26. Cohen, *Les Conseillers*, p. 60.
27. François Mitterrand, *Réflexions sur la politique extérieure de la France* (Paris: Fayard, 1986), p. 34.
28. Ibid., p. 40.
29. Cohen, *La Monarchie*, p. 57.
30. He becomes formally the Chef d'état major des armées, which is charged with the operational responsibility for directing French forces.
31. Samy Cohen, "Le centre d'analyse et de prévision du Ministère des Relations Extérieures," *Revue Française de Science Politique* 6 (December 1986).
32. *Liberation*, April 1987.
33. The IHEDN (Institute for Higher Defense Studies) has been an important socialization mechanism to ensure broad consensus among the elite. The French are so impressed with its role that they helped to create an IHEDN on the European level to enhance elite consciousness of Europeanism as well.

4. Italian Arms Control Policy

1. After the U.S. State Department overcame some objections from a Pentagon worried about a diversion of attention from the central front.
2. For a brief discussion see Michael M. Harrison, "Government and Politics," in *Italy: A Country Study* (Washington, D.C.: American University and Department of Defense Country Handbook Series, 1987, forthcoming via the Library of Congress).
3. F. Accame et al., *Pace e Sicurezza: Problemi e Alternative, Problemi del Socialismo* (series) (Milan: Franco Angeli, 1984), p. 182.

4. See the criticism in Eliseo Milani, *Rapporto di Minoranza della a Commissione Permanente (Difesa)*, sulla parti de competenza del disegno di legge n. 1504 e sullo State di Previsione del Ministero della difesa 1505, tabella 12. Atti Parlamentari, Nr. 1504 e 1505-A/1-bis, IX Legislatura, Disegni di legge e relazioni. Documenti.

5. For a brief description of these bases see Congressional Research Service, "U.S. Military Installations in Italy" (Washington, D.C.: Library of Congress, mimeo). In late 1985 an Italian source (*L'Espresso*, November 10, 1985) asserted that through 1984 there were a total of 220 sites where U.S. military personnel were located in Italy, of which about 40 were of some size or importance.

6. This estimate is made in P. Cotta-Ramusino et al., *Scienza, Armi e Disarmo: Quaranta Anni Dopo Hiroshima* (Bari: Edizioni Dedalo, 1986), specifically, the article by Franco Selleri, "I Sommergibili nucleari, la corsa agli armamenti e i rischi di guerra totale," pp. 87–102.

7. The first study, by IRDISP. was entitled "Quello che i Russi gia' sanno e gli Italiani non devono sapere," published in 1984; the second, by Marco De Andreis, was *The Nuclear Debate in Italy* (Rome: IAI, 1985); see also the estimate in W. Arkin and R. Fieldhouse, *Nuclear Battlefields* (Cambridge, Mass.: Ballinger, 1985). All the figures are reported in Paolo Cotta-Ramusino, *Il Controllo delle Armi Nucleari Americane in Europa* (Rome: Centro Studi di Politica Internazionale. Note and Ricerche no. 2, April 1985).

8. Even though studies are now appearing that calculate the effects of a Soviet strike on the main NATO military installations on the peninsula. See Andrea Ottolenghi, "Simulazione degli effetti a breve termine di un attacco nucleare di tipo 'counter-force' in Italia," in *Scienza, Armi e Disarmo*, pp. 127–58.

9. Senate Debate of April 11–12, 1984, quoted in Cotta-Ramusino, *Il Controllo delle Armi Nucleari Americane in Europa*, p. 17.

10. Author's interview with Giorgio La Malfa, PRI chairman of the Foreign Affairs Committee of the Italian Chamber of Deputies. All interviews cited here were held in Italy in January 1986.

11. See Archivo Disarmo, "Spese Militari: Bilanci Statali," B.S. no. 2, February 28, 1985 (pamphlet). Also, Maurizio Cremesco, *La Pace Dal Terrore al Disarmo: Le Forze in Campo. Armi, Governi, Movimenti* (Italy: Adnkronos, 1983). Figures differ radically from source to source. According to the 1985 *SIPRI Yearbook*, Italy's volume increase in defense expenditure from a 1976–78 average to 1984 amounted to an annual average of 4.9 percent, the highest in NATO except for the United States.

12. This interpretation was suggested and confirmed in a number of interviews, particularly with military experts such as Stefano Silvestri and Maurizio Cremasco.

13. For this argument see my paper "The United States and Craxi's Activist Italy" (Washington, D.C.: U.S. Department of State, Bureau of Intelligence and Research, 1983, mimeo.) For an informed, up-to-date analysis of Italian politics see Frederic Spotts and Theodor Wieser, *Italy: A Difficult Democracy, A Survey of Italian Politics* (Cambridge: Cambridge University Press, 1986).

14. See Lelio Lagorio, *Indirizzi di Politica Militare. Relazione alle Commissioni Permanenti per la Difesa della Camera dei Deputati e del Senato della Republica* (Rome: Ministry of Defense, June–July, 1980).

15. Rome interview, January 1986.

16. The government was reconstituted as if it had never fallen. This longest-lived postwar Italian government did formally collapse in July 1986, but Craxi succeeded himself as prime minister and revived his former cabinet on August 1. The crisis was caused by domestic political infighting, which produced a tenuous agreement that Craxi would step down as prime minister in March 1987 and turn the post over to a Christian Democrat. On the *Achille Lauro* incident, see Frank J. Piason, *Achille Lauro Affair: Italian Policy Considerations and Implications for the United States* (Washington, D.C.: U.S. Department of State, Foreign Service Institute, the Senior Seminar, 28th Session, 1985–1986, March 1986).

17. See Luigi Caligaris, "La Condizione Militare in Italia," *Affari Esteri* 16, no. 65 (Fall 1984):433.

18. Angelo Panebianco, "The Domestic Origins of a 'Low-Profile' Stand," *Politica Internazionale* (English edition), 3, no. 1 (Spring 1983):14–20.

19. Interview with Claudio Martelli.

20. See Sergio Rossi, "Public Opinion and Atlantic Defense in Italy," in *The Public and Atlantic Defense*, ed. Gregory Flynn and Hans Rattinger (London: Croom Helm, 1985), esp. p. 196.

21. For examples of this view see the debate statements by Luciana Castellina, a PDUP (Party of Proletarian Unity) deputy, in Accame et al., *Pace e Sicurezza*, p. 57.

22. See Fabrizio Battistelli, *Armi e armamenti: Dagli esplosivi alle testate nucleari. Una possibili strategia di pace* (Rome: Editori Riuniti, 1985), p. 22.

23. Ibid., p. 18.

24. See Cotta-Ramusino et al., *Scienza, Armi e Disarmo*, especially the article by Roberto Fieschi, "La Logica della corsa agli armamenti," pp. 11–12.

25. Interview with Mr. Bernini in Rome, January 1986.

26. de Voto article in *Rinascita*, December 29, 1984.

27. In Accame et al., *Pace e Sicurezza*.

28. Interview with Giancarlo da Novi, then director-general for political affairs in the Ministry of Foreign Affairs.

29. See Enea Cerquetti, *Relazione di Minoranza su: Disegni di Legge:* Disposizioni per la formazione del bilancio annuale e pluriennale dello stato (lege finanziaria 1985) (2105). Bilancio di previsione dello Stato pel l'anno finanziario 1985 e bilancio pluriennale per il trennio 1985–1987 (2106). Stato di Previsione del Ministero della difesa per l'anno finanziario 1985 (tabella 12). Atti Parliamentari. Camera dei Deputati. IX Legislatura, Disegni di Legge e Relazioni, Documenti.

30. See Milani, *Rapporto di Minoranza della a Commissione Permanente (Difesa)*, 1505, tabella 12.

31. Interviews with various authorities.

32. Quoted by Giorgio La Malfa in the *Washington Post*, November 6, 1985.

33. See Umberto Cappuzzo, "The New Italian Perception of Security," *International Spectator* 19, nos. 3/4 (July–December 1984):134–35.

34. Ibid., p. 136.

35. Statement to the Chamber of Deputies Defense Committee, October 13, 1981.

36. See Ministero della Difesa, *La Difesa, Libro Blanco*, 2 vols. (Rome: Ministry of Defense, 1985).

37. Ibid., p. 44.

38. Ibid., p. 56; The white book discusses two kinds of rapid action forces, one for "civil" actions and another for national and possibly international missions. Information here also from various interviews.

39. Quoted in Cremasco, "Italy: A New Role in the Southern Flank?"

40. Information drawn from various interviews.

41. The Defense Ministry does have more detailed information available but plays only an advisory role because the foreign minister dominates actual policy-making as well as the makeup of Italian delegations.

42. See ISTRID, La Difesa dell'Europa (Rome: Instituto Studi e Ricerche Difesa, 1985).

43. Interview with the consultant who made the proposal.

44. For example, Craxi was responsible for trying to upgrade Italy's presence as an observer at the Vienna MBFR talks by naming the former army chief of staff, Capazzo, as head of the delegation, a move which was imposed on a reluctant Ministry of Foreign Affairs.

45. See ISTRID La Difesa dell'Europa, p. 61.

46. See Rinascita, February 2, 1985.

47. See Gianluca de Voto, La Questione della Deterrenza: Considerazion; sulla strategia nucleare e sulla sicurezza (Rome: CESPI, Note e richerche no. 4, June 1985). Some general PCI expert views can be gleaned from Centro studi de politica internazionale del PCI, Il Dibattito Strategico in Occidente: Alcune Aspetti, no. 8, November 1982 (mimeo).

48. Ibid., p. 15.

49. See Cremasco, La Pace Dal Terrore al Disarmo; also Marco Favale, "Gli Stati Uniti e la Ripresa dei Negoziati sul Disarmo," Affari Esteri no. 65 (Winter 1985):3–12; ISTRID, La Difesa dell'Europa.

50. See Battistelli, Armi e armamenti, p. 141.

51. See Mario Capanna et al., Disarmo o Sterminio? L'Umanita al bivio del 2000 (Milan: Gabriele Mazzotta, 1983), p. 122.

52. Under a recent NATO agreement, this facility will be closed by 1992, and refurbished stocks will be held in the United States for deployment in Europe only during a crisis; Washington Post, May 23, 1986.

53. See Enrico Jacchia and Francesco Amadei, La Guerra Chimica: Incubo Sull' Europa (Milan: Sugar Co. Edizioni, 1984).

54. Ibid., p. 89.

55. Quoted in Vincenzo Tornetta, "Il Dibatto Sulla 'guerre stellari,'" Rivista di Studi Politici Internazionale no. 2 (April–June 1985):179–94.

56. From U.S. embassy (Italy), translation of the Andreotti speech.

57. See arguments in Luigi Caligaris, "Dubbi e Prospettive dello scudo stellare," Affari Esteri 17, no. 67 (Summer 1985):317–44; and Vincenzo Toretta, "Lo Spazio ed il Controllo degli Armamenti," Affari Esteri 16, no. 63 (Summer 1984):293–313.

58. See Paolo Vittorelli, "Rapport," Deuxième Conference des Partis Socialistes des Pays Europeens Membres de l'Alliance Atlantique, Bonn, November 27–29, 1985 (mimeo). Public opinion polls in September 1985 found that Italians were gener-

ally supportive of sdi research and were somewhat less inclined to fear that sdi would endanger arms control efforts than the public in other West European countries. (From a confidential but widely circulated usia research memorandum dated November 20, 1985.)

Index

Contributors

Barry Blechman   Dr. Blechman is president of Defense Forecasts, a Washington-based consulting firm. He was deputy director of the Arms Control and Disarmament Agency during the Carter administration and is a well-known specialist on Western security policies. He has written numerous books and articles in the arms control field.

Cathleen Fisher   Ms. Fisher is a Ph.D. candidate at the University of Maryland who is currently finishing her dissertation while in residence at the Center for Eurpoean Studies at Harvard University. She is a specialist on West German domestic politics and has worked with Dr. Blechman on a wide variety of security-related issues.

Michael Harrison   Dr. Harrison was the associate director of the Program for Strategic and International Security Studies at the Graduate Institute of International Studies in Geneva, Switzerland. Dr. Harrison wrote widely on European security issues, specializing in French and Italian affairs. He died early in 1989.

Robbin Laird   Dr. Laird is director of the Soviet and West European Security Program at the Instititue for Defense Analyses in Alexandria, Virginia. He has published several books and articles on Soviet and West European foreign and domestic policies.

Dinah Louda   Ms. Louda is a Paris-based specialist on French and European domestic politics. She has worked with *L'Express* in Paris and is currently working with *Business International* while completing her dissertation on French security policy at the Center for European Studies at Harvard University.

David Robertson   Dr. Robertson is professor of politics at St. Hugh's College, Oxford University and is a specialist in Western domestic and defense policies. He has written several books and articles dealing with British elections politics as well. He is currently a fellow with the Institute for East-West Security Studies in New York.

Library of Congress Cataloging-in-Publication Data

West European arms control policy / Robbin Laird, editor.
(Duke Press policy studies)
Includes index.
ISBN 0–8223–0955–6
1. Nuclear arms control—Europe. 2. Arms
control.   I. Laird, Robbin F. (Robbin Frederick), 1946–
II. Series.
JX1974.7.W46 1990   327.1′74′094—dc20   89–16819 CIP

DATE DUE